Dread and Pente~ ~ ~ ~

Dr Robert Beckford is currently a post-doctoral research fellow at the University of Birmingham. He was formerly the Tutor in Black Theology at the Queen's College in Birmingham.

Robert has been at the forefront of developing Black theology and Religious Cultural Criticism in England. His first book, *Jesus is Dread: Black Theology and Black Culture in Britain* (Darton Longman & Todd, 1998) was a groundbreaking text.

Aside from writing and lecturing, Robert has also contributed to television and radio programmes, including the widely acclaimed, *Untold – Britain's Slave Trade* (Channel 4, October 1999).

This book is dedicated to my parents,
Naomi and Leonard Beckford.

Dread and Pentecostal

A Political Theology for the Black Church in Britain

Robert Beckford

WIPF & STOCK · Eugene, Oregon

Wipf and Stock Publishers
199 W 8th Ave, Suite 3
Eugene, OR 97401

Dread and Pentecostal
A Political Theology for the Black Church in Britain
By Beckford, Robert
Copyright©2000 SPCK
ISBN 13: 978-1-61097-513-1
Publication date 6/1/2011
Previously published by SPCK, 2000

Contents

Introduction

We Know Where We're Going, 'Cause We Know Where We're From: Diaspora, Politics and the Black Church

The establishment of the Black Christian Civic Forum, UK is a response by Black Christians to the need for the Black-Majority churches in Britain to get more involved in politics and to speak clearly and prophetically on social and racial justice issues.

Black Christian Civic Forum promotional flyer

This book is concerned with developing a political theology for the Black Church in Britain and finding a viable context for its development and expression. The birth of the Black Christian Civic Forum in the Winter of 1998 reveals a 'wind of change' among second and third generation Black Christians: they are willing to get their political hands dirty. This emerging political voice requires a critical theological support. This text, therefore, is also a challenge to the emerging Black Christian body politic. In short, it offers a theological resource for a Black British political theology. In this introduction, I want to outline some central terms, ideas and methods.

DEFINITION OF TERMS

Before I can begin to address my central themes it is important to define key terms. All definitions of the Black Church emerge from particular situations and tend to be biased. Think of how self-definitions of Black people have changed since the 1950s! Also definitions are not easy because no one definition can fully encompass the complexity of what is being described. For example, not all churches or Black people are the same, so no one definition can capture the Black Church or Blackness – the concepts and experiences associated with being Black. Here, I want to define three concepts: 'African Caribbean', 'Black' and 'Black Church'.

'African Caribbean' and 'Black'

This study is primarily but not exclusively concerned with African Caribbean people in Britain. In this case, 'African Caribbean' refers to a specific experience of post-war migrants from the Caribbean. The people of the Caribbean are heterogeneous – not all the same. Therefore, here African Caribbean refers primarily but not exclusively to the descendants of African slaves, the largest ethnic group in the Caribbean. However, African Caribbean people are often referred to as 'Black people' in the British context. The concept 'Black' is a complex ethnic-political description. On the one hand it is a synonym for dark-skinned people, that is, Africans, African Caribbean and Asians. On the other hand, it can encompass those who are not White or those engaging in resistance to domination or what I call here counter-hegemonic resistance.[1] For example, Black nationalist philosophy in the 1960s in Britain was a movement dominated by African Caribbeans and Asians but it also incorporated a few Whites.[2] The concepts of 'African Caribbean' and 'Black' have implications for describing church identities.

'African Caribbean Christianity'

First, while this study is concerned with the broader Black experience in church life, it focuses on African Caribbean Christian experience in particular. African Caribbean Christianity is one tributary that flows into the co-mingled Black Christian experience in Britain. 'African Caribbean Christianity' refers to the particular Christian heritage and experience of Caribbean people in Britain. As I will show later in this chapter, African Caribbean Christianity is a religious system which emerges from the fusion between African religious traditions and European Christianity in the Caribbean. However, it includes African Caribbean Christians beyond denominational boundaries.[3] In most churches with large numbers of Black people in the congregation, elements of African Caribbean Christianity will be evident. After all, much but not all of Black Pentecostalism in Britain would be considered generic worship and theology in parts of the Caribbean.

'Black Church'

In this study, churches where the leadership and members of the congregation are predominantly African or African Caribbean are described as 'Black churches'. This term incorporates the multifarious mix of 'Black' people gathered from Africa, the Caribbean and Asia and even the presence of a minority White membership.

In terms of theological content, the term 'Black Church' refers to a particular theological and cultural orientation. Here, the Black Church is understood as having characteristics similar but not identical to African Caribbean Christianity. A church is considered a Black Church because it exhibits a style of worship and liturgy consistent with African Caribbean Christianity as outlined below and within the body of this study.

The term 'Black Church', therefore, applies to churches within any denomination and not just to Black Pentecostal churches; it can be applied to specific churches within traditional English denominations such as the Methodist, Anglican or Baptist.

'Black Pentecostals'

Black Pentecostal churches are churches with distinctive Black Pentecostal *roots* (origins) and *routes* (developments) that will be outlined later. For now it is necessary merely to say that Pentecostalism is a movement consisting of many denominations. The common feature of all Black Pentecostal churches in Britain is the baptism in the Spirit.[4] At my Pentecostal church in Handsworth, Birmingham, this aspect of our faith is central. As a youth I learned during many discussions with other Black Christians on the top of buses going home from school that baptism in the Spirit was a central distinguishing mark. Black Pentecostals had a vocabulary that other Christians did not have. We talked about 'sanctification', 'speaking in tongues' and 'baptism in the Spirit'. Later, in Chapter 5, I will explore some of the theological and functional commonalties among Black Pentecostals. But for now, I want to outline some of the differences.

While a plethora of minor issues separate numerous churches, arguably the central doctrinal distinction among Black Pentecostals is that which separates 'three-stage' and 'two-stage' churches. Put simply, 'three-stage' Pentecostalism recognizes three stages in the process of salvation. These are justification by faith, sanctification and baptism in the Holy Ghost. Three-stage Black Pentecostals in Britain include the two largest Black-led churches: The Church of God of Prophecy and the New Testament Church of God.[5] 'Two-stage' Pentecostalism believes sanctification and justification happen at the same time, followed by baptism in the Holy Ghost. Two-stage Pentecostals are predominantly White in Britain.[6] However, Oneness

Black Pentecostalism advocates the same understanding of sanctification as the two-stage camp from which many Oneness traditions have
their origins. What makes Oneness different is the use of the 'simple
formula' during water baptism (Acts 2.38). However, the use of this
formula developed into an understanding of the Godhead and a focus
for establishing difference between Oneness Christians and all others.[7]
This theological standpoint is often described technically as a mod-
alistic trinity.[8] However, in Black Pentecostalism the Spirit is understood more as a force or power rather than part of a Trinitarian system.
Consequently, many Oneness adherents would argue that those not
baptized in Jesus' name and filled with the Spirit, evidenced in speaking
in tongues, are not considered to have a full understanding or
experience of salvation.[9]

This study focuses primarily upon Black Pentecostal churches. This is
because in my opinion Black Pentecostalism offers the best focus for
developing a political theology. Black Pentecostals represent the largest
group of African Caribbean Christians and Black Pentecostals have
been the most effective African Caribbean Christian tradition in Britain
to date.[10] But there is another side of the defining process that must be
considered.

As Stuart Hall has shown, identity formation is always 'constructed
through difference'.[11] Therefore it is necessary to say something about
two terms which stand in tension and relation to 'Black' and 'African
Caribbean Christianity'. These are the terms 'White' and 'English
Christianity'.

The term 'White', like 'Black', has an ethnic-political resonance
associated with Caucasian British identity and experience. This term
may apply to indigenous English people or to European or Euro-
American people who have settled in Britain. Hence 'White' is concerned with a particular historical experience of Caucasians. 'English
Christianity' refers to the distinctive, historic churches in England.
'English Christianity' is a fluid term. This is because White people do
not dominate all English churches of the historic traditions. There are
Black churches which are Anglican, Methodist and Baptist and therefore
sit between African Caribbean and English Christian experience.

HALLMARKS OF THE BLACK CHURCH

At this point it is necessary to define some of the broad theological hallmarks of the Black Church. I learned from my earliest

undergraduate days that while traditional European ecclesiology (theology of the Church) has been deeply influenced by the Reformation,[12] it has rarely been concerned with theological thought within Black history and Black experience. Therefore, as a Black Christian and Black theologian searching from resources from within Black people's experience and culture, I want to find a contextual way of defining our ecclesiology. I would like to define the Black Church in a way that enables us to explore dimensions of its life and ministry that are theological and sociological.

Theological Hallmarks

I want to describe the Black Church as a 'shelter' or 'rescue', a place of radical transformation, driven by the Spirit and a family.

The earliest pioneers of the Black Church in Britain viewed themselves as establishing centres that would rescue the 'lost' West Indian and hopefully, indigenous population as well. The Hebrew word for 'rescue' (*yasa*) means 'saving' or 'salvation'. Hence, the Black Church here is understood fundamentally as a centre concerned with salvation/rescue. Roswith Gerloff suggests that the theme of rescue and shelter was manifest in names given to churches in the Black community in Britain.[13] The idea of shelter means that the Black Church should also express a concern for what happens outside the Church in Black communities as well as being concerned with the 'saved' inside the Church. Later, I will show that there is a tension between those who feel that that the Church should look inward and those who believe it should look outward.

Second, the Black Church is understood as a community concerned with radical transformation. The Black Church in Britain from its outset preached (*kerygma*) about human renewal. This is its message to the world. This is why 'fire and brimstone' themes of repentance are still a major topic in Black churches. At the heart of the Black Church is a desire to transform and empower. Radical personal transformation, then, is what the Church is about and what it is called to do (*diakonia*) in the world. As a Black theologian, I am concerned with the broader and more complex way of describing radical transformation as liberation.[14] As we shall see later, particularly with the illustrations from two London churches, Ruach and Mile End, critical issues include 'who is being transformed' (rescue) and 'for what purposes' (the nature of salvation). The latter concerns the relevance of the Church – whether its transformative work enables full emancipation or mere 'survival'.

Third, the Black Church must also be characterized as a centre driven by the Spirit. This third-person ecclesiology emphasizes the birth of the Church with the outpouring of the Spirit at Pentecost (Acts 2). Communion with the Holy Spirit forms a major part of the worship traditions of the Black Church – worship is subject to the 'moving' of the Spirit. The constant use of terms such as 'getting the Spirit', 'sensitivity to the Spirit' and 'the filling of the Spirit' all bear witness to the centrality of the Spirit. The Spirit renews, directs and inspires the Church. However, a critical issue concerns the focus of the theology of the Spirit or pneumatology. As James Cone has argued in the African American context, the pneumatology of the Black Church cannot be simply geared towards keeping the status quo. This is especially important in contemporary Britain where racialized subordination and White supremacist ideology are still prevalent. In opposition, pneumatology must be concerned with radical holistic change.[15] What I am suggesting here is that talk of the Spirit cannot be divorced from social change, critical analysis or tough decisions in the quest for racial justice. Therefore I will later suggest that in order to be responsive to the holistic impulse of the Spirit, the Black Church must take seriously political theology in the form of a 'dread' theology of the Holy Spirit.

Finally, the Black Church in Britain can be understood as a family. There are several layers of understanding. First, many of the Black churches were established by groups of families for the sake of fellowship and support (*koinonia*). That is, kinship networks were used to recruit new members. On another level, the Black Church is also family-oriented in that it has always preached values that sustain and nurture families. As Deotis Roberts has shown in the African American context, the family orientation has been an enduring feature of the Black Church in the northern hemisphere.[16] Also the Black Church is a family in the sense that each member is considered a brother or sister upon becoming a Christian. All have the potential to join the family or household of God, although profession of catholicity does not always result in a multi-cultural church or culture in the Black Church. The Black Church is a family in the sense that all those that enter the Church as members are called to serve as one body. The Black Church is also the 'body of Christ'.

Some Sociological Hallmarks of the Black Church

However, anyone who has been a member of a Black church knows well that church life is also a social space and church service a social event. Consequently, as well as the theological hallmarks of the Church, I would like to add another angle. I would like to suggest that we view the Church as an *association* or social network. This is because alongside the theological understanding of the Church, there are also sociological understandings, which are important for this analysis. This idea can be deduced from descriptions of the Christians in scripture. For example Matthew 18.20 describes a social relationship of 'two or three gathered together' as constituting a sacred space. Association can also be used to describe networks of people who interact for particular moral, social or political reasons. If we view the Church as an association how might we describe its mission? In order to answer this question, I turn to the sociological studies of social movements by Manuel Castells.

Manuel Castells argues that associations can be viewed as new patterns of political action and organizations that develop out of the decline of old industrial orders in overdeveloped urban situations.[17] He refers to these new movements as Urban Social Movements (USM). USM in many cases have become the new opponents of the prevailing social order. For example, the growth of Black protest groups concerned with education, housing or prison reform away from mainstream politics are examples of the rise of USM. The Black Church is to some degree an USM. This is because the Black Church, by offering an alternative lifestyle, provides a critique of the status quo. However, it is not a strong critique because it is not explicit.

If the Black Pentecostal Church is seen in a weak form as a post-war, post-industrial USM, then we are able to better assess its utility as a social, political and cultural force. However, it would be unfair and inaccurate to see the Black Pentecostal Church as primarily a simply socio-political creature without a moral and spiritual centre. Therefore, I want to explore briefly its religious character, to provide more insight into the Black Church as an USM.

The American sociologist Herbert Bulmer provides a useful conceptual framework for exploring how religion provides the motivation for USMs. Bulmer outlines a process that makes room for the force of ideas, motives and experiences. He distinguishes between three sorts of social movements; general, specific and expressive.[18] Expressive movements, while not always being concerned with directly challenging the social order, release expression and create meaning systems that change the lives of individuals and groups and thereby affect the social order.

Despite the inability of Castells and Bulmer to acknowledge Black experience within their intellectual frameworks, we can still make critical use of some of their ideas. Hence, here I want to view the Black Church as an expressive social movement; this allows us to address its theology (worship, song and preaching) as systems of meaning that have the power to effect change in the world, that is they have 'material force'. Hence, while recognizing the distinctive ecclesiology of the Black Church, I also see the Black Church as an expressive Urban Social Movement.

THE IMPORTANCE OF DIASPORA FOR A BLACK POLITICAL THEOLOGY

The Exodus event in the Old Testament is a defining feature of Israel's identity and Israel's understanding of God as well as being central to Israel's social development.[19] It is no surprise that Black and other liberation theologies have tended to focus heavily upon the theme of Exodus because of its theological and socio-political underpinnings for action against oppression of marginalized peoples today, and in particular, divine sanction of socio-political liberation within the context of oppression.[20] While the concept of Exodus has some resonance for African Caribbean people in Britain, because of the centrality of our history of migration, I want to suggest that the concept of diaspora is more significant.

For Israel, diaspora becomes vitally significant during and after the Exile. As many Hebrew scholars have shown, issues of cultural borrowing, religious purity, historical roots and memory become central themes of the diasporan community in exile: such relationships are central to diaspora. Similarly, issues of cultural syncretism, 'ethnic' purity and history are also important themes in contemporary Black British life. Diaspora is also political.

In *The Postcolonial Bible*, several scholars demonstrate that exilic/ post-exilic Old Testament texts do not negate concern for freedom or justice.[21] Justice and liberation were important themes in the exilic and post-exilic Israel. This means that focusing on the diaspora as a trope or unifying principle for the Black Church does not negate the need for justice and transformation in the present.

Rather than focusing on the Exodus, as has been the case in many liberation theologies, in this study the theological significance of diaspora will influence the starting point of a Black political theology in Britain. That is to say, we must begin by understanding that African Caribbean Christianity in Britain is part of a diasporan experience.

There are numerous biblical points of challenge on which the Black Church could be confronted with the question, 'Why should African Caribbean Christians from the Black Church be concerned with explicit political articulation and engagement?' I want to start with compelling contextual reasons that have theological importance. This is because theological thought is shaped and influenced by the social context.[22]

In the rest of this chapter I want to show how as part of the African Caribbean diaspora and in response to the efficacy of contemporary Black mobilization, a Black political theology is necessary. The strength of my argument can be tested through two themes: diaspora and mobilization.

Diaspora

The Black settlers arriving in post-war Britain from the West Indies were also conduits of an African Caribbean Christianity. African Caribbean Christianity is a part of and related to diasporan experience. Therefore, a Black Church serious about its contexts must take seriously the issues that emerge from the experience of this diaspora.

It is difficult to define diaspora, and any formulation must be open to change and adaptation. Bearing this in mind, a useful starting point is with definitions by William Safran.[23] He defines diasporas as expatriate minority communities

- that are dispersed from any original centre to at least two peripheral places;
- that maintain a memory, vision or myth about their original homeland;
- that believe they are not – and perhaps cannot be – fully accepted by their host country;
- that see the ancestral home as a place of eventual return, when the time is right;
- that are committed to the maintenance or restoration of this homeland; and
- whose consciousness and solidarity as a group are importantly defined by this continuing relationship with the homeland.

Here, I want to suggest that the African Caribbean diaspora in Britain can be analysed through Safran's six criteria, more closely identifying with the first three criteria and less so with the last three. Through an analysis of Safran's criteria, I shall aim to demonstrate theological-political concerns of the African Caribbean diasporan experience.

Dispersal from any Original Centre

What is of concern here is the historical fissures (fractures) that shape African Caribbean migration. The presence of the African Caribbean diaspora in Britain is a product of British colonial history; put simply, we are here because they were there!

Caribbean labour was repeatedly exploited by British capital, a development that begins in the context of slavery.[24] Three centuries of colonial rule in the Caribbean left the emancipated islands in 1834 bearing the psychological and social disfigurement of colonial exploitation. As Dilip Hiro shows, the English-ruled islands were generally left in economic ruin, facing the dual scourges of underdevelopment and overpopulation. Hence, a migration or 'push' became necessary. Commenting on Jamaican migration, Dilip Hiro states:

> By the 1860s migration had become a part of the island's life. Jamaicans went to Panama to build railways and then to assist in survey work and construction of the Canal. At one time or another 68,000 Jamaicans participated in these projects. Jamaican labour was engaged to boost sugar-cane production in Cuba after the United States had dislodged Spain as the imperial power in 1898. Later, Jamaicans were recruited to develop coffee and banana plantations in Honduras and Costa Rica, and Venezuela tapped this source of labour for its oil exploration ... But despite these temporary and permanent migrations ... the Jamaican population leapt ... The pressure to migrate kept rising.[25]

However, these 'push' factors should be tempered by the fact that despite the huge economic pressures for migration, wherever possible West Indians stayed at home.[26] As well as the 'push' of migration, the dispersal of West Indians was also influenced by 'pull' factors. Reasons for the pull towards Britain were varied. First, migration to Britain became more acceptable after 1954, when the US government restricted Caribbean migration to a trickle.[27] The second pull was the labour shortage in Britain. The post-war industrial labour force was understaffed. Although White European labour was preferred, Black labourers were able to enter as commonwealth citizens.[28] It was not long before many large corporations and State-owned industries recruited heavily in the Caribbean to meet the post-war labour shortage.[29] The third pull was the intimate colonial link between Britain and the West Indies. As a colonial force in the region Britain had cultivated a mythical image of a 'mother country' protecting and serving her colonies. It is now well-documented that many West Indians, as loyal colonial citizens, viewed migration as a sort of 'homecoming'.[30]

Regarding the place of the Black Church within this dispersal, African Caribbean Christianity was part of the cultural heritage that West Indian migrants brought to Britain. Numerous historical waves of missionary activity shaped this Christian tradition before its replanting in England. These waves of activity are the African slave religious heritage, eighteenth-century European missionary activity and twentieth-century Pentecostal mission from North America to the Caribbean.

The first wave of activity begins with the arrival of Africans as slaves to the New World. As Barry Chevannes demonstrates,[31] Caribbean religion is dramatically affected by the religious traditions which enslaved Africans brought with them. Despite the variety of tribal and religious backgrounds, African religions carried distinctive theological hallmarks[32] some of which, Albert Raboteau suggests, retained some influence as African slaves encountered Christian religion and society in the Caribbean and Americas.[33] Despite many African Caribbean Christians being unaware of the fact, or unwilling to accept it, African traditional religion formed an interpretative framework for the slaves' reception and decoding of Christianity.[34] This leads to another issue: the missionary activity of European Christians in the West Indies.

The West Indies experienced three key invasions by Christian missionaries that provided theological material for religious syncretism between African religious retentions and European Christianity.[35] Taking Jamaica as an example, the Society for the Propagation of the Gospel (SPG) initially taught rudimentary Christian doctrine to slaves in the Caribbean from 1701. Some debate has taken place about how effective these initial missionary endeavours were.[36] The second invasion grew out of the evangelical revival in Europe and the Great Awakening in North America in the mid-eighteenth century. These revivals resulted in a renewed and sustained missionary effort from Europe (Methodists, Moravians) and North America. Of particular importance during this wave is the arrival of the Black Baptist in the form of George Liele, a freed slave from North America (1783). The work of Liele and Moses Baker led to the development of a distinctive Black Caribbean Christian Protestant tradition.

The third invasion of missionary activity occurred in the early part of the twentieth century, when both Black and White Pentecostal denominations from America began to evangelize and establish churches in the so-called West Indies.[37] As I will demonstrate later, Iain MacRobert, Roswith Gerloff and Valentina Alexander have all shown how African Caribbean Christianity with distinctively African roots, for a variety of social and religious reasons that will be discussed in full later, flourished among working-class West Indians after the Second World War.

In short, missionary activity left the Caribbean a highly religious populace, part of a transnational network of Christian experience theologically related to both European and American Christian religion. In addition, Caribbean Christianity retained a distinctive African theological and anthropological core. Even today, Black Christian worship in Britain has a liturgical genealogy which goes back to the heart of African traditional religion, symbolizing what Kortright Davis entitles the 'African soul' within the Caribbean religion.[38]

Issues of dispersal, fissure and faith transportation have theological implications. As Roswith Gerloff states, it is the transnational movement and organization that defines the African Caribbean Christian tradition.[39] Therefore faith shaped by historical fissures requires serious analysis, as the example of African American church history has shown.[40] Of particular importance is the excavation of ideas, theologies and experiences that arise from the transnational movement of Black people. As Black feminists have shown, excavating Black history also nurtures the re-emergence of hidden knowledge or what one feminist calls the 'insurrection of subjugated knowledge'.[41] Similarly, such a process also identifies powerful ideals about freedom and liberation. Hence, Black church leaders today searching for resources for a Black political theology could mine this history in order to discover what Cornel West calls pre-hegemonic or residual critical perspectives that exist unconsciously within African Caribbean Christian cultures.[42]

Therefore, to understand what it means to be 'Church' in the service of God in a African Caribbean diasporan situation, the Black Church must examine and explore the theological-political significance of its history of migration. To fail to do so is to deny the theological importance of what God has done within our experience of migration.

Maintaining a Memory

When talking about memory, I am concerned with history. One of the areas rarely explored by Black church leaders is the issue of African Caribbean Christian history. The neglect is partly due to ignorance. As a consequence, some wonderful and beautiful things are overlooked. In response, this study is primarily concerned with second- and third-generation African Caribbean Christians. The reworking and restoration of 'memory' of the African and Caribbean past is of great importance.

Here I am concerned with deep persistent memories or psychohistory of African Caribbean Christians. This memory is a process shaped by profound historical connections mentioned in the previous section, namely, how cultural mixing or syncretism enabled cultural memories and historical references from Africa to survive in slave and colonial societies in the Caribbean.[43]

What I want to suggest is that the experience of post-war migration to Britain from the Caribbean has not totally erased the memory of Africa. Scholarly opinion for some time has described a tension between African and European traditions in Black (North) Atlantic cultures. W. E. B. DuBois described the African/European tension as a struggle between two souls, in *The Souls of Black Folk*. In recent years, building upon DuBois' analysis, Paul Gilroy has called this struggle the 'inner dialectics of diaspora identification'.[44] Gilroy's analysis is important because he provides an understanding of memory as a 'flow, exchange and in-between'[45] suggesting that memory cannot be fixed or static, but is always subject to change and transition – hence Gilroy's use of Iain Chambers' notion of 'roots' and 'routes' as a means of understanding the transportation of memory.[46] In short, the journeys (routes) as well as its African beginnings (roots) have shaped contemporary African Caribbean Christianity in Britain. This idea will be explored more fully later in this study.

There are differing views on the strength of African cultural retention among African Caribbeans in Britain who are now twice removed from Africa. On the one hand, Kobena Mercer *argues* for a view of diaspora where identity, culture and consciousness cannot privilege African origin or centrality.[47] This position is known as the anti-essentialist position. Anti-essentialists argue against any notion of a Black essence that unifies all Black people or cultures. On the other hand, James Clifford has demonstrated that it is possible to hold in tension historical rupture (journey) and African memory (origin). This process he calls 'changing same'.[48] This position is often referred to as the anti anti-essentialist position.

In this study, I side with Clifford – displacement has not totally stripped the African Caribbean diaspora of its distinctive sense of community or culture. However, I take seriously Mercer's concern that we recognize the influence of local and global networks which work on, challenge and transform Black cultures and views of the past (historical memory) so that Black culture is on a journey. That is, 'memory' is reshaped by experiences of migration, displacement and adaptation.[49]

The issue of 'memory' has implications for the theology of the Black Church, namely, how and in what form have African religious traditions been retained in African Caribbean Christianity? As we shall see later, studies of the Black Church suggest that African traditions live on in muted forms. Another issue for the Black Church to consider is that theological memory has political significance. Memory is an important asset in Black Nationalist thought. For example, both Marcus Garvey and Malcolm X argued that the 'whitewashing' of Black religious memory was part of White hegemony (domination) over Blacks in slavery and colonialism.[50] In response to the challenge of Garvey and X, Black theologians in America have attempted to unearth religio-political concerns from the theological memory of the Black Church in America.[51] It would naturally follow that African Caribbean Christianity contains similar traditions. This is not a new idea. For example, outside theological circles, Horace Campbell demonstrates that one dimension of Jamaican Christianity is its politically active past.[52]

Second, because 'memory' is informed and reworked by diasporan networks, the Black Church as a Black North Atlantic institution must take seriously the dialogue between African American and African Caribbean Church networks. Again this is not a new idea: as I have demonstrated in *Jesus is Dread*, worship in Black churches in Britain is influenced by numerous African American inflections (influences).[53] However, what is new, is that so far the Black Church in Britain has failed to have serious dialogue with the Black political experiences of African American Christianity. What I am suggesting is that it is dangerous for the Black Church in Britain to borrow uncritically music, worship traditions and styles from America without investigating their socio-political context.

Never Accepted by Their Hosts
My father never 'left' Jamaica despite being in England for over 30 years. I once ventured to ask him why he had made such little effort to settle in England. He responded by saying that it was not that he had made no effort, but that he realized that England would never accept him as a Black man. Here I am concerned with adaptation, in particular the ways in which Black people have adjusted to not being fully accepted in their host country. The experience of discrimination has been documented in numerous texts that explore the history of race relations in Britain. In quantitative terms this study has been dominated by a vast array of sociological studies. A central theme remains Black responses to racism:

What has been central to the experience of Black people in Britain has been neither the 'idea' nor the 'politics' of 'race' as the 'idea' or the politics of 'racial difference'. Rather, it has been racism and other forms of oppression. It is racism that has determined the manner in which their 'communities' have been policed; it is racism, which assaults their humanity in psychiatric hospitals; and it is the effects of racism too, that have been internalised. In short, it is racism against which the struggle has to be fought.[54]

Two recent studies illustrate the continued struggle against racism in Britain. However, these studies outline what might be termed utopia/ dystopia tensions. That is to say, Black people have used a variety of means to thrive and some have been more successful than others. For example, a recent study published in 1998 identified the success of Black women in the world of employment. This study showed that Black professional women were higher earners than their White counterparts and Black men. One implication is that Black women were doing well academically and therefore economically in Britain. In contrast Dr Tony Sewell's analysis of Black male academic struggle in English schools, *Black Masculinities and Schooling: How Black Boys Survive Modern Schooling*, identified the alternative picture of Black male educational struggle and limited life opportunities.[55]

Another recent study commissioned by 'Operation Black Vote' (August, 1998) revealed that despite a high degree of political awareness, African Caribbean people were less optimistic about the future of race relations in Britain and less likely to participate in party politics through voting.[56] One implication of this study is that Black people are still uncertain about their position and opportunities in Britain.

Racialized oppression and Black response has also played a role in the emergence of African Caribbean churches in Britain. For example, Anita Jackson's discussion with Black pastors in the 1980s revealed a history of rejection by White churches of the first Black settlers from the West Indies.[57] This rejection led many to start their own churches as early as 1952. However, this is not the full picture. In contrast, another school of thought puts forward a religio-cultural argument for the formation of Black churches in Britain; it suggests that Black Christianity was socially, culturally and theologically qualitatively different from English Christianty.[58] Therefore, it was inevitable that Black people would form their own churches once in England. However, I would like to add to this second school.

I want to suggest that the traditions of resistance or pre-hegemonic cultures of resistance were present within the African Caribbean

Christianity that emerged in Britain. The Black Christian 'difference' found among first-generation West Indians was in part the product of a long history of resistance to European domination. What I am suggesting is that Black churches contained cultures of resistance and celebration that would inevitably lead to conflict with the post-colonial English Christianity found in post-war Britain. Therefore the racism and culture arguments are in some ways related: both racism and resistance to racism forged in the context of racial subordination in the Caribbean were catalysts for the emergence of African Caribbean churches in Britain.

However, the lives of Black people have not been totally inhibited by racialized oppression. That is to say, utopia/dystopia tensions are present in African Caribbean diasporan cultures. Black people in Britain have struggled to carve out existences that dispute, disrupt and overturn racist ideologies. As Les Back so clearly shows in *New Ethnicities and Urban Culture*, Black people have mobilized cultural forms to criticize capitalism and create alternative spheres for developing consciousness.[59] Moreover, Claire Alexander has brilliantly demonstrated in *The Art of Being Black* the ways in which Black cultural identities are switched and manipulated to ensure Black advancement.[60] In short, a dynamic and varied representation of Black cultures has been one way in which Black people have represented ourselves as varied and complex and thereby contested racist representations of Blackness.

Similarly, the Black Church has also engaged in cultural resistance. For example, Nicole Rodriguez Toulis suggests that the Black Church has provided a space for the development of Black identities that challenge and subvert negative racialized images of Black people.[61] However, cultural resistance in the Black Church transcends Black members; the Black Church has always maintained a universal mission. Hence, one of the second-generation African Caribbean pastors who was interviewed as part of this research identified the importance of empowering all who attended his Pentecostal church in south London:

> One of my aims is to build a multi-cultural church but I do not apologize for reaching my [Black] people . . . We are in a White country and we have a lot of Black people who have some needs . . . If I as a Black person and leader I don't address and show some interest who will do that . . .?[62]

Issues of adaptation have implications for the contemporary Black Church, namely, the nature of its resistance. As I will discuss under the heading of 'mobilization', there is a strong view of the Black Church as politically passive and in need of an explicit political engagement. If this is the case, then it becomes difficult, for the Black Church to claim to be 'full gospel' or holistic without considering Black politics within the context of diaspora.

As mentioned above, definitions have to be flexible and open to change. Hence I suggest that in response to Safran's six points, the second set of three criteria is less relevant to the African Caribbean diaspora in Britain.

The Ancestral Home as a Place of Eventual Return

It is important to redefine what is now meant by 'return'. A documentary in 1997 on Channel 4 explored the idea of return among second- and third-generation Black British. While no statistical evidence was provided, the producer of the programme, Claire Hines, stated that 'for most Black British the notion of returning home is not a reality. England is home, but we are part of a wider network.' Similarly, in an interview for this study, Davey Johnson, minister of the Mile End New Testament Church of God, says: 'While we can't deny our roots ... most of us are saying that we are here to stay.'[63]

The ancestral homeland is not necessarily a place of return for the vast majority of Black people in Britain. Even so, the documentary revealed that, among second-generation immigrants, return to Africa or the Caribbean was a limited option for those with financial resources or professional aspirations that are more likely to be realized outside the UK.

Restoring the Homeland

For the majority of African Caribbean people, Safron's fifth point is best understood as a psychological, cultural and political statement of identification. One of the legacies I have from my Jamaican parents is the political and psychological connection to the Caribbean I feel as a second-generation Black British person. Hence for me 'maintenance' and 'restoration' may mean supporting the West Indies cricket team, supporting the Jamaican soccer team, or retaining an interest in the politics and needs of the homeland. As mentioned above, as part of a global network, the African Caribbean diaspora in Britain is in constant dialogue with the 'homelands' so that maintenance is often a form of cultural exchange. The Black Church has maintained links with the homeland through its theology.

Group Solidarity

As mentioned above, a diasporan network between continental and diasporan Black subjects continues to inform the African Caribbean diaspora in Britain. Paul Gilroy has identified the dialogic nature of Black life in Britain through his analysis of music.[64] Elsewhere, I have shown that the same might be said for Black British gospel as this tradition also internalizes styles and forms from the same Black North Atlantic networks.[65] Therefore, subconsciously the Black Church is renewed and reformed by its significant position on the diasporan network. As I have noted above, this position necessitates dialogue beyond the superficiality of borrowing simply styles, genres and fashions.

In conclusion, African Caribbean Christianity in Britain is part of a wider diasporan experience and network. It must therefore take seriously the historical fissures, memories and adjustments that have influenced its emergence. Without careful analysis its theology runs the risk of two limitations. These are historical amnesia – forgetting where we have come from, and political naïvety – being unsure of what we must do.

Mobilization

I remember reading the autobiography of Malcolm X in the third year of secondary school. I was 14 at the time and the book 'blew me away'. Here was the life of someone who was able to combine religious commitment, political struggle and Black liberation. In other words, the contextual concerns of the Black community were a resource for theological reflection. As mentioned in the previous section, as part of the African Caribbean diaspora in Britain, African Caribbean Christians who are concerned with addressing contextual issues (that is, issues that emerge from Black life in Britain) are compelled to take diasporan concerns seriously. One issue identified above in the discussion of racism was 'adaptation'. In order to adapt and make sense of the new situation in Britain, African Caribbean people have had to organize themselves. This process of organization I will call *mobilization*.

Mobilization is a model or paradigm. It is the holistic psychosocial relationship between internal and external human action. Internal mobilization deals with the psyche, the raising of consciousness. For the diaspora, this has been traditionally viewed as the process of 'mental' or 'intellectual decolonization'. Fans of reggae music will be well aware of a vast canon on this subject! In its external manifestation, mobilization is opposing oppressive social structures that operate both inside and outside Black communities through individual and/or group activity.

The concern here is to place the Black Church within the rubric of Black mobilization in Britain, so that through a process of comparison and contrast we can identify its political character. In order to do this, first it is necessary briefly to outline aspects of Black mobilization. I want to focus on the historical specificity and the diverse nature of Black mobilization.

We have been struggling against racialized oppression since we arrived in large numbers after the war. But it is important to recognize that Black mobilization is historically specific. This means that mobilization is likely to differ within each historical period. This does not mean that prior developments are less important than new ones, but they play a limited role as new forms of mobilization occur. Harry Goulbourne's thesis is that Black mobilization is concurrent with the social history of Black immigration. In other words, the type of mobilization present corresponds with experience in Britain: 'West Indian organizations and modes of participation in British politics generally correspond: entry/expectation, settlement/frustration, consolidation/engagement/participation within mainstream political institutions.'[66]

Goulbourne suggests that entry/expectation was characterized by the mobilization of welfare/cultural groups. Historical studies by Ron Ramdin and Dilip Hiro identify a plethora of cultural/welfare organizations that emerged in the late 1940s and early 1950s to assist the migrants' initial concerns.[67] The second phase of settlement/frustration is characterized by the emergence of 'broker' organizations such as the West Indian Standing Conference (WISC) and the Commission for Racial Equality (CRE). These organizations were established to deal with structural changes that needed to take place in order to accommodate and negotiate a better deal for West Indian immigrants.

The third phase, consolidation/engagement/participation, is characterized by the emergence of political organizations and associations that articulate the interests of Black people. These groups were concerned with identity politics and political rights during the late 1960s and mid-1970s. For example, those of us who had some of our teenage years in the 1970s will remember the emergence and proliferation of Black Nationalist groups and anti-racist organizations, marking the beginning of an explicit second-generation Black political engagement and mobilization in Britain. These groups were concerned with developing a sense of belonging. In many cases the emergence of political organizations also facilitated the emergence of 'organic intellectuals', that is, an educated Black elite concerned with articulating the struggles of Black people. As shown above, I see this new politics as operating outside the mainstream, concurrent with the USM.

One implication of viewing mobilization as historically specific is that it provides a framework for analysing the growth and development of the Black Church in Britain. Hence, the Black Church as an USM cannot be excluded from political analysis. Neither can Black Christians view themselves as not having any political 'value' within the Black mobilization continuum.

On my British birth certificate, I am defined as a 'Jamaican boy'. In my junior school reports, I am described as 'West Indian' and in my secondary school reports, 'Afro-Caribbean'. As an undergraduate I called myself, 'Black British'. These changes in description suggest that within each phase of mobilization identity formation is reworked. Stuart Hall articulates this view suggesting that the phases of Black political mobilization also contain overlapping expressions of a changing Black identity. Once more, new forms of identity do not dismiss prior ideas, but they become the backdrop against which new ideas can be worked out. In the first phase, roughly the first twenty years of migration, the Black person was perceived as a West Indian. Settlement was characterized by hostile reception and the emergence of a more militant outlook in the late 1960s. In the second phase (1970s) West Indians became an ethnic minority, among other minorities. The 1970s and 80s witnessed the emergence of a Black identity concerned with political and cultural resistance. In this new phase, Black identity or 'new ethnicity' is understood as being grounded in neither nature nor citizenship, but in sense of belonging and commonality of experience.[68] Here, Black identities are viewed as a construction and heterogeneous.

Hall's analysis has several implications for exploring the Black Church. It suggests that the Church can be understood as an arena in which 'new ethnicity' is worked out as new generations determine what it means to belong, based on new presuppositions about being Black. It also means that the cultural politics of the Black Church must be scrutinized as part of an ongoing struggle of being Black and British.

Regarding the third phase of mobilization, characterized by political activity, it is necessary to say more about its diverse nature.

Because Black identities are plural, it follows that Black political mobilization will also express a range of views. Because Black mobilization is diverse, there are numerous options available for the Black Church. In the African American context, Cornel West has identified four political traditions in contemporary African American communities.[69] In contrast, in the Black British context, Leyton-Henry and Studlar articulate five overlapping models of Black political engagement.[70] I will summarize their main arguments below.

First, Leyton-Henry and Studlar suggest that Black people will gradually integrate into the class structure of British politics. Second, and in contrast to the first possibility, Black people withdraw from the political process and form *nationalist* alliances based on race because of prejudice and hostility; they remain a constant force in society leading to significantly high levels of discrimination because of their withdrawal. A third possibility is that Blacks will be connected to the political order through organizations based outside their respective communities. This 'broker' approach has a history in Black Britain, as the State or other organizations have played a leading role in governing race relations through the establishment of broker organizations such as the Commission for Racial Equality (CRE). Fourth, it is possible that Blacks will withdraw from the political process due to growing disenchantment and alienation. Many Black organizations have been criticized for doing this, especially by social scientists in the 1970s.[71] Finally, the fifth and most likely possibility is that Blacks will choose a variety of relationships with the political process. That is, individuals and groups will adopt a variety of strategies to maximize their influence. Here, the general idea appears to be that resistance is fashioned to suit prevailing aspirations. Consequently, a spontaneous and varied resistance is most likely.[72]

Where do we place the Black Church within this analysis? There are two schools of thought on this matter. Some White social scientists and a few Black cultural critics suggest that the Black Church has 'withdrawn' from the 'hustle and bustle' of Black political mobilization in Britain. This school argues that apart from a few isolated incidents there has been no meaningful mobilization. However, as will be shown later, this school fails to consider the *internal* or *survival* traditions of the Black Church. According to the second school of thought, the Black Church is more willing to be engaged in State-run or 'broker' organizations. This is because its conservative theology nurtures a respect for governments and social order and seeks ways to empower its members. For example, many Black Christians and Black churches have been willing to participate in lower tiers of government and State apparatus.[73] In this sense, the Church as an USM maximizes resources (housing, jobs and grants) for its adherents.[74]

However, here I would like to suggest a third way of conceiving the mobilization of the Black Church that is not represented in the analysis above. I want to construct a theology for the Black Church based on diasporan sensibilities and concerns and the concrete political realities of Black mobilization.

Such a third way must begin with explicit engagement in the political arenas of life, this is one of the central concerns of a political theology. Such a task requires an alliance between theory and practice. That is to say, theology must be developed in commitment to the concrete concerns of the wider community. In this case a Black British theology must address the problems of the Black worlds and Black identities, particularly issues of marginality, struggle, diversity and overcoming.[75]

The theological underpinnings for a political theology are varied. However, two scholars provide us with central ideas. First, within the European theological academe, Jürgen Moltmann has done much to develop political theology. For Moltmann, a view of the future hope in God as a present reality (historical eschatology) is a central model.[76] Because Jesus overcomes, Christians today must also be a part of God's plan for holistic change in the world. Second, Jon Sobrino, writing from the Latin American context, has shown that the cross and resurrection as symbols of freedom are integral to an understanding of Jesus. Here Jesus is the one who brings about total freedom in the world.[77] Christians must do likewise – work for social, political and spiritual freedom. All of these are part of the plan of God in the world.

Political theology has its critics. Arthur McGovern has identified as a central methodological flaw the danger of theology becoming ideology – that is, forcing Christian theology into a particular ideological position or perspective.[78] In defence, Alistair Kee, while cognizant of McGovern's concerns, suggests that political theology is unavoidable because of the nature of the gospel message:

Christianity begins with a man on his way to the cross. The cross was not an altar for divine sacrifice, but the prescribed instrument by which the Romans tortured to death those who would not submit to them and who encouraged men to put their ultimate loyalties elsewhere. If Christianity is about incarnation the question is not whether political theology is still theology, but whether anything that is *without* political significance deserves the name 'theology'.[79]

From this statement I want to argue that all theologies are 'political', embodying an implicit or explicit relationship to the political order. This fact is often ignored in British theological establishments, where many still believe their theological perspectives are neutral and objective. However, Black people have learned that claims of objectivity and neutrality are just another way of maintaining the power-base of White scholarship. This is because with no recognition of bias, oppression or racism, there is no need for revolutionary change.

Therefore, the critical issue for the Black Church and a Black political theology is not about *becoming* political, but being honest about where political loyalties lie. To discuss Black political theology further, I want to engage in a Black Atlantic exchange by turning to the Black North Atlantic experience of African Americans.

In Black North Atlantic cultures, the clearest articulation of 'Christian' political theology has emerged in African American Black liberation theologies. Black theology in the USA originates from the civil rights struggle in the 1960s. As James Cone told an audience in Birmingham, England, Black theology was a product of the dialectic between the theology of Martin Luther King and the Black power philosophies of Malcolm X.[80] After two decades of development, according to George Cummings, Black liberation theology in the USA, in its modern form focuses on religio-cultural and socio-political liberation.[81]

Religio-cultural perspective is concerned with the relationships between Black religion and American culture; its religio-cultural political agenda is concerned with the problem of racialized oppression that occurs in theology. Euro-American hegemony in many aspects of intellectual and cultural life meant that Black theologians in academe were trained in dominant White systems of thought. However, the social and political turmoil of the 1960s demanded that Black theologians discover what the gospel of Jesus had to say to the Black condition.

While all Black theologians have not arrived at the same conclusions, or adopted similar approaches, *a postiori* religio-cultural analysis postulated that it was necessary to make an epistemological break with White Euro-American theologies and opt for the theological sources found within African American religious traditions.[82] As George Cummings has shown, this process resulted in a break with White theological interpretations of Jesus Christ, the Church, eschatology and liberation.[83]

On a smaller scale, a similar argument has been articulated within the Black British context. In their 1992 publication, *A Time to Act*, Raj Patel and Paul Grant adopt a theological approach that emerges from the contexts of Black life rather than the dictates of the White theological academe.[84] However, Grant and Patel failed to discover a Black theological method.

The socio-political agenda within Black political theology in America is premised upon the theological belief of God's presence among the marginalized. Rejecting Karl Barth's warning against identifying God's activity in the world with particular political and ideological concerns, Black theologians set about constructing a theological system based on Black concerns. Initially, their theology focused on the need for Black civil rights and on responding to the emergence of Black nationalist movements. Today, political theology is concerned with greater multi-dimensionality – exploring and challenging all that inhibits human life.[85]

The Black theological political agenda has its critics. Initially, both Black Nationalists and Black clergy in America found fault with explicit political expression and the Church's identification with Black power.[86] Some Black Nationalists believed that all theology was too 'White' to make a valid contribution to the Black struggle. Also many Black clergy still thought, despite the life setting of struggle, that it was not the place of theology to fight political battles.

Second, Black religionists questioned the theological paradigms at work in Black theology. For example, William R. Jones' classic text, *Is God a White Racist?* (1973), posed questions that have not been fully addressed today.[87] Jones asked whether the idea of a God of liberation is consistent with Black experience of suffering. If God is a liberator why do Blacks still suffer? As Jones could see no evidence of divine liberation on behalf of Blacks, he sought an alternative starting point in order to eradicate what he termed 'divine racism'.[88]

Third, from the viewpoint of South African Black theology, Black political theology (USA) lacked the class analysis found in Latin American liberation theologies.[89] Itumeleng Mosala argues that without a class analysis of their contexts, Black theologians whether in the USA or elsewhere run the risk of indirectly supporting dominant systems of thought.[90]

So what then can be learned from the African American experience? There are two issues. First, Black political theology for the British context must address the doubters in the Black Church, especially those who refuse to acknowledge the importance of 'race' and subscribe to a 'colour blind God'. Second, a Black political theology must be multi-dimensional, exploring issues of race, class and gender as interlocking

systems of oppression. Multi-dimensionality will assist in the development of a holistic theology – that is, a theology concerned with every
aspect of life. This is of major importance for a Black political theology
in Britain. The example of the Black Christian Civic Forum provides a
useful example. A newspaper stated:

> The recently launched Black Christian Civic Forum which aims to champion
> political justice issues concerning the Black community, has appointed its
> executive body. Members comprise chairman Dr. Friday Nwator, general
> secretary Abraham Lawrence and Geoffrey Brandt as treasurer. Davey
> Johnson and Ron Nathen serve as executive members. David Muir the
> founder of the BCCF, will be executive director.[91]

The lack of female representation within the first executive of the Black
Christian Civic Forum suggests that despite the organization's desire for
political equality, it has failed to recognize the importance of gender
equality as integral to the Black political struggle.

Finally, the African American experience teaches us that political
theology must address the most pressing needs in Black communities;
it cannot avoid the struggles of everyday Black people in search of
esoteric or ivory-tower recognition. In other words, such a theology
must emerge from and be owned by Black communities.

Towards A Black Political Theology in Britain

We Black British are not a homogeneous group. Therefore it is
impossible to find a singular understanding of what it means to be
Black and British. However, here I want to define Black British as
incorporating numerous influences from Black Atlantic cultures in
America, the Caribbean and Europe. Ted Polhemus has demonstrated
how Black identities in Britain exhibit such a synthesis.[92] American,
Caribbean and British theological, social, political and cultural forces
past and present are woven together in Black British political theology.
Just as with Black British musical forms such as 'Acid Jazz', 'Jungle' or
'Drum and Bass', this 'Black British' study 'cuts and mixes' resources
from other Black contexts and frames them in accordance with issues,
themes and concerns from Black life in Britain. Such a process is an
integral part of being Black and British in the latter part of the twentieth
century.[93] It is the location of the researcher and study within the social
and political geography of Britain that ultimately makes this study
British.

Previous studies have given muted expression to the desire for a Black political theology for the Black Church. Studies of African Caribbean Christianity have shown briefly the lack of politics within the Black Church. These studies fall into two types. First there are academic studies. The majority of these studies are concerned with recording and analysing oral accounts or histories so as to document beliefs and practices of Black churches. Studies by Malcolm Calley (1965), Roswith Gerloff (1992), Nicole Rodriguez Toulis (1997) and Iain MacRobert (1989) are examples of this first type. Because these 'empirical' studies are primarily descriptive, they lack the prescriptive critical acumen necessary by transforming the contexts they analyse. In contrast, a second cluster of critical writings is concerned with prescribing alternative pathways for African Caribbean Christianity. The critical writings of Elaine Foster (1988), the eclectic studies by Raj Patel and Paul Grant (1990, 1992) and my own religio-cultural analysis *Jesus is Dread* (1998) all critically interrogate African Caribbean church life in order to offer alternative theologizing. However, this second group of studies lacks the analytical depth of the first group and their ability to challenge the status quo is restricted. Therefore a third process is necessary which should draw from the analytical weight of the first group and the prescriptive or prophetic acumen of the second group. This is the task of this study. It is now necessary to outline a methodological framework.

This body of research is theoretical. It is concerned with explaining findings within a conceptual framework. The research undertaken collects data from secondary sources. In other words, it is a processing of existing research. In addition, in order to 'ground' central theoretical ideas, illustrative material gathered from primary sources will be introduced. The researcher is both a participant in and an observer of African Caribbean churches.[94]

Illustrative material is used in a minor but significant way in order to provide 'real life' British verification of the mainly Black Atlantic theoretical construct that appears within this study. According to Glaser and Strauss, researchers should seek to link theory with real life in order to achieve a 'grounded' theory.[95] Hence, this study uses illustrative material from the Black Church experience in order to explore and test the strength of the theories. As Bulmer has argued, such an approach enables a 'mutual interdependence' between theory and research.[96] In this case it is the relationship between intellectual ideas and the worship experience of Black church life.

The use of illustrative material also fulfils another purpose. Mutual interdependence provides potential for change within the social situation. For example, Jürgen Habermas suggests that relating theory to real life provides a context for political action. Such 'critical-emancipatory' approaches ensure that issues of domination, coercion and oppression are identified in the quest for understanding.[97] There are some general and specific areas that constitute a grand conceptual framework.

This study gives special weight to Black Atlantic ideas and resources, in response to the ideological and cultural bias of traditional Western theology in Britain.[98] This contextual approach legitimates the use of intellectual resources from the Black Atlantic traditions to provide an opportunity for hidden or 'subjugated' knowledge to arise.

In contrast to some Germanic schools of theology, I understand all theology as emerging from particular socio-political situations, and therefore subject to bias.[99] I do not believe that theology is neutral or objective. Such myths in White Christianity in Britain have acted as smoke screens which maintain White male elitism. How else is it possible to live in a multi-cultural society yet ignore the 'Other' once one enters academic institutions and theological departments? Could it be that unwitting, institutionalized racism is also at work within England's theological colleges and universities? My experience demands a response in the affirmative!

In terms of research methodology, this point encourages a critical interrogation of theological ideas, concepts and terms, including my own biases. I am a male, African Caribbean Pentecostal, and my values must be subjected to scrutiny. One way of doing this is to include personal pronouns within the body of research in order to identify the researcher within the group being studied as well as placing the personal experience of the researcher within the text.[100] Also, where possible, I shall seek a better understanding by comparing theological systems which develop in different contexts.[101]

I draw critically from Cone's definition of theology that relates theological inquiry to context and justice: 'Christian theology is a theology of liberation. It is a rational study of the being of God in the world in light of the existential situation of an oppressed community, relating the forces of liberation to the essence of the gospel, which is Jesus Christ.'[102] This definition makes theological inquiry inseparable from a commitment to 'liberation'. By liberation, I mean complete emancipation from all forces that deny full existence or being. It also views theology as contextual and ideological – it is related to the particular interests of a group. Theology cannot be seen as neutral but

28   *Dread and Pentecostal*

is always partisan. Furthermore, Cone's methodology prioritizes experience so that Black existential concerns engage in dialogue with what is defined as the gospel of Jesus Christ. What I am suggesting here is that theology, like Habermas' notion of critical theory, is at its best when constantly brought back to real life concerns.

Overview

This study is concerned with developing or moving towards a political theology and finding a home for it in the Black Church.

In Chapter 1 I will analyse five major studies of the Black Church in Britain, and will show how Black churches articulate political resistance and what sort of political theology emerges from these studies.

Chapter 2 begins the first of two historical sections. It traces the antecedents of White racism. In response Chapter 3 explores the antecedents of African Caribbean resistance. I suggest that it contains resources for a political theology. By outlining the antecedents of racism and resistance to racism, this chapter aims to identify how Black people have responded to racialized oppression. This chapter is concerned with retrieval and memory. Of particular importance is the role of religion within the antecedents of Black resistance. Chapter 4 attempts to derive specific methodological tools from Chapter 3.

After these historical and analytical sections, the next two chapters focus on theological development. In order to apply the methodological framework developed in the previous chapter, Chapter 5 outlines a 'dread' Pentecostalism; it seeks to give theological content to the framework provided in the previous chapter. Chapter 6 builds a theological system. This system is a political theology based on 'dread' Pentecostalism. Particular reference is made to Christology (study of the Christ of faith). I have chosen Christology because of the importance and centrality of Christology in Black churches and also in the studies of Black churches.

I conclude by exploring where a Black political theology can develop and challenge injustice in Britain.

Notes

1. Hiro, D. *Black British, White British: A History of Race Relations in Britain.* London: Paladin, 1991, p. viii.

2. Ramdin, R. *The Making of the Black Working-Class in Britain.* London: Gower, 1987, p. 483.

3. Wilkinson, J. *The Church in Black and White.* Edinburgh: Saint Andrew Press, 1993, pp. 101ff.

4. See Hollenweger, W. *The Pentecostals.* Minneapolis: Augsburg Publishing House, 1972.

5. See MacRobert, I. *Black Pentecostalism, its Origins, Functions and Theology.* PhD thesis, University of Birmingham, 1989, p. 288.

6. Ibid., p. 291.

7. Gerloff, R. *A Plea for British Black Theologies: the Black Church Movement in Britain in its Transatlantic cultural and Theological Interaction.* Vol. 1. Frankfurt: Peter Lang, 1992. The Oneness or Apostolic tradition, emerged out of the 'new issue' controversy within the early Pentecostal movement in the USA.

8. MacRobert, I. op. cit, p. 295.

9. Ibid., pp. 292–4.

10. Beckford, R. *Jesus is Dread: Black Theology and Black Culture in Britain.* London: DLT, 1998, p. 7.

11. Hall, S. and Du Gay, P. (eds), *Questions of Cultural Identity.* London: Sage, 1996, p. 5.

12. McGrath, A.E. *Christian Theology: An Introduction.* Oxford: Blackwell Publishers, 1999, pp. 461–90.

13. Gerloff, R. op. cit., pp. 221–6.

14. See Evans, J.J. *We have been Believers: An African American Systematic Theology.* Minneapolis: Fortress Press, 1992, p. 135.

15. Cone, J. *Black Theology and Black Power.* San Francisco: Harper & Row, 1989, pp. 56–61.

16. Roberts, J.D. *A Black Political Theology.* Philadelphia: Westminster Press, 1974, p. 177.

17. See Castells, M. *The City and the Grass Roots.* London: Edward Arnold, 1983.

18. Bulmer, H. 'Social Movements'. In: Lyman, S.M. *Social Movements: Critiques, Concepts and Case-Studies.* London: Macmillan Press, 1995, pp. 76–9.

19. Weems, R. In: Gottwald, N.K. and Horsley, R.A. (eds). *The Bible and Liberation: Political and Social Hermeneutics.* New York: Orbis, 1992, p. 42.

20. For example, Cone, J. *God of the Oppressed.* San Francisco: Harper Collins, 1975.

21. Sugirtharajah, R.S. *The Postcolonial Bible.* Sheffield: Sheffield Academic Press, 1998.

22. Cone, J. op. cit., pp. 39–45.
23. Safran, W. 'Diasporas in Modern Societies: Myths of Homeland and Return.' *Diaspora*, 1991, 1 (1), pp. 83–99.
24. The European capital exploitation of the Caribbean begins with its discovery by Christopher Columbus in the fifteenth century. The tropical environment of the region was exquisite for agricultural development. However, such development required a large, cheap, adaptable workforce. The inefficacy of indentured Europeans and indigenous Indians made African labour desirable – Africans being better suited to the climate. Hence, tens of thousands of enslaved Africans became the economic fuel for the agricultural economic development of the region.
25. Hiro, D. op. cit., p. 14.
26. In short, migration was only a prospect in islands where there was limited opportunity to secure work. Hence, Trinidad, a traditional importer of labour from surrounding islands, did not experience uniform migration as happened in pre- and post-war Jamaica and Barbados. In the islands, once job opportunities arose in the tourist industries (bauxite in Jamaica and oil in Trinidad) the desire to leave diminished, particularly amongst the middle and upper classes that were able to benefit more readily from the economic development.
27. Hiro, D. op. cit., p. 15.
28. Solomos, R. *Race and Racism in Britain.* 2nd ed. London: Macmillan, 1993, pp. 56–7.
29. For example, the National Health Service and London Transport made serious efforts to attract Black labour from the Caribbean.
30. Hiro, D. op. cit., pp. 19ff.
31. Chevannes, B. *Rastafari: Roots and Ideology.* New York: Syracuse University Press, 1994, p. ix.
32. See Mbiti, J. *Introduction to African Religion.* 2nd edn. Oxford: Heinemann International Literature and Textbooks, 1991.
33. Raboteau, A.J. *Slave Religion: The Invisible Institution in the Antebellum South.* Oxford: Oxford University Press, 1978, p. 8.
34. See Hood, R.E. *Must God Remain Greek? Afro Cultures and God-Talk.* Minneapolis: Fortress Press, 1990.
35. Wilkinson, J. op. cit., pp. 69ff.
36. Some scholars claim that these churchmen and women were primarily concerned with appeasing the religious needs of the ruling elite or 'plantocracy'. See John Wilkinson, op. cit.
37. Wedenoja, W. 'Modernization and the Pentecostal Movement in

Jamaica.' In: Glazier, S.D. (ed.). *Perspectives on Pentecostalism*. Washington, DC: University Press of America, 1980, p. 30.

38. Kortright, D. *Emancipation still Commin: Explorations in Caribbean Emancipatory Theology*. Maryknoll, NY: Orbis, 1990, pp. 50–67.

39. Gerloff, R. op. cit., p. 57.

40. Gayraud Wilmore and Vincent Harding and womanists Emilie Townes and Katie Canon reveal that Black church history is a necessary resource for the theology of the Black Church. See Wilmore, G. *Black Religion and Black Radicalism: An Interpretation of the Religious History of African Americans*. Maryknoll: Orbis, 1988; Harding, V. *There is a River: The Black Struggle for Freedom in America*. San Diego; New York; London: Harcourt Brace Jovanovich, 1981; Canon, K. *Black Womanist Ethics*. Atlanta, Georgia: Scholars Press, 1988; Townes, E.M. *Womanist Justice, Womanist Hope*. Atlanta, Georgia: Scholars Press, 1993.

41. Collins, P.H. *Black Feminist Thought: Knowledge, Consciousness and the Politics of Empowerment*. London: Routledge, 1990, pp. 67–90.

42. West, C. *Prophesy Deliverance: An Afro-American Revolutionary Christianity*. Philadelphia: Westminster Press, 1982, pp. 188–221.

43. Burton, R.E. *Afro-Creole: Power, Opposition and Play in the Caribbean*. Ithaca and London: Cornell University Press, 1997, pp. 4–5.

44. Gilroy, P. *Black Atlantic: Modernity and Double Consciousness*. London: Verso, 1993, p. 23.

45. Ibid. p. 190.

46. Gilroy, P. 'It's a Family Affair.' In: Dent, G. (ed.). *Black Popular Culture*. Seattle: Bay Press, 1992, p. 303.

47. Mercer, K. *Welcome to the Jungle: New Positions in Black Cultural Studies*. London: Routledge, 1994, p. 63.

48. The notion of 'changing same' is the hermeneutical focus for defining 'tradition' among the African Caribbean. See Clifford, J. *Routes: Travel and Translation in the Late Twentieth Century*. Cambridge, Mass.: Harvard University Press, 1997, pp. 267–8.

49. Mercer, K. op. cit., pp. 63ff.

50. See Karenga, M. *Introduction to Black Studies*. 2nd edn. Los Angeles, California: University of Sankore Press, 1993.

51. For examples of the use of memory, see Cone, J. *The Spiritual and the Blues*. New York: Orbis, 1970.

52. Campbell, H. *Rasta and Resistance: From Marcus Garvey to Walter Rodney*. London: Hansib Publications, 1985, p. 26.
53. Beckford, R. op. cit., pp. 136–42.
54. James, W. and Harris, C. *Inside Babylon: The Caribbean Diaspora in Britain*. London: Verso, 1993, p. 3.
55. Sewell, T. *Black Masculinities and Schooling: How Black Boys Survive Modern Schooling*. London: Trentham Books, 1997, pp. ix–xvii.
56. Operation Black Vote. 'Ethnic Minorities and the British Electoral System.' www.Charter88.org.uk/democratic/obv/docs/anwar.
57. Jackson, A. *Catching Both Sides of the Wind: Conversations with Five Black Pastors*. London: British Council of Churches, 1985, pp. ix–xxi.
58. MacRobert, I. op. cit.
59. Back, L. *New Ethnicities and Urban Culture: Racisms and Multiculture in Young Lives*. London: UCL Press, 1996, p.184.
60. Alexander, C. *The Art of Being Black*. Oxford: Oxford University Press, 1996.
61. Toulis, N.R. *Believing Identity: Pentecostalism and the Mediation of Jamaican Ethnicity and Gender in England*. Oxford; New York: Berg, 1997.
62. Francis, J. Interview with author, 6 March 1998.
63. Johnson, D. Interview with author, 6 March 1998.
64. Gilroy, P. *There Ain't No Black in the Union Jack*. London: Unwin Hyman, 1987, pp. 153ff.
65. Beckford, R. op. cit., pp. 136ff.
66. Goulbourne, H. (ed.) *Black Politics in Britain*. Aldershot: Abeury, 1992, p. 87.
67. Ramdin, R. op. cit., pp. 371ff. Also Hiro, D. op. cit., pp. 37ff.
68. Hall, S. 'The New Ethnicities.' In: Donald, J. and Rattansi, A. (eds). *Race, Culture and Difference*. London: Sage, 1992, p. 254.
69. West, C. op. cit., ch. 3.
70. Leyton-Henry, Z. and Studlar, L. *Black Mobilization in Britain*. University of Warwick, 1983.
71. Rex, J. and Tomlinson, S. *Colonial Immigrants in a British City*. London: Routledge and Kegan Paul, 1979, pp. 244–5.
72. See Leyton-Henry, Z. and Studlar, L. op. cit.
73. See Milwood, R. *Liberation and Mission: A Black Experience*. London: African Caribbean Educational Resource Centre, 1997.
74. For a fuller discussion, see Castells, M. *The City and the Grassroots*. London: Edward Arnold, 1983.

75. Forrester, D. *Theology and Politics.* Oxford: Blackwell, 1988, pp. 60–3.
76. Moltmann, J. *Religion, Revolution and the Future.* New York: Charles Scribner's Sons, 1969, p. 66.
77. Sobrino, J. *Jesus the Liberator: A Historical-Theological Reading of Jesus of Nazareth.* Kent: Burns and Oates, 1991, pp. 233–54.
78. McGovern, A. *Liberation Theology and its Critics: Towards an Assessment.* New York: Orbis, 1994, pp. 160–4.
79. Kee, A. (ed.), *A Reader in Political Theology.* London: SCM Press, 1974, Preface.
80. Cone, J. *Malcolm, Martin and Theology.* Lecture at Queens College, Birmingham, May 1996.
81. Cummings, G. *A Common Journey: Black Theology (USA) and Latin American Liberation Theology.* New York: Orbis, 1993. p. 38.
82. See, for example, Cone, J. *A Black Theology of Liberation.* New York: Orbis, 1986.
83. Cummings, G. op. cit., p. 39.
84. Patel, R. and Grant, P. (eds). *A Time to Act.* Nottingham: Russell Press, 1992, p. 1.
85. See Douglas, K.B. *The Black Christ.* New York: Orbis, 1994.
86. Cone, J. *My Soul Looks Back.* New York: Orbis, 1991, pp. 54ff.
87. Hopkins, D. *Black Theology USA and South Africa.* New York: Orbis, 1990, pp. 52ff.
88. Jones, W.R. *Is God a White Racist?* Boston: Beacon Books, 1998, pp. viii–xvi.
89. Cummings, G. op. cit., pp. 62ff.
90. Mosala, I. *Biblical Hermeneutics and Black Theology in South Africa.* Grand Rapids, Michigan: William B. Eerdmans, 1989, p. 21.
91. *The Voice* newspaper, 15 February 1999.
92. Polhemus, T. *Street Style.* London: Thames and Hudson, 1994.
93. See Gilroy, P. *The Black Atlantic: Modernity and Double Consciousness.* London: Verso, 1994, pp. 2–3.
94. See Gold, R. 'Roles in Sociological Field Observation.' In: McCall, G. and Simmons, J. (eds). *Issues in Participant Observation: A Text and Reader.* London: Addison Wesley, 1969.
95. See Glaser, B. and Strauss, A. *The Discovery of Grounded Theory.* Chicago: Aldine, 1967.
96. Bulmer, M. 'The Role of Theory in Applied Social Science Research.' In: Bulmer, M. *et al. Social Science Social Policy.* London: George Allen and Unwin, 1986, p. 208.

97. See Habermas, J. *Knowledge and Human Interests*. Cambridge: Polity Press, 1989.
98. Bevans, S. *Models of Contextual Theology*. New York: Orbis, 1992, p. 5.
99. See Cone, J. *God of the Oppressed*. New York: Orbis, 1975, pp. 39–45.
100. Fraser, N. *Unruly Practices: Power, Discourse and Gender in Contemporary Social Theology*. Cambridge: Polity Press, 1989, p. 113.
101. Baker-Fletcher, K. and Baker-Fletcher, G.K. *My Brother My Sister: Womanism and Xodus God-Talk*. New York: Orbis, 1997, p. 16.
102. Cone, J. *A Black Theology of Liberation*, p. 1.

1 Ragamuffins and Respectables

Contemporary Black Churches and Political Mobilization

I was 'born' in church. My earliest memories of my family are from church. In the early 1970s the Black church was a centre of my community in Northamptonshire. My family, like many others, had reproduced and reconfigured church life from the Caribbean in Britain. This was because a large percentage of the so-called West Indian migrants who arrived in Britain between 1948 and 1965 were church-goers. Church attendance in the Caribbean formed an integral part of communal living and in some places as many as 98 per cent of all West Indians attended church. The arrival of church-going West Indians in Britain raised a fundamental question: would these migrants be integrated into the English churches, many of which were established on the Caribbean Islands during slavery? As I have shown in the discussion of diaspora, the combination of 'back home' and 'new home' made integration within Britain's existing churches problematic for the majority of the pioneering West Indian generation.

The major concern of this chapter is a critical examination of aspects of the theology and practice of Black church life in Britain. Five major studies of the Black Church are examined, chosen because they are extensive studies that explore theology and practice.[1] I am concerned with the Black Church's engagement with the political world. To explore and clarify this I turn to the Latin American educationalist Paulo Freire.

MODELS OF CHURCH POLITICS

Although there are numerous frameworks for analysing the Black Church, I want to employ a specifically political model. Freire provides three models of church engagement with the political order. Although his focus is Latin America, his models are useful for the Black Church context in Britain.

His first model is that of the *traditional* church. These churches are characterized by a rejection of the world. Their reality is dualistic: the church is good, the world is bad. This is an enduring but only partly accurate view of the Black Church. Naturally, these churches are a haven for the masses – an opiate for the people.

The second model is the *modernizing* church. Unlike the traditional churches, these churches engage with the world, but are concerned with popular structural change and avoid radical social change. In short, they deal with social welfare but not social reform. As will be demonstrated below, the Black Church emphasizes welfare more than reform.[2]

Finally, the third model is the *prophetic* church. This model is a church that is radically committed to the struggles of the oppressed. In so doing, the prophetic churches pursue radical social transformation in order to achieve the necessary social change.[3] Naturally, as I am concerned with political theology, the prophetic church model is presented in this study as the ideal model for Black churches wishing to develop a political theology; they must embrace a holistic approach to theology that is concerned with prophetic change in every aspect of human life.

For each of the five studies of the Black Church described here, I will ask, first, how does it interpret the relationship between the Black Church and politics? Second, what sort of political theology (traditional, modernizing or prophetic) emerges from it? Then I will use two contemporary Black churches to illustrate and challenge some of the questions raised by these academic studies.

Major Studies of the African Caribbean Church in Britain

Malcolm Calley

In the 1960s many sociologists and anthropologists began to take their first serious look at the Black Church. Possibly influenced by the Civil Rights struggle in America, White analysts wondered whether there was a framework for Black social transformation germinating within England's shores. The most significant study was Malcolm Calley's *God's People: West Indian Pentecostal Sects in England* (1965). Writing from the perspective of a social anthropologist, he analysed the rise of

Pentecostal 'sects' in England.[4] First, I will survey his principal ideas, then I shall analyse his findings.

There are two themes within this book: that what he pejoratively calls 'sect' behaviour is a response to a hostile environment, and that the purpose of the 'sect' is to alleviate pressure, providing 'satisfaction'.

Regarding the first theme Calley states that all 'sect' worship is 'human response to prevailing environmental forces, albeit economic or social'.[5] Hence, 'sects' are related to the West Indian's inability to integrate into English society. But 'For a long time yet,' he says, 'there will be a large residue of migrants unable to adjust, and these will seek refuge in small, world-renouncing, uncompromising sects.'[6]

Calley has little time for the idea that prejudice of White church leaders in any way influences sect formation. He does not recognize racism as a major or significant factor in the formation of the Black Church, although he does acknowledge that there may be some prejudice among a few church members.[7] As I will demonstrate later, Gerloff, MacRobert, Alexander and Toulis challenge this view.

The second aspect of Calley's study concerns the concept of 'satisfaction'. In his final analysis the principal function of these sects is their ability to satisfy the individual. Calley places 'satisfaction' in Pentecostal sects within the historical context of West Indian Christian experience. He begins with two religious responses to oppression.

First, there is what he calls the 'religious-political' action. Here, social reform and Christian belief go hand in hand. He cites the philosophy of Marcus Garvey, Paul Bogel, Anthony Bedward and Ras Tafari as examples of this tradition but does not elaborate on their theological systems. Second, there is a rejectionist tradition that sees this world as irredeemable and wicked and therefore seeks habitual disengagement from the socio-political reality. Here 'magico-religious' solutions are sought to help people cope.[8] It is within this second tradition that Pentecostal sects are located. Describing this tradition, Calley states:

> Pentecostal sects (like many others) offer members a new set of values and a new self-respect. The meaningless drudgery of a life devoted to finding enough to eat becomes less in the service of God, or takes on a new significance as an apprenticeship for the hereafter. Members who lack ... are persuaded that such things are unimportant ... In their devotion to him [God] members make a virtue out of necessity, rejecting the values of the world which anyway they could not hope to achieve.[9]

For Calley, rejection of this world provides sect members with an opportunity to feel superior to it. This gives them a sense of 'satisfaction'. He does not see any embryonic relationship between the religious-political and the magico-religious traditions. Consequently he is unable to identify any positive strands within the former which may produce the latter. Later we will see that there is a complex interplay between these two traditions in African Caribbean history.

Calley's analysis leads to an understanding of Pentecostal 'sects' as something abnormal. Nowhere is this view more clearly seen than in the term 'sect' which, even within Ernst Troeltsch's framework, implies marginality and pathos. This view of Black religion has a long past and a durable present. As Dale Bisnauth has shown, White colonialists and their church leaders 'demonized' Black religious forms in the Caribbean among indigenous Indians and African slaves from the earliest times.[10]

This view is not exclusive to White research. In contemporary Britain the Black British 'dub' poet and political activist Linton Kwesi Johnson, writes of Black religious conversion as a retreat from adverse social conditions: 'w' en wi can't face reality, wi leggo wi clarity'.[11] In contrast, I would add that Calley, like many others even today, fails to assess accurately the inner or psychological liberation that Black church life offers in contexts of racial subordination. Moreover, I would contend that even satisfaction has limited value in a hostile climate that dehumanizes Black life.

As for the sort of political theology that emerges from this study, Calley's research suggests that the Black Church has no political praxis or vision except withdrawal, because its church–world dialectic regards the world as evil and without redemption. Such an apocalyptic vision shuns political involvement and produces limited socio-political awareness. In short, following my use of Freire's models, according to Calley, the Black Church is a *traditional* church.

Roswith Gerloff

By the beginning of the 1980s the Black Church had gained respect. As Black people began to claim full citizenship, and many cities erupted in response to State oppression and police brutality, the Black Church stood out as an alternative and sustaining mode of Black existence. It was clear that, like Black people, the Church was here to stay and that it provided resources for family and community development.

In response, analysts set out to prove that there was a form of liberation operative within the Black Church that was obscured by Calley's racist lenses. One such study was Roswith Gerloff's *A Plea for British Black Theologies: The Black Church Movement in Britain in its Transatlantic, Cultural and Theological Interaction* (1992). Although her text was published later than MacRobert's, Gerloff's research was conducted in the early 70s and 80s, so it reflects an earlier stage of analysis of Pentecostalism, particularly the Oneness tradition.[12] Here, again, I shall begin with a brief survey of the main arguments, after which I will evaluate the findings. Gerloff's study is vast and complex and cannot be covered in full in this study. I want to focus on what I consider to be her central theme.

In contrast to Calley, Gerloff is not shy in admitting the history of racism within the development of the Oneness tradition. Her historical analysis of the 'new issue' controversy that gave birth to the Oneness tradition in the early Pentecostal movement reveals how racist ideas underpinned the controversy:

> ... the racial components, if not more than equally significant as the theological factors in the controversy, as theology is always done in a particular context and as racial, cultural and socio-political questions can, or even must, take on board theological language and experience ... In other words, the 'new issue' brought to light a basically different approach to doing theology between Black and White – between those whose theology is a life language, not done outside a particular racial, cultural or socio-political context, and therefore, a possible means for racial redemption and those who theology is impoverished, a language of argument outside and above the harsh realities of a segregated society, and therefore a possible vehicle for self-promotion and oppression.[13]

Already one can note a rejection of the 'relative deprivation' and 'psychological maladjustment' theories of Malcolm Calley: Gerloff is willing to take seriously the complex historical, social and cultural forces that shape African Caribbean Christianity. In other words, she is moving from the idea of a *traditional* to that of a *modernizing* church. This movement is partly due to her reliance on the affirmation of Pentecostalism in the work of Luther Gerlack and Virginia Hine.[14]

Gerloff identifies a distinctive theological system that draws on elements retained from African roots. This is of vital significance for two reasons. First, it enables a broader historical analysis of the Black Church. Second, it provides an African–European Christian mix or syncretistic theology as a framework for analysis. These African elements are:

- *The experience of God.* This refers to an understanding of a living God involved in the affairs of Black people. God is therefore not a philosophical proposition but an experienced life-giving source. In the Black Church, faith is based on a living, breathing, walking, talking relationship with God. When Black Christians ask, 'Do you know Jesus?' we seek an experiential answer.
- *Narrativity of theology.* This in Black Christianity, the spoken word and voice is as important as the written text.[15]
- *The power of the Spirit.* This describes the interaction with the Spirit world – the ability to reckon with superhuman forces, and to be 'possessed by the Spirit'. In Black Christian communities this means taking seriously the power of the Spirit of God, the supreme spiritual force in the universe.[16] This experience is manifest in a variety of ways. 'Touching and falling, weeping and laughing, dancing and speaking in tongues thus become quite natural vehicles of understanding the world, not only with one's intellect but with one's whole self'.[17] I want to affirm this observation, because she makes a link between the power of the Spirit and the ability to transform both the individual and society. Later, I will try and demonstrate more clearly a political pneumatology.
- *Worship as empowerment.* Going to church is central to Black faith. Gerloff focuses upon the experience of worship as a communal, life-giving experience. She interprets the life and ministry of the Church as healing, both physical and social: 'It is an emotional as well as historical experience, integrating home and family, people and society, God and universe.'[18] The music, rhythm and dance are all ways in which the Spirit can descend.
- *Agents of healing.* The Black Oneness Church consists of communities of people concerned with redemption, renewal and transformation. The self-supportive, self-sufficient nature of these congregations makes them a powerful movement in Britain. Gerloff suggests that the African elements reveal an ability to mobilize people through training and decision-making, and provide an opportunity for expression. Such a theology is truly contextual as it is 'owned and lived out in factories, kitchens, buses, hospitals, restaurants or offices'.

There are limitations and problems in Gerloff's African-centred framework. While making connections with the African origins, she does not explore the complex nature of the syncretism which results from European influence. As I have demonstrated above in the study of diaspora, it is vitally important to focus on the origins or *root* and the journey or *route* of African Caribbean experience. How has the journey itself shaped the Black Church? Without exploring this, Gerloff runs the risk of describing the Black Church as essentially 'glued' to African retentions, when in reality its cultural-theological complex is constantly undergoing change and transformation.

Despite the limitations of Gerloff's work, and in dramatic contrast to the work of Calley, the Black Church movement cannot be branded as escapist or withdrawn, but is a 'socio-political answer to the conditions under which they emerge'.[19] It affirms self-respect and dignity 'as people discover themselves as being part of creation, as well as of the African diaspora', and thus enables 'a kind of Christian Black power' similar to the mobilization of Pan-Africanist and Black Nationalist groups.[20] At this point it becomes clear that Gerloff is engaging in some serious exaggeration. First, when we consider the political complexity and dynamism of Black liberation movements in America and South Africa as identified by Dwight Hopkins,[21] it is clear that Gerloff's Black Church Black power pales in significance. I would also suggest that Gerloff has focused on the inner or internal liberation, which is 'radical', but such a claim cannot be made of her description of the Black Church's limited external political articulation or protest.[22] She blames the lack of explicit politics on colonial history:

> Undoubtedly, this is due to the damaging effects of colonial history, especially the history of Christian fragmentation and 'otherworldliness' projected by the slave masters and certain streams of White Christianity. Clearly, it is also the consequence of the fact that for too long fundamentalist institutions, and not the critical academic schools, have opened their doors and resources to Black students.[23]

Unlike Calley, Gerloff does not represent the Black Church as 'magico-religious'. Neither does her analysis suggest that it is committed to 'religio-political' concerns. Instead, she charts a middle path that describes a movement providing cultural and religious resources to meet practical problems.

So how does Gerloff represent the relationship between the Church and politics? She suggests that the Apostolic (Oneness) tradition she observed responds *indirectly* to racism by providing each believer with a powerhouse experience that propels them to fulfil their potential as human beings. (Later we shall see that Valentina Alexander terms this indirect challenge 'passive resistance'.) However, while this evaluation was useful in describing the first generation of the Caribbean diaspora, she does not explore its usefulness for second- and third-generation Black Pentecostals in Britain. I would argue that Gerloff, as an outsider looking into the Church, fails to see the conflict and struggle over issues of identity and change and politics. Her African-centred analysis fails to identify contemporary political forces that challenge the Black Church's reworking of its African identity. For example, little space is provided in her study for the concurrent emergence of Black Nationalism, Rastafari and the Black women's movement alongside the history of the Black Apostolic tradition in Britain.

It is clear that the theology of the Church from Gerloff's perspective is deeply influenced by African religious ideas. However, she is keen to show that while racism, oppression and disadvantage have played a role, it is the cultural and theological forces that define, organize and propel this tradition. This means that the Black Church is a *modernizing* church, which strives for social welfare projects or 'healing' of the community but fails to address the underlying structural forces that shape the socio-political environment.

Iain MacRobert

The late 1980s marked the emergence of 'UK Black' in popular culture as a recognizable, articulate, self-defined Black British community. Likewise, the Black Church tradition also began to take seriously the need for thinking about its role and its theology in Britain. One study that captures this new mood is Iain MacRobert's *Black Pentecostalism: Its Origins, Functions and Theology* (1989). This is a historical study that takes more seriously than any previous study the diasporan journey of Black faith from Africa to the colonial contexts of the Caribbean, primarily Jamaica. I will begin by outlining the central arguments, and then judge it by my theological-political criteria.

MacRobert anchors Black Pentecostalism in Britain in the religious syncretism of the African diaspora in the Americas. He calls this the Black *leitmotif*. However, whereas Gerloff focuses upon the Oneness Pentecostal Church, MacRobert focuses upon the emergence of the Pentecostal Trinitarian movement. Particularly relevant to this study is MacRobert's work on the function and theology of Black Pentecostalism.

MacRobert subsumes a plethora of functions under the main heading of 'counter ideology'. Counter ideology is an alternative view of the world, which affirms Black life within the Church. It stems from the 'implicit ideology' of the Black Pentecostalism forged in worship:

> For Black Pentecostals the primacy of encounter and experience lies at the heart of the hermeneutical process. Once God has been pneumatically encountered and experienced in love and power within the worshipping community, faith and hope have a foundation upon which to rest ... the Spirit produces a new way of interpreting the world and a new perception of self and community.[24]

Black worship is part of a counter ideology. Worship affirms the equality, self-dignity and self-worth of African Caribbean people and is particularly relevant in Britain's racist society. This counter ideology assists in the construction of a new Black identity and self-image that challenges the negative stereotypes that reside both inside and outside Black communities. Self-critically, he goes on to argue that, given the multiple oppression of Black Pentecostals, the adherence by some to White American theology, the internalization of White images of Christ, and a theology that forbids explicit theological reflection on politics, the effects of this counter ideology will always be limited.[25] Furthermore, MacRobert provides a prognosis: for Black Pentecostals to develop an explicit political theology involves an admission that oppression is 'more than an eschatological sign of the end times' and therefore something to be bypassed.[26]

  The second significant area of analysis in MacRobert's study concerns the theology of Black Pentecostals. He argues that there is a huge discrepancy in Black Pentecostalism between the explicit and implicit, the stated and latent. These dichotomies he attributes to the Black leitmotif in Black Pentecostal theology. 'From the earliest days of slavery in the Americas there is evidence of a disjunction between outward profession and inner meaning'.[27] Therefore in order to get to 'real' Black Pentecostal theology, it is necessary to get to the substratum of implicit theology. This theology lies in what is said and done.[28] Like Gerloff, MacRobert believes that implicit theology relies upon a literal interpretation of the Bible. However, for MacRobert, 'the Black Pentecostals do not primarily have a hermeneutic of the Bible but an incarnation'.[29] Implicit theology is therefore experiential theology. This is 'a theology of doing; a theology of life and Spirit rather than one of the written word; a theology that grows out of encounter with the God of Moses and of Jesus'.[30]

  I would argue that there is an inherent danger within MacRobert's analysis of implicit theology. Such analysis can imply that the relationship between the rational and the experiential is dialectical (tension) rather than dialogical (relational). Without awareness of the dialogic, MacRobert's argument can be used to support the myth that Black Pentecostal theology is less intellectual by virtue of being more experiential.[31] This was one of Calley's assertions about Black worship. I suggest that implicit theology is partly a misreading; it does not take seriously the cognitive component in the history of the construction of Black Pentecostalism.

A pattern emerges in the work of Gerloff and MacRobert. According to MacRobert the theology of the African Caribbean plays a central role in empowering its adherents to cope with and make sense of life. Implicit theology, despite its potentially racist overtones, focuses on the inner person and his or her experience of God. Such a theology counters, with varying degrees of success, the forces of oppression in the social world. MacRobert, like Gerloff, sees implicit theology as limited in its ability to develop a political theology that analyses and confronts social injustice because of the multiple forms of White oppression that limit the prevalence and significance of the Black leitmotif. Therefore, a multi-dimensional analysis is necessary.

MacRobert's study shows that implicit theology cannot provide sufficient resource for a political theology. As with Gerloff, the Black Church is still a *modernizing* church unable to cope with explicit political analysis.

Valentina Alexander

Probably the most important text from my perspective is Valentina Alexander's study *'Breaking Every Fetter': To What Extent Has the Black Led Church in Britain Developed a Theology of Liberation?* (1997). As the first Black British, African Caribbean author to approach the subject of the Black Church, Alexander brings an insider's evalua-tion of Black church life and theology. Moreover, this unpublished thesis takes us a stage further than the work of Gerloff and MacRobert and attempts to address 'theological liberation and how it is both interpreted and utilised' by African Caribbean Christians in Britain.[32] Alexander is concerned with the Black Church as an institution of holistic transformation. Whereas Gerloff and MacRobert draw on the Black religious and cultural heritage as a means of explaining and defining the theology of the movement, Alexander's central evaluation is liberation theology. I shall begin with a brief survey of her central ideas, and then assess her study from the two concerns of this chapter.

There are two stages to Alexander's work. First, she constructs a measure or heuristic for evaluating the Church. Second, she engages in a critical examination of what she terms the 'Black Led Church' according to this framework or heuristic. The three most important issues she raises are found within her conclusions about the concepts of 'liberation', 'theology' and 'liberation theology'.

Regarding liberation, she opts for a holistic understanding where liberation is both internal and external:

> The internal is characterised by certain features nurtured by the structures of the Church which combine to provide a pragmatic and holistic spiritual identity for its members. The external refers to the way in which the Church has, through this spiritual identity, attempted to identify and respond to the social needs of its congregations and their communities through a range of self-help services.[33]

For the Black Church to be concerned with liberation, it must be concerned with every aspect of human life. This includes engagement with the socio-political world.

Regarding theology, she draws on the work of those, including James Cone, who suggest that theology is 'human speech about God'. This is a significant appropriation because it places the construction of theology within the sphere of human experience. That is, theology is a human development and therefore subject to critical inquiry.

Regarding 'liberation theology', Alexander defines a six-point measure for liberation theology:

1. Is it contextual theology?
2. Is it holistic theology – concerned with a range of oppression?
3. It must engage with social analysis.
4. It engages in critical reflection on liberating praxis – making sure that liberation is linked to a spiritual source.
5. It must be dialogical and ecumenical.
6. It must be practised at professional, pastoral and popular levels.[34]

Unlike Gerloff and MacRobert, she seeks to understand the Church in response to strict categories of liberation theology. This facilitates a more sophisticated analysis of the relationship between politics and the Black Pentecostal Church in Britain. However, her heuristic does not arise from the Black British context, but from a synthesis of African American and Latin American theological ideas. On the one hand, such an approach creates a broad alliance between marginalized people. On the other hand, she (and also I as a result of using Freire) fails to make space for a distinctive Black British theological framework for analysis which emerges from this specific context. As a consequence, some might suggest that her research could be considered a partial, non-Black Atlantic importation.

The next concern in Alexander's work is to measure the Black Church in response to her six measures of liberation theology. Four of these points are central to understanding her arguments. First, liberation theology as contextual theology. Here Alexander argues that a sense of community, identity, encouragement, personal development, direction/authority and incentive/hope are central products of contemporary Black Pentecostal churches' contextual theology.[35] Second, regarding her measure of liberation theology, as holistic theology, she identifies the numerous projects through which the Black Led Church has attempted to operate so as to counter oppression at every level. She makes it clear that the respondents to her questionnaires viewed oppression as both a spiritual and a structural force. However, as in the work of Gerloff and MacRobert, the predominant explanations were spiritual.[36]

In my opinion the most important aspect of her work concerns her third point, about 'social analysis as a facilitator of liberation theology'. There are two models of social analysis, *passive radicalism* and *active radicalism*. Regarding passive radicalism, like Gerloff and MacRobert, Alexander suggests that analysis within the Black Led Church (BLC) is implicit in so far as it offers a means of confronting the forces of oppression through liberation spirituality:

> The Church's engagement with social analysis is inextricably intertwined with its manifestation of liberational spirituality. This spirituality which has been understood as holistic and fundamentally connected to the social experiences and realities ... is the overriding medium through which, at pastoral and popular levels, the BLC interprets and analyses the social context of those believers. Liberational spirituality is, therefore, the key epistemological tool at these levels. The contextual development of the Church means that it has most often been, however, essentially an implicit tool enabling believers to identify, challenge and overcome the various levels of their ideological and material oppression without necessarily seeking out its socio-historical source and without making an explicit theological alignment with that liberational process. To the extent that this manifestation of social analysis within the BLC would seem to represent yet another paradox, it has been identified in this study as *passive radicalism*.[37]

Like Gerloff and MacRobert, she recognizes that implicit theology is internally liberational, but lacks the historical criticism that would facilitate a structural analysis of context.[38]

Finally, her fourth point, 'critical reflection in liberation praxis as a facilitator of liberation', explores the failure of the Black Led Church to articulate the holistic liberation that she calls 'active radicalism'. Active radicalism makes explicit experiential and cognitive liberation spirituality by seeking to:

> ... broaden the scope of social analysis, providing it with a multi-dimensional insight into social transformation and allowing for the possibility of an historico-analytical element to be added to its method of interpreting the social world ... it is now able to more effectively undermine the oppressive hegemonic practices of society which in its latent state it could only attempt to *cope with* and *survive* under. Believers are able to recognise therefore that liberation must address structures of oppression as well as provide personal empowerment for individual advancement.[39]

Furthermore she provides an outline for this process:

> It begins with the personal conviction that the individual is made in the image of God and therefore of worth and value. It continues through the exploration of Biblical hermeneutics in which believers are able to understand that God is 'no respecter of person'. It then comes to fruition with a conscious theological understanding of God's alignment with the struggles of the oppressed and the conviction, therefore, that the Church has both a divine calling and a social responsibility to speak out against oppression in the Church and in society.[40]

I would suggest that Alexander's analysis of passive and active radicalism is the most important intellectual construct in the socio-political analysis of the Black Church in Britain. Passive radicalism is consistent with the framework of the *reforming* church, outlined in brief above. Alexander also provides us with a model of the *prophetic* church namely, active radicalism. However, she is unable to provide a theological system consistent with active radicalism and therefore only suggests a socio-political perspective for the Black Church. Any meaningful Black British political theology must take active radicalism seriously but provide it with a holistic theology to replace the vague liberational spirituality Alexander describes.

As was the case with Gerloff and MacRobert, Alexander sees a partial form of liberation operating within African Caribbean Christianity. She suggests that the Black Church is characterized by a passive radicalism: it is a *reforming* church.

Nicole Rodriguez Toulis

Despite Alexander pushing the analysis of the Black Church in a new direction, the old ideas about Blackness as survival and passivity remain. Nowhere are these themes more evident than in my last review *Believing Identity: Pentecostalism and the Mediation of Jamaican Ethnicity and Gender in England* by Nicole Rodriguez Toulis (1997). Toulis' central thesis is that the Black Church is a social space in which Black identities are constructed and reconstructed so as to counter negative racialized images. Drawing on insights from cultural studies, she argues that the Black Church enabled first-generation African Caribbean people in general, and women in particular, to make sense of identity in a complete cultural environment – the tension between being African Caribbean and British. The sociological tools that influence the study are concerned with identity rather than religion, culture or liberation. Examples are the application of 'race formation' (Paul Gilroy) and 'new ethnicities' (Stuart Hall) to the context of Black Pentecostalism.[41]

Toulis begins by showing that what she calls the 'African Caribbean' Church is not necessarily a 'Black' only church. This is because Pentecostalism promotes through conversion a particular religious identity:

> Any assumption that Pentecostalism is ethnic expression ignores the gains made from the analysis of conversion and Pentecostal participation: the transformation of the individual with received categorical identities to an individual with a self-ascribed and self-achieved identity as a Christian. Several episodes suggest that there is no simple congruence between ethnicity and faith for the members.[42]

In contrast to her analysis of the Black Church, Toulis argues that within Rastafari there is an unbreakable link between Blackness and religion.[43] However, I would suggest that her conclusions about Rastafari are also true of the Black Church. In African Caribbean experience, identity is closely but not exclusively connected to religious belief.[44] In Black churches, as in all churches in Britain, religion and ethnicity are interwoven. Toulis' claim must be challenged because it is not possible to make a total separation between faith and ethnicity. Unlike MacRobert, Toulis has not grasped the difference between the latent and the stated, outward confession.

Having established the dominance of religious identity, Toulis argues that by adopting 'religious' identities such as 'saints' and 'mothers' older Jamaican women constructed an identity that is empowering and sustaining.

> By explicitly drawing the boundaries of identity around that which is religious rather than that which is ethnic, members assert their right to self-representation. This does not mean that the painful and unavoidable facts of racism and disadvantage in Britain are denied within the church ... the church offers a way of transcending the suffering engendered by such forces.[45]

Like Alexander, Toulis sees the Black Church as providing particular empowerment to Black women. However, whereas Alexander focuses on internal politics of the Black Church, Toulis shows that it is with the world outside the Church that Black female identities are concerned. Identity formation among this older generation is primarily concerned with a challenge to the status quo:

> While African Caribbean Pentecostalism embodied in this denomination may not be waving the yellow, green and black flag of resistance, this does not mean that members are not engaged in controlling and redefining their situation. Paradoxically the right to self-determination in the politics of representation is achieved through relative passivity. African-Caribbean Pentecostalism enables members to deal with the non-negotiable facts of racism by providing them with the means necessary to control their own thoughts regarding themselves.[46]

Toulis is regurgitating the 'passive resistance' thinking from the work of Gerloff and MacRobert. However, it is not clear in her work what is meant by 'controlling their own thoughts regarding themselves' in a context of racial subordination. The African American historian Gayraud Wilmore[47] would argue that this type of resistance is simply 'survival' techniques that form the basis of greater resistance in the future.

Toulis also believes that identity formation has implications for the wider society: the emphasis upon religious rather than ethnic identity reveals a people concerned with the heart and not the colour of skin. In this way, she argues, the Church offers a moral critique of racism.[48]

There are two dangers with Toulis' conclusions. First, she does not discuss the possibility that the rebuke of racism within the Church is

inadequate without structural action and transformation. She does not
explore the traditions of liberation within the broader Black faith.
Second, in my opinion, Toulis' emphasis upon internal or symbolic
empowerment is limiting. Her analysis is very close to Calley's concept
of 'satisfaction'. For example, commenting on the symbolic nature of
Black church life, Toulis states that 'members transform the Symbolic
code of the wider secular society in which they are disadvantaged and
replace it with a new spiritual code in which they are advantaged'.[49]
Here, religion becomes a form of compensation for social maladjustment. It should be no surprise that there is such an undercurrent in
Toulis' thinking because she relies upon Malcolm Calley's *God's
People* as the prime socio-religious resource for evaluating Black
Pentecostalism. Consequently, religious worship and participation is
mainly viewed as a form of social amelioration – adjustment or
compensation for social underachievement and underattainment –
what Calley called 'satisfaction'. Probably, the most important statement
made by Toulis is what she has omitted in her research. Toulis' study
fails to fully acknowledge alternative assessments of first-generation
African Caribbean Pentecostalism as outlined in the work of Gerloff,
MacRobert and Alexander. Despite her text being concerned with Black
church life, none of these studies is referred to or acknowledged. Her
failure to acknowledge recent developments in analysis of Black faith
means that aspects of her study are twenty years behind contemporary
scholarship.

Toulis promotes identity formation as the focus through which
African Caribbean Christians of the first generation negotiated their
political resistance in England. Like all the preceding studies, she
identified a passive but practical approach to resisting oppression.
The type of political theology that emerges from this study is the
traditional church model where religious 'Christian' identity is so
constructed as to reject the racism and disadvantage of the world
outside.

Contemporary Political Paradigms of the Black Church: Respectables and Ragamuffins

What has emerged from the major studies of the Black Church is the
overrepresentation of the *traditional* and *modernizing* Church models.
The *prophetic* model is yet to be identified within Black church life.
Therefore, at this point I will show that there are some elements of the

prophetic within contemporary Black church life in Britain. I will identify these elements with a brief survey of how contemporary Black churches are articulating political ideas. Two churches have been selected, representing two progressive second- and third-generation Black churches in London. They provide important insights into the contextual issues that concern this study. Also, there are important theological and sociological differences between them. However, these churches cannot be viewed as representative of all Black churches in London or even Britain; the material is illustrative and is used to ground theoretical ideas. I will say something about the context of each church, and then provide a brief analysis of its mission. The discussion of mission will include excerpts from interviews with each church's leader. This is because the leadership plays an important role in shaping the vision of the church. As Mark Johnson's analysis of Black church leadership reveals, the vision, attitudes and perceptions of the leader will shape and inform the social and political praxis of the congregation.[50] Finally, I will attempt to clarify the political paradigm at work, drawing on insights from the five studies above.

Ruach Ministries

Ruach Ministries at the time of this study was located at 'The Brix' theatre in Brixton. The Brix is part of a converted Anglican church (St Matthew's) that also houses a main sanctuary and numerous meeting rooms. On Sunday mornings most of these rooms are let to a variety of Black churches for morning worship. As one travels up the main stairwell, it becomes apparent that each floor is occupied by an African or African Caribbean church singing songs, praying in unison or listening to the dynamic theological utterances of a preacher. One of these congregations is Ruach Ministries.

The Brix is located on the intersection between Brixton Road and Brixton Hill. Brixton Road is a busy shopping throughfare. Banks, music shops, fast-food restaurants, offices and a cinema are all located on Brixton Road. A thriving market selling cultural artefacts and domestic groceries is situated on Electric Avenue off Brixton Road. The Brix is a block away from Railton Road and other 'front line' sectors of one of Britain's historic Black cultural and political communities.[51] To talk of Brixton is to talk of the African Caribbean community in Britain. This is why Brixton was the target of a racist bombing in the spring of 1999.

Ruach ministries began in December 1992. The church grew quickly, primarily through street witnessing and the formation of a choir that became a vehicle for advertising the church and 'saving souls' (recruiting converts). The mission of the church is expressed in its ministries. These are activities geared towards educating and empowering existing members and also evangelistic endeavours to reach non-Christians. As well as several services on Sundays, midweek Bible studies, prayer meetings, membership classes and a Bible school, the church regularly engages in street witnessing. The church also runs a counselling centre where individual members can receive guidance from qualified staff. At the time of my study, the church broadcasts its Sunday morning services intermittently on national cable television stations.

The growth of the church can also be attributed to the charismatic leadership of Rev. John Francis. Francis felt called by God to begin the church. However, the needs of the context soon began to shape the nature of the church's ministry. John Francis outlined his personal understanding of Ruach's mission:

> We came to start a church ... God said to me, 'Go to South London'. But we noticed that there were some issues with our own people as well as other people ... on drugs, trying to get their lives together, and we were attracting these people. But we did not know how to help them. We had people come to our church who were openly speaking about their problems. Do I refer them to a rehabilitation centre? ... only to find out that there is not one Black rehabilitation centre ... It got me to look at the whole issue of what the church should be doing. I feel that there is more to it [worship] than just having a service and having a good time. It's great to know there are people in the church who have fought and got through the system and have good jobs, but wait, there are people here who need more, so it kind of forced me to look into the vision of the church and start directing my thoughts and aims to meeting the whole of man.[52]

Here, mission is guided by the needs of the situation. As with the first generation of Black churches, there is a need to provide a spiritual centre for Black people that will counter negative social and psychological forces in the community.[53]

The result is a mission to the marginalized to produce productive members of society. The combination of radical action or praxis – mission to the marginalized – and conservative theology, producing stable members of society, results in a creative tension. The critical issue is the degree to which Ruach is willing to explore human transformation so as to engage in a broader analysis of the human condition for the sake of a politically motivated social justice. This is the movement from passive to active radicalism. This concern for political action can be further explored by a more elaborate analysis of Francis' personal mission statement. There are three areas of concern.

First, Ruach is committed to a social ministry geared towards individual empowerment, equipping people to become successful Christians and emotionally stable members of society. Here the emphasis is upon personal psychological liberation. According to Alexander, such analysis 'is primarily geared towards creating and nurturing strategies of survival which serve to challenge the effectiveness of oppression in the lives of the believers. It does not, therefore, seek to dismantle systems of oppression but merely to develop appropriately resistant *responses* to them.'[54]

An opportunity for a broader or multi-dimensional analysis occurred locally when Ruach attempted to purchase a derelict warehouse to convert into a multi-purpose church building on Brixton Hill. After several planning requests were turned down, Francis and his congregation began to challenge the decision and delay by speaking to councillors and other officials. This event 'conscientized' the church concerning the lack of Black involvement in local politics (there was only one Black councillor, despite the locality's large Black community). On more than one occasion, members of the church attended council meetings to observe the progress of the building plans. After the property was secured, with the blessing of Francis and the church officials several members of the congregation explored the possibility of running for election at the local level. This raises several points.

It identifies a reactive engagement with the political: involvement was a response to the immediate problem of lack of access to land and space for worship, rather than being a challenge to the structures of oppression in general. Even so, the issue of the new building unmasked a potential active radicalism:

> The only way we will be able to change things in the community is to have local people joining these councils and going to the meetings . . . that is how we will really affect . . . It's about penetrating government areas.[55]

In my opinion, this form of reactive, active radicalism reveals a partial acknowledgement and awareness of the *prophetic* model of the church. However, it is limited. This is because it is not clear whether the glimpse of the prophetic model is a veneer for church ambition or a modicum of Christian altruism.

A second thing that emerges from Francis' personal statement is the recognition of the church's responsibility to multi-cultural ministry including African Caribbean concerns. He states:

> One of my aims is to build a multi-cultural church but I do not apologize for reaching my [Black] people . . . We are in a White country and we have a lot of Black people who have some needs . . . If I as a Black person and leader I don't address and show some interest who will do that . . .?[56]

Multi-cultural ministry means enabling Black, White and Asian Christians to feel welcome and participate in the ministries of the church. As Roger Hewitt showed in the mid-1980s, interracial contact where Black cultural forms, particularly language, are the norm led to the development of group solidarity and anti-racism among the Whites.[57] This was also the case at Ruach where the emphasis upon Black worship culture enabled interracial solidarity and the development of a particular type of anti-racism among White members.

However, the emphasis upon multi-culturalism did not undermine a concern for Black African Caribbean people. First, the church had a witness to Black social outcasts. There is a ministry to street people, a prison ministry and also programmes to reach Black men with drug problems and those who are unemployable. Second, alongside the nurture of the marginalized is a programme to empower those who have professional or material success. Such class-based social responsibility encourages collective action that, James Cone states, will make possible non-classist ministry within Black communities.[58]

The tension between multi-culturalism and African Caribbean British concerns was balanced by the creation of a deracialized ideal 'self' or 'Christian identity' at Ruach. As Nicole Rodriguez Toulis has shown, collapsing a racial identity into a spiritual one enables the construction of identities that counter negative Black images from the social world.[59] The process of constructing a variety of identities that are manipulated according to context (situational ethnicity) Claire Alexander calls the 'art of being Black'.[60] At Ruach, Black identities were submerged beneath a spiritual identity (Christian) so that while not totally ignoring Blackness, a universal Christian identity united the various racial and cultural groups within the church. Black issues did not dominate the worship experience because in this context Black people are ultimately Christian people, made in the image of God. As Francis states, 'the way that I teach my church, they do not have to feel inferior about who they are'.

The final aspect of Francis' personal mission statement explores the needs of 'the whole of man'. While *man* is used in the generic sense (humankind), the exclusive use of language raises the issue of the role of women within the congregation. Exploring women's roles is important because, as Elaine Foster suggests, leadership patterns are indicative of women's progress in patriarchal Black churches.[61] Foster and Toulis both suggest that women collude in male domination for a variety of reasons, including the need to allow Black men status in a society that seeks to treat them less than fully human.[62] Valentina Alexander suggests that women's collusion must be understood in a more complex manner: women in the church have developed ways of retaining control and influence without occupying positions of status.[63] In my opinion, the status of women can be a litmus test for the nature of sexism and awareness of systems of oppression within the Church.

At Ruach the leadership – the Eldership Board – dominates the church government. This board consists of the pastor, ministers and elders. It is predominantly male. Hence women are underrepresented at the highest level. In contrast, at the lower levels of church organization, women dominate numerically and in terms of roles. Hence, structurally Ruach Ministries conforms to Elaine Foster's 'inverted pyramid' of male domination.[64] Men dominate the powerful apex while women are overrepresented at the base.

At Ruach, the leadership legitimates male participation at every level by referring to the social context:

> Right now our eyes are set on our men at the moment because if you really want to affect the community, being in Brixton where the Nation of Islam is, you can't really basically avoid programs geared towards men.[65]

The focus on men is also given biblical justification. For example in one sermon on Genesis chapter 2 Francis states:

> Blessings will never come upon the church until men have taken their rightful place. I am not chauvinistic, I believe in women preaching and women pastors. But God ordained you [men] first to look after what I [God] have created. God had it in mind that we should rule and take charge ... The church will never move on until the men take responsibility.[66]

This logic suggests that strong dynamic men will attract similar types into the church. However, the fact that strong dynamic men have always dominated Black church leadership in Britain weakens this argument. Women in the congregation permit this overemphasis on male recruitment and 'positive discrimination' because they too recognize the need for greater male participation at every level of church life. Hence, rather than opt for a greater female participation at the top, they collude with the plan for male affirmation. Some women that I spoke to thought that the male domination was a passing phase that would be changed. One young sister said at a Wednesday night meeting:

> There are still a lot of things to be done in the body of Christ, and I see more and more people entering the church and I see a trend towards more liberty and more females becoming more powerful and having more dominant roles.[67]

The danger for Ruach is that the emphasis on male participation will simply reconfigure patriarchy and maintain male domination at the top. But the numerical strength and localized female domination of management of church projects means that the influence of women is experienced throughout the congregation. However, the power relations between the Eldership Board and its auxiliaries have determined that male influence in the end will always dominate. Hence, there is an inability to reckon with structural oppression. In this area Ruach fails to be *prophetic*.

'Ragamuffin' is a Jamaican musical genre. It describes a movement away from traditional reggae into a more hard-core, offbeat tradition. While there are many negative associations,[68] one positive association is its appeal to streetwise Black 'hustlers'. What I would like to suggest here is that Ruach exhibits ragamuffin traits.

Ruach is streetwise because of the nature of its mission and ministry. It attempts to transform the lives of marginalized Black people of working class and working poor backgrounds. The homeless, drug-dealers, prostitutes, single parents and disaffected are the main missionary arena. While there are professional and aspiring professional people in the congregation, the focus of the church is with the less well-off. By providing emotional support and psychological empowerment, the worship and ministry of the church is geared towards mental and material stability. The social analysis employed at Ruach is a reactive active radicalism. This is because multi-dimensional analysis of the social context is only employed in response to direct challenges to the existence or expansion of the church.

Ruach is *Black* only in the sense that the pastors make no apology for their explicit ethnic identity and also the Afrocentric musical traditions and cultures within the worship. The members are concerned with developing a sense of group identity in a situation where Black identity is subordinate to Christian identity.[69] However, the avoidance of the political significance of Black Christian identity further limits the ability to make concrete socio-cultural issues the focus for an investigation of the Bible and a critique of church life.

The *hustler* focus in Ruach is related to their transforming action or praxis. Expressive worship and dynamic outreach ministries are aimed at the level of the 'street' in order to transform or 'hustle' the lives of marginalized people into a confrontation with the person of Christ. The Christ at work is one that is not afraid to get his hands dirty by mixing with the lowest of the low in Brixton. This is what it means to 'hustle'. However, this transforming praxis, while focusing on the interests of men and their numerical absence – ignores the potential inherent sexism and other structural discrimination. For a less reactive active radicalism, hustling at Ruach must be multi-dimensional exploring marginalization and disadvantage at every level of church life.

Mile End

Mile End New Testament Church of God is situated in the East End of London. Bordering on Bow and Hackney, Mile End is a racially mixed area, with a large Bengali community. The church is situated in a residential area bordering newly renovated Georgian terraced houses. Some of the housing is considered desirable and in recent years young professionals have moved into the area, joining working-class Whites and Bengalis. The current building was acquired several years ago and converted. Today it houses a well-designed main sanctuary, kitchen, offices and classrooms. Mile End has a longer history than Ruach and belongs to a large denomination. Furthermore, while Ruach has a large number of single people, Mile End is a church of many families and young married couples. Even so, Mile End is considered experimental in its denomination, because it is the 'rebel' church, with a history of going against the grain of its denomination.

As was the case with Ruach, the pastor, Davey Johnson, is male and a product of the Pentecostal church tradition. Davey Johnson went to East End schools, grammar school and university. Whereas African American Christianity impressed Francis, White charismatic and evangelical Christians at the Christian Union challenged Johnson at university. He states, 'So when I came back to my local church it caused me to rock the boat at times because I had a broader view of things'.[70] Like Francis he worked under the leadership of the church as someone with a gift for ministry. Both men are therefore products of the Black church 'ministerial apprenticeship scheme'.

On the wall in the sanctuary is the church's mission statement. It reads:

> This church welcomes all people. We are committed to a Relationship with God, through faith in Jesus expressed in worship, witness and the development of a Christian lifestyle. Our purpose is to equip and enable our members through the work of the Holy Spirit to serve each other and the wider community.

As a part of the New Testament Church of God, Mile End has an established congregation with families of several generations making up its membership. In contrast, rather than being concerned with building a church from scratch, Mile End concentrates on maintaining and developing its members. Therefore, mission is not driven by the socio-cultural location, but instead is driven by the needs and aspirations of the members. Whereas mission at Ruach is an 'outward-inward' project focusing on bringing people into the church, at Mile End it is primarily 'inward-outward' concerned with internal personal development as a tool for mission outside.

As was the case with Ruach, there was universal mission directed to all people in the community. However, there was also recognition of the African Caribbean heritage and focus of the church:

> We can't deny our roots. As a majority Black church, it is not that we are negating our past or our history, but most are saying that we are here to stay. And the realities of what it means to be here, the reality is that the Black community is becoming much smaller here so ... we consider ourselves, although mainly Black, we do not consider ourselves to have a church that only considers a Black ethos. We see ourselves as a community church here to stay and meeting people of all races and colours.[71]

However, like Ruach, despite claiming to be explicitly multi-racial, the ethos, membership and style of the worship and ministry was African Caribbean. As in Ruach, what is happening is strategically important: building a multi-cultural or ethnic church from a Black context.

Regarding the role of women, the result of a decade of progressive ministry at Mile End was a thinking ministry concerned with informed, enlightened Christianity that nurtures openness and education:

> Real Christians are people who are liberated in their thinking. It's actually quite scary because freedom and liberty actually requires much more

responsibility than just keeping people in captivity. Many of the churches in our denomination do keep people in captivity. 'This is the line, you walk in it and don't question it and that is the way it is going to be.' Here, you can think differently and if you do we are not going to throw you out, we are going to walk with you and see where you are coming from and see what the Bible has to say about it ... But it has been liberating because it has caused people to fight against the status quo and experiment with their liberty especially with things like the dress code and also as regards attitudes towards women.[72]

In contrast to Ruach, Mile End has opted for a critical analysis of male domination:

We think that there are major anomalies as regards the role of women within our denomination. You can have a pastor who is a woman, but on a pastor's council you can only have men. We believe that that is rather weird. But we have tried to get around that by appointing additional members to the council ... who carry as much weight. We believe under God that this is right ... We don't need to get to heaven before we experience 'there is neither male or female'.[73]

A similar development has occurred in the treatment of single parents:

We now ensure there is a woman within the women's leadership who is a single parent ... so we can understand what it is that single parents are going through. We have not marginalized them in terms of church life ... they are actively involved.[74]

What these statements suggest is that, in contrast to Ruach, there is an explicit concern to address the historic marginalization of women in the Church. The extent to which this concern is translated into missionary strategy is not noticeable from a surface viewing of the worship at the church.

In short, the progressive enlightened ministry has nurtured an educated congregation, with many people pursuing degrees in higher education as well as holding respectable jobs in the public and private spheres. This does not mean that less materially and professionally qualified people do not attend the church. As at Ruach, there is a commitment to ministering to marginalized people in the Black community, but there are no active programmes geared towards street people, prostitutes or drug addicts as is the case with Ruach. It is more likely that members are encouraged through their personal networks to achieve this goal; mission was primarily a witness by internal example rather than external action.

Another aspect of the inward-outward mission is the need to be open and honest or 'real' in one's life – being open about where one is 'at' and having a desire for spiritual enrichment. Spiritual development was a feature of every ministry at Mile End. At the end of a sermon the worship leader added:

> God is saying to us that ... he has been calling us to higher highs ... new and richer experience of him. Calling us to be better parents, friends, persons ... whether in our relationships, our homes ... better employers or employees.[75]

Relationship with God was also expressed in a quest for holiness. As Iain MacRobert has shown, the Holiness tradition is a major contributor to the emergence of Pentecostalism.[76] Toulis has shown how the Holiness tradition was absorbed and mobilized by the first generation of African Caribbean Pentecostals in Britain.[77] On one occasion, a young man advertising a 'rap' gospel concert talked of 'uncompromising gospel music', implying an essentially puritanical form of the genre. Such a distinction can be related to retaining a sense of 'purity' in a genre associated with the profane. Similarly, in one prayer an African Caribbean elder said:

> Nothing in our hands we bring but simply to the cross we cling ... wash us, cleanse us, purify us, Lord, oh Jesus, don't let us steal or commit adultery ... he expects each and every one of us to be holy, commit ourselves to God.[78]

What is important here is that the idea of individual holiness or Christian lifestyle is also part of the inward-outward missionary strategy, so the relationship with God leads to a transformation of lifestyle.

However, the emphasis on holiness and the talk of service did not manifest itself in modest dress or a detachment from materialistic concerns. On the contrary, church members seemed to be caught up in the quest for material possessions and professional success. As one young barrister said to me at a church social event, 'I've always wanted to get ahead, that is why I go to church.' In my analysis of the preaching and practice, the rhetoric of holiness did not always manifest itself in a quest for simpler lifestyles, participation in projects of justice or a critical attitude to capitalism. Instead the members talked about 'service'. Johnson states:

> We believe that our life change is supposed to make a difference in the community. We are embracing political involvement . . . When people think about this church . . . it's a church that is dealing with the real issues.[79]

There were many dimensions to service at Mile End, often geared towards helping its members improve their spiritual and educational capacity. Hence, whereas Ruach was concerned with getting its message on the streets, and creating a great beginning for people with little hope, Mile End was more interested in running seminars and educating children in a Saturday school in order to break the glass ceilings imposed upon its members.

Mile End displayed a form of active radicalism in its mission. However, because its field of concern was primarily the church, its influence and potential were limited. It displayed a weak active radicalism that I would like to describe as 'respectable' Pentecostalism. It is respectable because of the location and aspirations of the majority of its membership. For those on the margin, the church provided a glimpse of what is attainable and also a supportive environment where they would be 'encouraged to be all that they can be'.

Respectable African Caribbean Christianity is radical because of the open-minded, human-centred ministry which nurtures Black advancement. However, it is limited in that its preaching and teaching still relies upon a traditional, apolitical approach to the understanding of the Bible, the relationship with the world and the limited political involvement.

Hence, while moving beyond a passive radicalism, they have moved into a weak form of active radicalism. Here, there is a willingness to acknowledge political issues but not organize so as to provide the framework for political change. The church will inform members of what political parties stand for, or join in Racial Justice Sunday, or be part of social-concern ecumenical/inter-faith groups but not (when this study was conducted) provide a concrete structure for socio-political engagement or mobilization.

I have attempted to show that contemporary Black Pentecostalism has a range of political outlooks ranging from reactive active radicalism to weak active radicalism. Using the framework defined by Freire, it is clear that these churches at their core are still *modernizing*, but have the potential to be *prophetic*.

CONCLUSION

This chapter has demonstrated how scholars have analysed the political theology of African Caribbean churches. All studies identified internal liberation of various types operating within the African Caribbean churches. Theologically, Alexander, MacRobert, Gerloff, and Toulis suggest that the African Caribbean Church exhibits a powerhouse theology which through worship enables the individual to encounter the liberating power of God. An ideology of resistance or 'liberation spirituality' undergirds a hermeneutical process that uses the Bible like a guidebook for human concerns. In Freire's terms, the Black Church is a *modernizing* church. One reason for this, as Toulis shows, is that religious identity supersedes 'ethnic' identity and consequently the individual's spirituality is more important than collective ethnicity.

Both MacRobert and Alexander suggest that the Church must move beyond a spiritual interpretation and engage with socio-political analysis. As the examples of Ruach and Mile End show, some Black churches have moved beyond the passive to occupy reactive and weak forms of active radicalism. Hence, an explicit movement from passive to active radicalism is still required so that there is a more concrete link between the life of the Spirit (or 'pneumatic') and the political. Only then will the powerhouse theology mobilize a fuller resistance to oppression. Such a process must engage with structural oppression that inhibits Black life in the history of the African Caribbean diaspora. Such an investigation must take racial oppression seriously and see how it can be resisted in the Black Church.

To take MacRobert and Alexander's concerns seriously, it is necessary to analyse what Calley called the 'religio-political tradition'. Such a task will provide resources for a political theology. To this end, it is necessary to explore racialized oppression and identify responses to it among the African Caribbean diaspora. These are the aims of the next two chapters.

NOTES

1. I have chosen these studies on the grounds that they cover a wide range of theological, social and cultural issues relevant to the concerns of this study. However, I have had to omit other studies on the grounds that they overlap the foci of the studies included.
2. Beckford, R. *Jesus is Dread: Black Theology and Black Culture in Britain*. London: Darton, Longman and Todd, 1998, p. 13.

3. Freire, P. 'Education Liberation and the Church.' In: *Religious Education*. Fall 1984, 79.4 pp. 535–43.
4. He is aware of several groups and lists thirteen including both Oneness and Trinitarian traditions. Calley, M. *God's People: West Indian Pentecostal Sects in England.* Oxford: Oxford University Press, 1965, p. 39.
5. ibid., p. 3.
6. ibid., p. 8.
7. 'In 1961 I talked with more than thirty London clergymen ... whose churches stood in areas of dense West Indian settlements. I found none of them prejudiced against West Indians though some felt that members of their congregations would not welcome them in large numbers.' Ibid., p. 134.
8. ibid.
9. ibid.
10. Bisnauth, D. *The History of Religions in the Caribbean.* Trenton, New Jersey: Africa World Press, 1992, pp. 19ff.
11. Johnson, L.K. 'Reality Poem.' In: *Inglan is a Bitch*. London: Race Today Publications, 1981.
12. The Oneness tradition was a Pentecostal tradition that emerged from the Trinitarian Pentecostals in the early part of the twentieth century (1913–16). As Gerloff demonstrates, the Oneness grew out of a controversy over the use of a baptismal formula, but had ethnic and racial origins and motivations as well as theological. Gerloff, R. *A Plea for British Black Theologies: The Black Church Movement in Britain in its Transatlantic Cultural and Theological Interaction.* Vol.1. Frankfurt: Peter Lang, 1992, pp. 87ff.
13. ibid., p. 94.
14. ibid., pp. 13, 16, 20, 62.
15. ibid., p. 61.
16. Gerloff draws upon Gerlach and Hine's definition. That is, these phenomena are the 'revitalisation of the pan-human capacity for supra-rational, ecstatic experience' (ibid., p. 62).
17. ibid., p. 62.
18. ibid., p. 64.
19. ibid., p. 65.
20. ibid., p. 204.
21. See Hopkins, D. *Black Theology USA and South Africa: Politics, Culture and Liberation.* New York: Orbis, 1990, pp. 7–31.
22. Gerloff, R. op. cit., pp. 12–13.
23. ibid., p. 15.

24. MacRobert, I. *Black Pentecostalism: Its Origins, Functions and Theology*. PhD thesis, University of Birmingham, 1989, p. 458.
25. ibid., p. 464.
26. ibid., p. 467.
27. ibid., p. 498.
28. MacRobert states: '... the theology that really matters to Black Pentecostals can be heard in the oral narrative forms of the dramatic sermon, the testimony, the story, the proverb, the chorus, and even simultaneous individual praying and the account of the dream or vision. It can be seen as Black Pentecostals seek to live out the Bible in their congregations and in the wider society' (ibid., p. 503).
29. ibid., p. 505.
30. ibid., p. 509.
31. While the present book was being written, in the mid-1990s, a deep and bitter debate resurfaced in the US regarding the relationship between IQ and race. The 1994 publication of *The Bell Cure: Intelligence and Class Structure in American Life* by Richard J. Hernstein and Charles Murray claimed to offer 'scientific' proof of the inferiority of Black people in particular and poor people in general.
32. Alexander, V. *'Breaking Every Fetter'? To What Extent has the Black Led Church in Britain Developed a Theology of Liberation?* PhD thesis, University of Warwick, 1997, p. 1.
33. ibid., p. 29.
34. ibid., pp. 75–6.
35. ibid., pp. 163ff.
36. ibid., p. 186.
37. ibid., p. 227.
38. These are a uni-dimensional analysis and a lack of historical analysis (ibid., pp. 237–9).
39. ibid., p. 251.
40. Ibid.
41. Toulis, N.R. *Believing Identity: Pentecostalism and the Mediation of Jamaican Ethnicity and Gender in England*. Oxford; New York: Berg, 1997, pp. 170ff.
42. ibid., p. 168.
43. ibid., p. 169.
44. Alexander, V. op. cit., Chapter 6.
45. Toulis, N.R. op. cit., p. 209.
46. ibid., p. 207.

47. Wilmore, G. *Black Religion and Black Radicalism.* New York: Orbis, 1998.
48. Toulis, N. R. op. cit., p. 210.
49. ibid., p. 207.
50. Johnson, M.R.D. 'The Churches, Leadership and Ethnic Minorities'. In: Werbner, P. and Anwar, M. (eds). *Black and Ethnic Leadership: The Cultural Dimensions of Political Action.* London: Routledge, 1991, pp. 277–92.
51. Brixton is one of the most famous Black communities in London. It was one of the six areas where West Indian migrants settled in large clusters from 1958 onwards. Brixton became a unofficial arrival centre for West Indian migrants as early as 1948 when a local Labour MP encouraged a group of men from the *Empire Windrush* to consider Brixton their second home. Three decades of African Caribbean migration to England in general and Brixton in particular resulted in Brixton becoming the mythical spiritual and political centre of Britain's Black African Caribbean community. This was most evident during the early 1980s, when Brixton's second-generation Black African Carribbean community rose up in spontaneous acts of direct social action against oppressive police practices. One conclusion we can draw from analysis of the Brixton context is that the uprisings, and the subsequent inquiry conducted by Lord Scarman, made Brixton a barometer of Black second-generation responses and concerns over inner-city tensions in housing, employment and policing.
52. Francis, J. Interview with author, 6 March 1998.
53. See Bevans, S. *Models of Contextual Theology.* New York: Orbis, 1992.
54. Alexander, V. op. cit. p. 236.
55. Francis, J. Interview with author, 6 March 1998.
56. Francis, J. Interview with author, 6 March 1998.
57. Hewitt, R. *White Talk Black Talk: Inter-racial Friendships and Communication Amongst Adolescents.* Cambridge: Cambridge University Press, 1986, pp. 100–25.
58. Cone, J. *God of the Oppressed.* San Francisco: HarperCollins, 1975, p. 108.
59. Toulis, N.R. op. cit., pp. 200–11.
60. Alexander, C. *The Art of Being Black: The Creation of Black British Youth Identity.* D. Phil, Oxford University, 1992.
61. Foster, E. 'Women and the Inverted Pyramid of the Black Churches in Britain'. In: Saghal, G. and Yuval-Davis, N. *Refusing Holy Orders:*

Women and Fundamentalism in Britian. London: Virago, 1992, pp. 63–5.

62. Toulis, N.R. op. cit., p. 264.

63. Alexander, V. 'Mouse in a Jungle: The Black Christian Women's Experience in the Church and Society in Britain.' In: Jarret-Macauley, D. (ed.). *Reconstructing Womanhood, Reconstructing Feminism: Writings on Black Women.* London: Routledge, 1996, p. 93.

64. Foster, E. op. cit., p. 63.

65. Francis, J. Interview with author, 6 March 1998.

66. Francis, J. *Change My Name.* Taped sermon.

67. Joseph, J. Conversation with author, 18 March 1998.

68. See Back, L. *New Ethnicities and Urban Culture: Racisms and Multiculture in Young Lives.* London: UCL Press, 1996.

69. As mentioned above, Hall showed that Black identities in Britain are transformed by local and global influences so that identity and culture are constantly undergoing change and formation. Hall, S. 'Old and New Identities, Old and New Ethnicities.' In: King, A.D. (ed.). *Culture, Globalization and the World System.* London: Macmillan Press, 1991.

70. Johnson, D. Interview with author, 6 March 1998.

71. ibid.

72. ibid.

73. ibid.

74. ibid.

75. Worship leader, Sunday morning service, 6 April 1998.

76. MacRobert, I. *Black Roots and White Racism in Early Pentecostalism.* London: Macmillan Press, 1988, pp. 34–47.

77. Toulis, N.R. op. cit., pp. 80–120.

78. Worship leader, Sunday morning service, 13 April 1998.

79. Johnson, D. Interview with author, 6 March 1998.

2 Downpression
A Genealogy of Racism

My father used to say, 'History is the greatest teacher.' I would later learn as a post-graduate that retrieving Black history is a powerful resource for challenging the norm.[1] What my father did not mention was that being critical of the 'norm' when what is normal is often 'anti-Black' is fundamental to our survival!

This chapter briefly outlines the genealogy of British racism. (I use the term 'genealogy' because it explores influences and historical relationships.)[2] Study of such connections is particularly important because it reveals underlying assumptions that shape modern British racism.

I begin with the Greco-Roman period because this is the common foundational point for European values and civilizations. The Middle Ages are also important because they represent an evolution in representations from the imagined to the real. The Enlightenment is an important transformation of thought in European history, moving towards a critical examination of 'race'. Next comes the nineteenth-century emergence of pseudo-science, in an attempt to validate racism scientifically. Finally I will explore modern racism in Britain.

DEFINING RACISM

Racism is a difficult term to define. It began as a nineteenth-century pseudo-scientific concept; today, there is no one single definition in usage.

David Goldberg has shown that racism is based on presuppositions about racial hierarchy (classification), difference (differentiation) and limitations (restriction) which are deeply embedded in institutional practices (regulation).[3]

I am particularly concerned with racism as an inferior 'fixing' of Black people. As Homi Bhabha has shown, fixity is a feature of the colonial construction of the Black 'Other'.[4] Fixing enables a people to be viewed as homogeneous or all the same. Fixity then allows negative characteristics to be ascribed to the group.

Then, as Black Atlantic cultural critics such as Kobena Mercer and Michelle Wallace have demonstrated, racialized oppression can be evaluated through an exploration of representation.[5] To take representational politics seriously, I will also take account of the use of the concept of Blackness within each context.

By beginning with White racism, I make White history the starting point for an evaluation of Blackness.[6] A critique of 'Whiteness' is important because Black political liberation is related to an understanding and critique of White oppression.[7] Therefore, aspects of Whiteness cannot be ignored.

Again, there is a danger that by evaluating White racism I demonize it by suggesting that everything associated with White people is bad. This is not my intention, however. White racism is not seen as the product or property of all European civilizations or peoples. Therefore this study will also identify anti-racism in European civilizations in order to avoid racial reasoning (Black is good, White is bad) or stereotyping.[8]

THEOLOGY AND RACISM

As well as being concerned in this chapter with sociological descriptions of racism, I am also concerned with the theological problems associated with racism. I want to argue that racism contradicts two central biblical doctrines, the creation and the incarnation.

The creation event in Genesis (Genesis 1.27) places humanity at the centre of God's creation. One result of being made in the likeness of God or *imago Dei* is that human beings not only have the capacity to relate to the divine but are also created equal. When we treat people as innately inferior we call into question God's creative act. Hence, racism is a form of idolatry because it makes 'race' the central focus of creation.[9] To refute racism is to affirm the image of God in all humanity.

Racism also stands against the doctrine of incarnation. One theme of the incarnation is that God became flesh (John 1.14) so that all of humanity is called into a relationship with God. All people through the incarnation can have fellowship with God through Christ. Racism distorts the incarnation by suggesting that the message of salvation privileges a particular human form. Racism is therefore heretical because it denies the universal message of the gospel in the incarnation. To refute racism is to affirm the universality of the incarnation and ultimately the universality of salvation: God became flesh to redeem all of humanity.

However, the idolatrous and heretical nature of racism has not prevented its persistence within the history of the Christian Church both ancient and modern.

GRECO-ROMAN CIVILIZATIONS

As Jan Nederveen Pieterse has shown, any discussion on Greek attitudes to Africans should first note Greek attitudes to Europe's savages. The traditions of the 'wild man' and 'barbarian' provided a framework demeaning those who were different from Greeks.[10] This process I refer to as *dialectical Othering*, placing the 'Other' in opposition to the 'White Self'.

Greek civilizations were varied in their culture but there were general impressions of Africans. (It should be noted that the term 'African' did not always mean Negroid. It included people of dark skin in the regions of ancient Africa – Egypt, Ethiopia and Nubia – that became known to Greeks and Romans.) Although Greek societies did not have a concept of 'race' based on biological type, they developed ways of conceiving of other peoples.

There are two schools of thought on African representation. On the one hand, there is sufficient evidence to suggest that Africans grew to be negatively represented in Greek cultures. In support of this view one might begin with the earlier Greek literature of the sixth century BCE, where there were negative images of Black 'creatures' with Negroid features and large genitalia.[11] Such imagery made links between eroticism, Blackness and African people.[12] As Stephen Small has demonstrated in *Racialised Barriers*, these themes remain today and have deep roots in Western thought.[13] Regarding the concept of Blackness, this school of thought also argues that Blackness was sometimes associated with moral character. There is evidence that darkness was negatively associated with the tragic, dread and terror[14] and associated white with triumph and good.

On the other hand, there is sufficient evidence to suggest that classical Greece's attitude towards Black-skinned people, and Blackness as a concept, was positive. Such a view must first acknowledge that any distinctive Greek ethnocentrism which may have entered the culture after the Greeks defeated the Persians in the fifth century BCE introduced a negative view of all foreigners and not just Africans. Given this possibility it is necessary to identify ways in which Greece paid respect to Black people within their general worldview.[15]

Frank M. Snowden suggests that as early as the sixth century BCE, Greeks were honouring Black citizens of Delphi, coinage depicting them with Negroid features.[16] Further, Blackness as a concept was used to define positive moral virtues in classical Greece. For example, bravery and courage were associated with being Black and dark-skinned.[17] In addition there is evidence to show that colour was not involved in cosmic battles or divine favour (white = good, black = bad). Therefore, this school would argue that what is at work in the Greek colour aesthetic is a fluid and complex tradition found in many cultures around the world.[18] Snowden's most significant claim is that African physicality, beauty and intellect was also the focus of adoration and acclaim. For example, Herodotus called Ethiopians handsome.[19] However, not everyone would agree with Snowden. For example, Cornel West argues that there is little evidence to suggest that Black cultures were central to the artistic and intellectual accomplishments in Greece despite evidence of Greek cultural and intellectual acknowledgement.[20]

Like Greek civilizations, Roman cultures were not homogeneous or fixed. Consequently when exploring African representation I am concerned with general ideas that emerge. While debates rage about Greek attitudes to Black-skinned people and the concept of Blackness, Robert Miles suggests that the Romans adopted a less ambiguous, more straightforward colour aesthetic. White was associated with good and Black with bad.[21] Furthermore there is evidence to suggest that moral value was accorded to skin colour in Roman society. Grace Beardsley's work suggests a two-pronged attack on people with Black skin. First there are pejorative representations of Africans in Latin texts beginning with Cicero (106–43 BCE), who begins a tradition of viewing the Ethiopians as stupid and docile.[22] Second, as well as the attack on intellect, there was a demeaning of Black sexuality. Romans exoticized African sexuality so that at certain times marriage across colour lines was taboo in Roman circles.[23] Again, from the earliest times, the minds and bodies of Black people have been ridiculed and exploited.

Pragmatism enabled the Romans to incorporate African technology and personnel into their imperial machinery, but even so, they had an ethnocentric view of the world and their Black aesthetic contributed to pejorative projections as they encountered Black people and Blackness.[24]

In summary, initially there was a general ambiguity towards Black people in the ancient world. Even so, any meaningful resistance strategy or emancipatory theology must take seriously the fact that negative evaluations of Blackness are etched deep in the Western psyche. In addition, the ancient world shows the emergence of a subtle relationship between skin colour and moral character. Consequently, resistance strategies must explore the tension between aesthetics and hegemony.

Early Christian Thought

A critical question that I want to raise at this point is whether Greco-Roman cultural aesthetics affected the colour symbolism of the New Testament. It is difficult to outline all the sources that contributed to the worldview of the first century. However, Cain Hope Felder suggests, in *Troubling Biblical Waters*, that the minds of authors were affected by some Greco-Roman influences of the day.[25] In order to see whether the Early Church was affected by Roman colour symbolism, we shall examine the use of Blacks and Blackness in the Hebrew scriptures and the Greek New Testament.

Professor Randall Bailey has shown that Black people occupied a variety of social positions in Old Testament times.[26] Moreover, Octavius Gaba has demonstrated that the Old Testament's use of the concept of Blackness has positive connotations. Here I make darkness synonymous with Blackness because in Black history the relationship between the two concepts has been generally indistinguishable. Gaba argues:

> The positivity of darkness in relation to the Hebrew Yahweh occurs in several passages in the Old Testament. In the Creation event (Genesis), the Exodus event (Exodus, Deuteronomy, Numbers), the words of the prophets (2 Samuel, Job, Isaiah, Jeremiah, Ezekiel, Daniel, Amos) and the words of the Psalmist we have indications of the positive participation of darkness in the being of Yahweh.[27]

In addition, Gaba shows in his reading of the creation myths and other examples that the Yahwist tradition rejects the notion that darkness negates the presence of God. Instead, the being of God incorporates darkness.[28]

However, what I am concerned with here is primarily New Testament thought. Some negative understandings emerge in the New Testament regarding Blacks and Blackness. Black scholars illustrate key concerns through two themes, the *presence* and *repre-sentation* of African people.

First, regarding the presence of Africans in the New Testament, in comparison to the Old Testament, the New Testament makes very little reference to Black people. There are isolated references to Black indi-viduals such as Simon of Cyrene (Matthew 27.32; Mark 15.21; Luke 23.26) and nations (Acts 2.7–11; Revelation 7.9), but the only book that makes multiple references to Blacks is Acts. Charles Copher states that in the twenty-seven books that constitute the canon, only Acts 8.26–39 and 13.1 contains references to Black persons and peoples.[29]

The way in which Black people are described in the New Testament also reveals much about how Blacks and Blackness were evaluated at that time. Black scholars are deeply critical of the portrayal of the Ethiopian official (Acts 8.26–40). Although most European scholars have acknowledged the African origins of the Ethiopian character, in European and Euro-American theological circles little effort has gone into exploring his theological significance.[30] Cain Hope Felder argues that the story of the Ethiopian is affected by a process of secularization, that is, the weakening of a religious concept (here, racial equality) by the weight of socio-political and ideological pressure (the need for Paul to get to the capital of the known world).[31] Felder compares the narrative of the conversion of the Ethiopian with that of the Roman Cornelius, arguing that the conversion of Cornelius is of more sig-nificance for the Lukan writer than the gospel being taken to the end of the world (conversion of the Ethiopian):

> The racial implication that I do wish to highlight is that Luke's editorialising results in a circumstantial de-emphasis of a Nubian (African) in favour of an Italian (European) and enables Europeans thereby to claim that the text of Acts demonstrates some divine preference for Europeans.[32]

I would suggest that Felder is stretching a point by basing a lot on the intention of the Lukan writer. Also, neither Martin nor Felder contrasts the Ethiopian with the role ascribed to Simon of Cyrene. The latter narrative might lead to a less pejorative role for African peoples in the minds of the New Testament writers. Simon of Cyrene stands as a symbol of Black African participation in the passion of Jesus. Furthermore, Simon represents African presence as a positive and redemptive influence in Christ's journey to the cross. We must not deny the potential theological significance of Simon of Cyrene today.

Regarding the concept of Blackness, it has been suggested that a form of colour symbolism that denigrated Blackness existed in the minds of the New Testament writers. Again, Octavius Gaba argues that varied and ambiguous views of the concept of darkness (Blackness) found in the Old Testament are replaced by a dualism in the New Testament. In the Greek scriptures, there is evidence to suggest that light is separated from the ontological concept of darkness so that darkness is 'demonized'. An example is found in Matthew, who interprets the revelation of God in terms of light (Matthew 4.16); also, Mark and Luke relate the being of God to light (Mark 4.22; Luke 9.28–36).[33] Similarly, the Gospel of John exemplifies the glorification of light (John 1.5).[34] Gaba suggests that Paul exemplifies the demonization of darkness:

> The price he [Paul] pays for using a language foreign to Jesus is what can be construed as the 'de-ontologization' of darkness. That which has being is denied being so that it may serve as the 'scapegoat,' the 'foil,' in contrast to that which has being. Light therefore is used to denote sinlessness and being in Christ. Darkness becomes sinfulness and that which is anti-Christ.[35]

I want to challenge Gaba on the grounds that he does not provide evidence to show that the negative association of darkness was projected onto people of dark skin in the writings of the New Testament. Although darkness is demonized, it does not directly affect the status of Black people in the New Testament world; the world of the New Testament did not always associated dark skin with evil moral qualities. Gaba's analysis is not conclusive.

It is clear that early Christian tradition may well have been affected by Greco-Roman colour symbolism, but the consequences are difficult to discern in the New Testament world. However, Robert Hood insists that a connection between the de-ontologization of Blackness and negative associations of Black skin can be found in the Apocrypha and the writings of the Early Church Fathers such as Jerome and Ambrose.[36] However, there is little evidence to suggest that the Blackness of Africans rendered them beyond salvation or made them less than human. There are some cases which suggest that the Early Christian traditions did not always make a direct association between Black people and the de-ontologization of Blackness. For example, the appointment of Black and African Popes in Early Church history weakens Hood's argument.[37]

THE MIDDLE AGES

The Middle Ages are an important period in this genealogy as they account for an evolution of thought that emerges from encounter.

While there are no precise dates for the start and end of the Middle Ages, we may regard them as dating from the collapse of the Roman Empire in the fifth century up to the fifteenth century. As was the case with our study of Greek and Roman civilizations, it is impossible here to present a total view of Blacks and Blackness within this period. Instead, I shall focus on significant issues and images pertinent to this genealogy. I will identify developments from the early, mid and high Middle Ages.

Blacks as Monstra

In the early Middle Ages, previous traditions about Black people from the classical period were collected and interpreted from the religio-cultural perspective of the Christian Church. The combination of medieval mind and Christian theology led to the generation of negative images of Blacks and Blackness. Robert Miles suggests that:

> The pre-Enlightenment view of the world was characterised by its irrational premises, static nature and parochial scope. Man's relation was fixed to God and to nature. The world was ordered according to God's will and true knowledge was available only to the Supreme Being ... In this world of fixed relations and limited experiences, irrational prejudices attached themselves to anything and everything out of the ordinary. In communities that were ethnically homogeneous, geographically isolated, technically backward, and socially conservative, prejudice and superstition were the natural response to the strange and unknown ... In the isolated, ignorant world of feudal Europe, Africans were often portrayed as devils, monsters or apes.[38]

According to Friedmann, in the early Middle Ages new phenomena such as deformed births or strange peoples in distant lands became known as 'acts of God' or *monstra*. In the early Middle Ages, *monstra* defined whole populations of people with physical appearances and phenotypes that differed from those found in Europe.[39] The most enduring interpretation of *monstra* was that they represented a group that had been cursed by God and were therefore physically disfigured, exiled and cursed.[40] Significant for Africans is the fact that skin colour was considered by some to be one form of *monstra*. When filtered through Christian belief, with its light/dark, good/evil symbolism, it was relatively easy to think of Blacks as *monstra*.[41] In short, there was a dramatic closing of the distance between negative views of Blackness and Black skin.

Islamic Other

The later Middle Ages witnessed a significant change in the evaluation of Black people and Blackness. The unprecedented development of knowledge in the late Middle Ages through the development of trade and travel, the establishment of universities, led to a shift away from the imagined to the encountered Black Other, first in the form of Islam and then in the beginnings of the slave trade.

The rise of Islam in the eighth century and the imperial aspirations of Muslims on Christian soil led to the development of an anti-Islamic tradition in European thought. For example, medieval art often represented the devil and the fallen angels as Black, with Negroid physical characteristics. Judith Wilson identifies a combination of factors:

> Southern Europe was brought face to face with dark-skinned peoples as Spain fell to the Moors. At first, thanks to the combination of Christian symbolism with its stark equations of good and evil with light and dark – and the tendency of conquered peoples to demonise their foes, medieval European art often represented Blacks as grotesque figures whose defining features were impossibly thick lips, bulbous noses, and receding chins, along with prominent cheekbones and curly hair.[42]

Even so, there is also evidence that Blacks and Blackness were not always negatively evaluated once Blacks were regularly encountered. For example, I suggest that any careful reading of the development of the Black warrior, Black Madonna and Black Magi traditions in medieval Europe can be seen positively, Blacks and Blackness representing sanctity and salvation.[43] Therefore, to argue that all Black peoples, whether African or Arab, were portrayed negatively at this period is to misrepresent something more complex.

Slavery

The high Middle Ages are significant because we see the enslavement of Blacks and the theological legitimation of slavery. The actions of the Church must be placed in the wider social and economic context, namely the rise of the merchant class and Protestantism. Both of these weakened the Catholic Church's ability to affect private morality, in particular the pursuit of individual wealth at the expense of Black exploitation.

There is strong evidence to identify the Church's complicity in the demonization of Blacks and Blackness. Initially, slavery was condemned by the Pope (Martin V) in 1425. However, Pope Nicholas V permitted it in a papal bull in 1454. Once the riches from the slave trade began to fill the coffers of both Church and State, it became increasingly difficult for the Church to oppose slavery.[44] Oppression required theological blessing. Hence, Christian theology was marshalled to support the trade in African people. Two theological themes emerged to legitimate slavery and colonialism.

First, prominent in England and America was the Curse of Ham theory. Ham in Genesis 19 is cursed by his father Noah and condemned to a life of servitude.[45] Because Ham signifies the Black race, it was deduced that Blacks were ordained to be subservient to all other races. A particular form of exegesis made it possible for the Genesis story not only to make Blackness and servitude synonymous, but also to suggest sexual impropriety as the reason for Ham's curse.[46] The relationship of divine disfavour, sexual immorality and Black skin, themes present from Greco-Roman times, are reworked for the present. Over the course of 200 years the Curse of Ham theory would take on several forms, but all focused on Black skin as a sign of disobedience and sin and the servile role of Black people in the divine plan.[47]

Second, many Church scholars argued that colonialism ought to go hand in hand with evangelism of the infidel. This was the view of Columbus on his several voyages, and also Ginés de Sepúlveda (c. 1490) who argued for war against the Indians of Latin America as a prerequisite for later evangelization. Here the gospel was subordinate to the political aspirations of the State and the Church. Therefore, violence against the Africans and Indians was justified because the Europeans, like the Israelites, had to conquer the 'heathen'.

However, not all Christians condoned slavery. In fact, there is strong evidence of Christian thinkers such as Fra Anton de Montesinos agitating to prohibit enslavement in the early sixteenth century.[48] Also, Bartolomé de Las Casas (1474–1566) argued that the Indian people of the New World were fully human and therefore should be accorded the rights of all human beings and not be enslaved. Controversially, Las Casas did not sufficiently obstruct the enslavement of Africans,[49] but later repented for this failure.[50]

In summary, despite the traditions that presented Blacks and Blackness positively, the medieval mind was still able to fix Blacks and Blackness in negative categories. Furthermore, as religion was a framework for evaluating Black people, Christianity stands accused as a major contributor to the exploitation and enslavement of Blacks. Despite this history of collusion, even today there has been no formal acknowledgement, apology or reparation to African or

Caribbean people for the Church's role. However, the anti-Black tradition in the Middle Ages was not the same as modern racism. Even though medieval Europe provides modern racism with major themes for the exclusion and oppression of Black people, there is no 'scientific' racial classification in this period.

The Enlightenment

Modern racism emerged in the Enlightenment,[51] that collection of intellectual, social and political forces of change that swept through Europe in the seventeenth and eighteenth centuries. A debate exists on *what* within the Enlightenment produced racism.

For a long time economic determinism was *en vogue*. For example, Peter Fryer argues that English racism emerged on the plantations of the Caribbean and became an established way of thinking in Victorian England.[52] Eric Williams, the Caribbean intellectual, expresses a similar view.[53] If we take Fryer and Williams seriously, then racism is reduced to economic necessity. However, the major problem with economic determinist arguments is that they cannot account for racist thinking in situations outside capital formation.[54] Hence the need to explore two other perspectives.

A prominent view has emerged with the African American Harvard philosopher Cornel West. He argues that it was categories of thought that produced racism.[55] David Goldberg also expresses this view.[56] They suggest that three intellectual developments that fuelled the Enlightenment also facilitated the emergence of modern racism. The intellectual developments are the scientific revolution, the Cartesian transformation of philosophy and the classical revival.[57] These historical processes transformed the 'metaphors, notions, categories and norms' (the 'structures of modern discourse') through which racism was articulated. The central thesis for this camp is that the re-emergence of classical cultural standards produced a measure by which scientific evaluations could be made. This 'normative gaze', as West calls it, was promoted by a variety of sixteenth-century scholars.[58] Therefore, the cultural context in which Black people were to be measured and evaluated in natural history had already accepted White supremacist standards, which were contingent within the categories of thought.[59]

If West is correct, then we must take seriously the belief that ideas and systems of thought are not value-free, but represent the interests of individuals and groups. Furthermore, racism is not accidental but is part of the structures. In some ways, West's analysis mirrors the crude Marxist idea that the dominant ideas are linked to the dominant material force. However, West's arguments do not add up when placed within a broader analysis of the Enlightenment framework. Let me explain by turning to Kenan Malik.

Kenan Malik suggests that the views of West *et al.* do not fully account for the diverse interpretations of Enlightenment thought. Malik argues that the Enlightenment also provided the intellectual foundations for human freedom and the banishing of ignorance and prejudice which was so prevalent in pre-Enlightenment thought.[60] Thus the categories of thought that emerged with the Enlightenment are not to blame for the emergence of racism. Instead, the focus of blame rests upon a fear of freedom, or social contexts unable to absorb Enlightenment values in a systematic or consistent manner.

Malik's thesis is based on the notion that Enlightenment ideas were an ideological pool for a variety of competing groups such as monarchs, merchant classes and the emerging bourgeoisie.[61] Revolution did not always occur because not everyone wanted to sweep away the existing social order. Where the conditions were right, however, Enlightenment ideas became a force for changing the established order. An example that I believe endorses Malik's arguments is the French revolution and also the Haitian (San Domingo) revolution of 1790 led by Toussaint L'Ouverture. These examples show that where there was sufficient force of will and radical action, the Enlightenment provided the intellectual basis and raw material for emancipation.

If we take Malik's argument seriously, then rather than exploring the categories of thought for racial bias as suggested by West, we need to be primarily concerned with the potential for racial subordination within any social system concerned with maintaining order. It is important to be aware of social change and in particular the ways in which racialized oppression can be legitimized through discourse supposedly concerned with maintaining the social order. Later I will show that immigration control in contemporary Britain provides us with an example.

After considering Fryer, West and Malik, my own suggestion is that any attempt to identify the emergence of modern racism must include a plethora of social, scientific and political changes that marked seventeenth-, eighteenth- and nineteenth-century European society. H.F. Augstein makes clear the complex forces that affected the rise of racial theory in the nineteenth century:

There is no single philosophy, no single movement or author who can be considered as having paved the way for nineteenth-century racial theory. Instead, it grew out of the combination of previously rather distinct traditions – a liberal, lay, anti-monarchical political outlook; the rise of the nation-state; biological and zoological investigations; phrenological and physiognomical fortune-telling; a political interest in finding a scientific justification for slavery; the philological investigation of languages as a mirror of national character. Nineteenth century racial theory resulted in a unification of the various approaches to the study of mankind which had evolved in the preceding age.[62]

Augstein's statement suggests an inclusive or a both/and approach to the ideas of West, Malik and Fryer.[63] In essence, the emergence of racism requires a multi-dimensional analysis. This is an important observation because challenging racism will also require a similar approach. For now, it is clear that these developments in the seventeenth and eighteenth centuries can be called racism because specific racial categories were used to define and differentiate groups of people.

PSEUDO-SCIENTIFIC RACISM

Pseudo-scientific racism was an attempt to find 'scientific' evidence of the inferiority of Black people. According to Kenan Malik, issues of social stability in the midst of social unrest were fundamental in influencing the ruling elite in Europe from the mid-eighteenth to nineteenth centuries – in particular the ability to understand 'the mob'[64] In order to maintain a spurious link between social libertarianism and social stability, science emerged as an important tool for gaining understanding. However, while scientific developments were used to improve social conditions, they were also open to misuse as tools for domination – a practice dubbed 'pseudo-science'. As Nancy Stepan suggests, pseudo-science maintained British hegemony in a time of rapid change and transition:

A fundamental question about the history of racism in the first half of the nineteenth century is why it was that just as the battle against slavery was being won by abolitionists, the war against racism was being lost. The Negro was legally freed by the Emancipation Act of 1833, but in the British mind he was still mentally, morally and physically a slave.[65]

Influenced by the racial hierarchy of Linnaeus' *Systema naturae* (1735),[66] so-called 'scientific discoveries' were used by some to validate British imperial rule in the eighteenth and nineteenth centuries.[67] Pseudo-science consisted of European and North American scientists working in various pre-anthropological disciplines, in order to construct biological, physiological and socio-biological evidence for White supremacy.

Biological arguments led to two schools of thought: *monogenesis* and *polygenesis*. While the former recognized a single human species, the latter, a minority view, argued for plurality of species, naturally with Whites superior to Blacks. The full horror of polygenesis was played out in some of the most brutal colonialist activity. For example, polygenesis theories gave intellectual support for genocide in America and Australia.[68]

Physiological arguments attempted to classify the Black body as inferior. Enlightenment aesthetics classified various grades of human intellectual ability. Working from a similar premise, pseudo-sciences such as craniology and phrenology in the nineteenth century supported the belief in the superiority of European character, culture and morality due to their superior skulls and facial features.[69] Phrenology justified the expansion of empire because it supported the concept of British rule over 'lesser' races: the African was lazy and in need of brutal subjugation for the best civilizing results. For example, Fryer links the cheapening of Black bodies in phrenology with the brutal repression of Paul Bogle and the Morant Bay rebellion in Jamaica in 1865.[70]

Socio-biological arguments for Black inferiority arose in the aftermath of the publication of Charles Darwin's *On the Origin of Species* (1859). Darwin's concept of evolution by natural selection was given a social interpretation. Social Darwinists[71] rejected much of Darwin's thinking about random change. They viewed aspects of the world, such as race, as fixed. 'Natural selection' was applied to the social world to justify the removal of the impure aspects of a race and nation.

In summary, I would like to emphasize that the representations of Blacks that emerge during the 'golden era' of racism, at best, fixed Black bodies as tools of labour, and people as destined to a life of servitude.[72] At worst, Black bodies were legitimate subjects of torture and annihilation. The remnants of scientific racism persist today. For example, the publication of *The Bell Curve* by Richard Herrnstein and Charles Murray (1994)[73] generated a firestorm debate over their arguments for the innate intellectual superiority of Whites in the North Atlantic. The notion of innate difference must be resisted.

Racisms in Contemporary Britain

It would be wrong to suggest that British post-war history is without traditions of anti-racism from the White English. From anti-fascist leagues in the 1930s to the activism of the Anti-Nazi League in the 1970s, White English people have played an important role in combating racism in Britain. However, despite these challenges the onward march of racism has continued.

I have demonstrated above that any discussion of racism must be historically specific.[74] Therefore rather than thinking of one racism, we must talk about the ways oppression based on colour or race is shaped in different contexts. I have also shown that racism is associated and disassociated with dominant systems of thought and practice. In other words racism, while being related to prevailing hegemonies, also takes on a life of its own. These issues will become more relevant in our discussion of racism in contemporary Britain.

Any discussion of racism in post-war Britain must first mention the racism against Jews and the Irish in nineteenth- and early twentieth-century Britain.[75] Also, the attempts to discredit scientific racism after the Second World War meant that racialized oppression was no longer tolerated within legal systems and structural practices. In short, racists would have to find other ways of articulating their creed. This shift from 'old' to 'new racism' can be explained in socio-psychological terms as a movement from *dominative* to *aversive* racism.[76] While dominative racism is overt White supremacy designed to subjugate Black people, aversive racism is more complex. Aversive racists can appear liberal, tolerant and even supportive of Black liberation, but this expression is just a veneer – beneath this outer appearance the aversive racist is keen to maintain his dominant position.[77] This shift can also be understood as a move from the law to the culture.

As we shall see below, old racism can be countered through legislation and training because it is primarily structural in its manifestation. In contrast, new racism operates at the level of culture and experience. It is encoded in attitudes and behaviour and is encountered in everyday interaction between people. Despite its clandestine nature, the new racism is as destructive and dehumanizing as old racism.

Old Racism

The old racisms (before the advent of new racisms in the early 1980s) are ideological racism, common-sense racism and institutional racism.

One of the best definitions of racism as an ideology occurs in the work of Miles and Phizacklea. Racist ideology, they say:

> identifies individuals as belonging to a group on the basis of some real or imaginary biological or inherent characteristic. It is common for the group to be identified by reference to some immediately evident physical characteristic(s) ... which is thought to be inherent in every member of the group. The group so identified by this biological or supposedly inherent characteristic is then so also defined as having some other social or psychological characteristic(s) which is regarded unfavourably. This combination of characteristics and evaluations is interpreted to indicate a difference, a 'race'. The ideology of racism additionally claims that all those who share these characteristics are necessarily deficient or inferior and so should be treated less favourably than other groups not so identified.[78]

As Samuel Kennedy Yeboah demonstrates in *The Ideology of Racism*, White racist ideology is an attempt to legitimate White supremacy and Black subordination.[79] However, racist ideology is not stable or true; neither is it scientifically valid, as it is based generally upon inaccurate interpretations of the social world.[80] However, some aspects of ideology may be true; ideologies are therefore inherently contradictory.

The second 'old' racism is common-sense racism. This emerges from life experiences, which inform us how the world works. According to Miles and Phizacklea, when we build a picture of how things should be they constitute an ideology. Ideology, when taken for granted, becomes common sense. However, common-sense reasoning is not consistent or systematic. Neither is it stable, as it may change when it is tested.[81] For example, Stella Orakwue's analysis of the emergence and progress of Black footballers in Britain, *Pitch Invaders: The Modern Black Football Revolution*, identified how common-sense reasoning on Black footballers has changed in two decades.[82]

The third and final form of 'old' racism, Robert Miles' analysis of institutional racism, takes two forms:

> First, there are circumstances where exclusionary practices arise from, and therefore embody, a racist discourse but which may no longer be explicitly justified by such a discourse. Second, there are circumstances where an explicitly racist discourse is modified in such a way that the explicitly racist content is eliminated, but other words carry the original meaning.[83]

As Paul Gilroy demonstrates in *There Ain't No Black in the Union Jack*, institutional racism is subtle. Once 'race' as a factor is silenced, it is possible to continue practices that exclude people.[84] As shown in the

Macpherson Report into the murder of Stephen Lawrence, institutional racism is clearest when the link between 'race' and practice is determined:

> The collective failure of an organization to provide an appropriate and professional service to people because of their colour, culture, or ethnic origin. It can be seen or detected in processes, attitudes and behaviour which amount to discrimination through unwitting prejudice, ignorance, thought-lessness and racist stereotyping which disadvantage minority ethnic people.[85]

I turn now to new racism.

New Racism

The social and political context of post-war, post-industrial Britain has led to a rearticulation and reconfiguration of British racisms. Post-war industrial and social decline was partly responsible for a crisis in the sense of nationhood in the later part of the twentieth century. This crisis was deeply felt in the 1970s when Britain went cap in hand to the International Monetary Fund and experienced the re-emergence of mass and structural unemployment. 1970s Britain produced a genera-tion of school leavers who believed there was 'no future' and 'no hope'. Such nihilism was articulated in popular cultural forms such as punk music.

These ideological and social shifts in British society occurred concurrently with the emergence of multi-cultural communities in Britain's cities. Although the Black presence was primarily the result of economic migration in the post-war years, many on the right of the political spectrum began to rethink what it meant to be British in response to post-industrial decline and the emergence of Black people in Britain. I agree with Anna Marie Smith's suggestion that Enoch Powell was a key spokesperson. Making Black people the 'enemy within', the 'alien occupation' and 'the foreigner on British shores', Powell rearticulated racism by reconfiguring the myth of the British nation as homogeneous and fixed.[86] Against this common-sense image, Black migration was presented as an aberration to the traditional British way of life. Here, institutionalized racism focused on the entry of Black people into a mythically homogeneous Britain.

The association between racism and the reconfiguration of 'nation' was continued during the election of Margaret Thatcher in 1979. However, whereas Powell was able to articulate racism through discourse on race, Thatcherism and the New Right developed strategies for articulated racism without mention of race. This development was at the heart of new racism. Below I want to outline two significant interpretations of new racism: as socio-biology and cultural racism. I will then explore the new racism in the Labour party of the late 1990s.

Martin Barker suggested that a new racism emerged with the Conservative Party in the mid-1980s. Factors such as anti-Europeanism and the continued fear of Black settlers led right-wing think tanks, prominent politicians and journalists to construct a racism underpinned by socio-biology – that is, the idea that by a form of natural selection people choose to be with their own kind. One implication of this thinking is that human nature determines who should be included and excluded from the 'nation'. Barker states:

> Human nature is such that it is natural to form a bounded community, a nation aware of its difference from other nations. They are no better or worse. But feelings of antagonism will be aroused if outsiders are admitted.[87]

Another way of describing this version of new racism is to look at how *territory* and *nation* became a part of national discourse under Margaret Thatcher's government.

As was the case with Enoch Powell, concern over *territory* was expressed in immigration controls and the attack on anti-racism as reverse racism. Immigration was viewed as an attack on the natural and homogenous White British nation, a corruption of her purity. Hence, immigration controls become a natural task. Anti-racism was re-interpreted as an attempt to force White Britons to conform to legislation that discriminated against the White *nation*. In both of these areas of racist discourse there was no need to mention 'race' or hierarchy. Instead, crude socio-biology was expressed in simplistic assumptions about human nature.

Socio-biological racism is not as new as Barker would have us believe,[88] but in my opinion what is new about this form of racism is that race is omitted from the discourse so as to present discrimination and exclusion as the natural right of the British nation.

A second definition of new racism in Britain comes from Paul Gilroy. Gilroy argues that new racism's primary focus is culture:

> Contemporary British racism deals in cultural difference rather than crude biological hierarchy. It asserts not that Blacks are inferior but that we are

different, so different that our distinctive mode of being is at odds with residence in this country.[89]

Cultural racists recast the language of cultural diversity in order to promote exclusion and hegemony. A useful way of describing what is happening is to say that cultural racism recodes racism. That is, cultural rationales are used to maintain political hegemony over Black communities by substituting the fixed language of race with the fixed language of culture:

> Culture is something you are born into, not something you acquire, the conservatives argue. Viewed in this fashion culture inherits the role of race in the nineteenth century, and history the power of biology. Culture becomes particularistic and exclusive, delineating a common past to which some can belong and some cannot. And that past becomes determinist and teleological, holding power over the present through tradition and rootedness.[90]

But the real problem for Black people according to this theory is that 'they are forever locked in the bastard culture of their enslaved ancestors, unable to break into the "mainstream" alternative'.[91] Gilroy also argues that Black people, particularly social workers, have adopted a similar conception of culture, which is equally as damaging.[92] However on this second point, while Gilroy's analysis of cultural racism provides important insight, he does not allow for a 'strategic essentialism' or a political Black unity for the sake of resisting attacks on Black life in contemporary Black Atlantic cultures.

My final task in this genealogy is to explore racism in the present, that is racism under the cultural and social ethos of Britain created and re-invented by the New Labour Party.

The 1997 election of the Labour Party in Britain under the leadership of Tony Blair represents a new stage of racialized discourse in Britain. The Labour Party has been historically the chief vehicle for political expression of African Caribbean people in Britain. Even so, the Labour Party has also held an ambivalent place in the post-war history of State race-relations. On the one hand it has been party to institutional racism by passing racist immigration laws in the 1960s and 1970s. On the other hand it has established State-sponsored race-relations bodies such as the Commission for Racial Equality and has been responsible for ground-breaking anti-discriminatory legislation.[93] In short, Labour has effected a two-pronged approach of 'keeping Blacks out' but 'improving race relations inside'. What I would like to suggest is that the Labour

Party is in the process of reworking new racism in the form of 'one-nation' racism. Let me explain.

The failure in the 1980s of Black Labour activists to achieve 'Black sections' within the Party, cleared the way for a general colour-blind approach to Labour Party policy by the beginning of the 1990s.[94] Hence, during the 'modernizing' of the Party under the late John Smith in the early 1990s and more recently under Tony Blair, Labour has been able to develop an additional form of new racism.

My concept of one-nation racism is related to Leslie Carr's analysis of colour-blind racism. For Carr, colour-blind racism is an ideology that denies the existence of Black people, inadvertently securing the inequalities of the status quo.[95] An example of this process can be seen in the British context when, under Blair's government, the concept of 'cool Britannia' recasts a mythical British homogeneous imperial past that disregards the complex ethnic relationships within its boundaries. Cool Britannia does not recognize colour, therefore it neglects national contradictions and inequalities as represented in such combinations as Black and British. Blair's new racism is predicated on the belief that Blacks will be assimilated into the mainstream of society and should not, all things being equal, have favours or advantages based on 'race' or 'colour'. That is, Black people will become a part of the one nation. Therefore, there were all-female short-lists for local elections, no such provision was made for prospective Black candidates. Hence, Black people are ignored and Black concerns are subsumed under general policy geared towards alleviating disadvantage.

In these forms of new racism the concept of race is encoded in language about territory and nation. Therefore, anti-racist strategies must be concerned with decoding racist concepts and cultural practices.

CONCLUSION

In this section I have attempted to explore a genealogy that leads to the development of racism in Britain. It is clear from this study that 'racism' is a highly flexible term and can be used to describe a multiplicity of concepts and practices from different historical periods, although the introduction of the concept of 'race' is the product of the Enlightenment. Consequently, what is important here is the historical specificity of racism and its fluidity and its relative autonomy. This last point will become increasingly significant as I explore Black responses to racism from an African Caribbean British context.

NOTES

1. See Sawicki, J. *Disciplining Foucault: Feminism Power and Body*. London: Routledge, 1991.
2. Anderson, V. *Beyond Ontological Blackness: An Essay on African American Religious and Cultural Criticism*. New York: Continuum, 1995, p. 84.
3. Goldberg, D.T. *Racist Culture: Philosophy and the Politics of Meaning*. Oxford: Blackwell, 1994, p. 47.
4. Bhabha, H. 'The Other Question: The Stereotype and Colonial Discourse'. In: *Screen*, 1983, 24, p. 4.
5. Mercer, K. *Welcome to the Jungle: New Positions in Black Cultural Studies*. London: Routledge, 1994. Also Wallace, M. *Invisibility Blues: From Pop to Theory*. London: Verso, 1990.
6. Anderson, V. op. cit., p. 91.
7. See Ani, M. *Yurugu, an African-Centered Critique of European Cultural Thought and Behaviour*. New Jersey: Africa World Press, 1994.
8. See West, C. *Race Matters*. Boston: Beacon Press, 1994, 23–32.
9. See Kelsey, G. *Racism and the Understanding of Man*. New York: Charles Scribner's Sons, 1965, p. 27.
10. Pieterse, J.D. *White on Black: Images of Africa and Blacks in Western Popular Culture*. New Haven and London: Yale University Press, 1992, pp. 30–2.
11. See Carpenter, T. *Dionysian Imagery in Archaic Greek Art: Its Development in Black-figure Vase Painting*. Oxford: Oxford University Press, 1986.
12. ibid., p. 19.
13. Small, S. *Racialised Barriers: The Black Experience in the United States and England in the 1980s*. London: Routledge: 1994, pp. 98ff.
14. See Kittel, G. (ed.). *Theological Dictionary of the New Testament*. Vol. 4. Michigan: Eerdmans, 1967, p. 549. In: Hood, R.E. *Begrimed and Black: Christian Traditions on Blacks and Blackness*. Minneapolis: Fortress Press, 1994, p. 33.
15. ibid., p. 29.

16. Snowden, F. *Before Color Prejudice: The Ancient View of Blacks.* Cambridge, Mass.: Harvard University Press, 1998, p. 49.

17. Irwin, E. *Colour Terms in Greek Poetry.* Toronto: Hakkert, 1974, pp. 147, 156.

18. Cf. Hood's analysis of the Massia, op. cit., p. 35.

19. Snowden, F. op. cit., p. 63.

20. West, C. *Prophesy Deliverance: An Afro-American Revolutionary Christianity.* Cambridge Mass.: Westminster Press, 1982, p. 64. Also Goldberg, D. op. cit., p. 22.

21. Miles, R. *Racism.* London: Routledge, 1989, p. 15.

22. Beardsley, G.H. *The Negro in Greek and Roman Civilisation: A Study of the Ethiopian Type.* Baltimore: John Hopkins Press, 1929, p. 119.

23. Hood, R.E. op. cit., pp. 41ff.

24. ibid., pp. 39–40.

25. Felder, C.H. *Troubling Biblical Waters: Race, Class and Family.* New York: Orbis, 1989, pp. 68–78.

26. Bailey, R.C. In: Felder, C.H. op. cit., pp. 165–86.

27. Gaba, O.A. 'Symbols of Revelation: The Darkness of the Hebrew Yahweh and the Light of the Greek Logos.' In: Bailey, R.C. and Grant, J. (eds). *The Recovery of Black Presence: An Interdisciplinary Exploration.* Nashville: Abingdon Press, 1995, p. 150.

28. ibid., pp. 150–3.

29. Copher, C.B. 'Three Thousand Years of Biblical Interpretation with Reference to Black People.' *JITC* Spring 1986, 13/2, p. 231.

30. Martin, C.J. 'A Chamberlain's Journey and the Challenge of Interpretation for Liberation.' In: Gottwald, N.K. and Horsey, R. A. (eds). *The Bible and Liberation, Political and Social Hermeneutics.* New York: Orbis, 1993, p. 494.

31. Felder, C.H. (ed.). *Stony the Road We Trod.* Minneapolis: Fortress, 1991, p. 129.

32. ibid., p. 143.

33. Gaba, O.A. op. cit., p. 154.

34. ibid.

35. ibid., p. 156.

36. According to Hood, Origen (185–245 CE) was almost alone in his positive appraisal of the Blackness of the bride in Songs of Songs. For Origen, the bride symbolized the gentile Church and is therefore a symbol of God's revelation to the world. However, other Church Fathers were not as sophisticated. For instance, Jerome

(342–420 CE) understood Blackness to be synonymous with 'carnal knowledge and erotic action' and in one commentary the Ethiopian represented the devil. Similarly, Ambrose (339–97 CE) associated Blackness with sin and the negative character of the Church. Hood, R.E. op. cit., pp. 73ff.

37. Van Sertima, I. *African Presence in Early Europe*. New Brunswick, USA: Transaction Publishers, 1993. p. 93ff.

38. Malik, K. *The Meaning of Race History and Culture in Western Society*. London: Macmillan Press, 1996. p. 43.

39. Friedman, J.B. *The Monstrous Races in Medieval Art and Thought*. Cambridge, MA; London: Harvard University Press, 1981, pp. 108–17.

40. ibid., pp. 88–103.

41. Miles, R. op. cit., p. 17.

42. Wilson, J. 'Getting Down to Get Over: Romare Bearden's Use of Pornography and the Problem of the Black Female Body in Afro-US Art.' In: Dent, G. (ed.). *Black Popular Culture*. Seattle: Bay Press, 1992, p. 107.

43. The Black Warrior tradition refers to the elevation of Black Christian warriors in European Christianity – for example, the eleventh-century cult of Saint Maurice, a Black Christian Egyptian martyr of the Diocletian persecutions, and the thirteenth-century myth of Prester John. Similarly, the Black Madonna cult was popularized in the twelfth century. It professed that Black Madonnas were capable of miraculous works. Finally, the Black Magi tradition became popular in the fourteenth century when several churchmen and scholars argued that one of the three magi was a Black African. Here, the African presence at the birth of Christ symbolized African participation in the biblical story and God's revelation to the world. See Hood, R.E. op. cit., pp. 100–13.

44. See Williams, E. *Capitalism and Slavery*. London: Chapel Hill, 1944.

45. The Curse of Ham theory argued that Black Africans by virtue of being descendants of Ham were condemned to a life of slavery. See Washington, J. *Anti-Blackness in English Religion 1600–1900*. New York: Edwin Miller Press, 1984.

46. Felder, C.H. op. cit., p. 132.

47. Hood, R.E. op. cit., p. 126.

48. For a discussion, see Prior, M. *The Bible and Colonialism*. Sheffield: Sheffield Academic Press, 1997, pp. 57ff.

49. See Gutiérrez, G. *La Casas*, New York: Orbis, 1994.

90 Dread and Pentecostal

50. Beozzo, J.O. *Humiliated and Exploited Natives*. In: Boff, L. and Elizondo, V. *1492–1992: The Voice of the Victims*. London: SCM Press, 1990, p. 87.

51. See Eze, E.C. *Race and the Enlightenment, A Reader*. London: Blackwell, 1997, pp. 1–4.

52. Fryer points to the Christianization of slaves as the field of discussion in which the debate about the human status of slaves was initially played out. The debate begins with the assertion of the sub-humanity of slaves by planters and merchants in the mid-seventeenth century to legitimizing the enslavement of African people. The next stage of English racism according to Fryer's schema is the written texts of the eighteenth century. Fryer focuses almost exclusively on the writings of Edward Long, and claims that Long's ideas were common among the English intelligentsia. However, other historians have disputed this point and suggested that Long was only marginal to the public bodies that shaped attitudes towards Black Africans. For Fryer, by the end of the eighteenth century British intellectuals were party to the development of a negative racial discourse. The final stage in Fryer's evolution of English racism is the advent of science in the nineteenth century.

53. See Williams, E. op. cit.

54. For example, Fanon explores racism outside the context of economics. See Fanon, F. *The Wretched of the Earth*. London: Penguin, 1990.

55. To prove this hypothesis, West argues that the classification of racist categories by François Bernier in 1684, Carolus Linnaeus in 1735 and Georges Louis Leclerc de Buffon in 1778, were all reinforced by classical ideas of beauty. In all of these classifications, Africans appeared lower on the evolutionary scale of development than Europeans. Similarly, the emergence of phrenology (the reading of skulls) and physiognomy (the reading of faces) in the eighteenth and nineteenth centuries also followed similar processes of using classical standards of beauty as the measure of all civilizations. If racism was contingent upon the building blocks of the Enlightenment, it should be no surprise that great Enlightenment thinkers such as Voltaire, Hume, Jefferson and Kant 'not merely held racist views; they also uncritically – during this age of criticism – believed that the authority for these views rested in the domain of naturalists, anthropologists, physiognomists, and phrenologists.' See West, C. *Prophesy Deliverance/An Afro-American*

Revolutionary Christianity. Philadelphia: Westminster Press, 1982. pp. 55–61.

56. Goldberg, D.T. op. cit.
57. The area of Enlightenment thought that West identifies as precipitating Enlightenment racism is the Scientific Revolution. The Scientific Revolution highlighted observation and evidence as the central foci for modern discourse. David Theo Goldberg suggests that the ultimate product of science was the significance of classification. The second category of thought that precipitated Enlightenment racism is the development of the scientific method of René Descartes (1596–1650). Descartes is significant because of his application of the inductive method of science, using science as a means of duplicating reality. According to West, Descartes provides a legitimacy for modern science. 'By demanding that notion was true until establishing grounds for doing so (I think therefore I am) he moved from subject to objects, from the veil of ideas to the external world, from immediate awareness to extended substances.' Finally, the third category of thought that precipitated Enlightenment racism was the classical revival initiated in the early Renaissance (1300–1500). The revival in classical learning reintroduced. 'Greek ocular metaphors and classical ideas of beauty, proportion, and moderation. This revival was of great significance because beauty became the measure of intelligence and ontological value so that natural qualities established virtues such as morality and nature. To possess classical values of beauty was to establish a place in the racial hierarchy and its perceived intellectual differences.' op. cit., p. 50.
58. West, C. op. cit., p. 55.
59. ibid., p. 54.
60. Malik reminds West *et al.* that the Enlightenment represents a surge towards equality: Not only did Enlightenment philosophers declare the unity of humankind, but they believed that all were potentially equal. 'Whilst we maintain the unity of the human species', wrote von Humboldt's brother, the naturalist and explorer Alexander, 'we at the same time must repel the depressing assumption of the superior and inferior races of men. Since men are made of the same clay,' he argued, 'there should be no distinction or superiority among them ... This belief in the unity of humanity and the equality of Man was held by virtually all Enlightenment thinkers.' See Malik, K. op. cit., p. 49.
61. ibid., p. 57.

62. Augstein, H.F. *Race, The Origins of an Idea, 1760–1850.* Bristol: Thoemmes Press, 1996, p. x.

63. While Malik is right to show that the Enlightenment ideas and concepts were related to the interests of monarchs, merchants and revolutionaries (anti-monarchical political outlook and the rise of the nation state), the nature of these categories also enables them to be readily available for oppression. For instance, the use of scales of hierarchical classification would almost inevitably lead to winners and losers on the human scale of progress (biological and zoological investigations), especially once classical standards of beauty were introduced as a measure of civilizations. As we have noted in the section on methodology, ideas and methods are not value-free. Hence, categories of thought developed in the Enlightenment must be scrutinized. Finally, Fryer is correct in showing that racism had its roots in the plantocracy's attempts to justify slavery.

64. Malik, K. op. cit., pp. 85–6.

65. Stepan, N. *The Idea of Race in Science: Great Britain, 1800–1960.* London: Macmillan, 1982, p. 1.

66. See Yeboah, S.K. *The Ideology of Racism.* London: Hansib Publications, 1997, p. 54.

67. Fryer, P. *Staying Power: The History of Black People in Britain.* London: Pluto Press, 1984, p. 165.

68. Yeboah, S.K. op. cit., p. 59.

69. Fryer, P. op. cit., pp. 166–70.

70. ibid., p. 177.

71. ibid., p. 180, for a list of social Darwinsts.

72. ibid., pp. 174–6.

73. Herrnstein, R. and Murray, C. *The Bell Curve.* New York: Free Press, 1994.

74. Hall, S. 'Racism and Moral Panic in Post War Britain.' In: C.R.E. *Five Views of Multiracial Britain.* London: C.R.E., 1978.

75. First, before the arrival of migrants from the Caribbean in the post-war years, Britain had recent experience of mobilizing against foreign migrants. Both the Irish and the Jews in the late nineteenth and early twentieth centuries experienced negative stereotyping and physical attack from the British working classes. Similarly, the State sponsored immigration law to restrict coloured seamen entering Britain in the early 1920s. Hence, the racialization of immigration, racist immigration legislation and negative stereotyping were a feature of British life before the so-called 'West Indians'

arrived in the late 1940s. Solomos, J. *'Race' and Racism in Britain*. London: Macmillan, 1993, p. 44.

76. Although these 'ideal types' (dominative, aversive) are fluid and internally varied and were initially applied to the US context, they have relevance to the post-war British context.

77. Kovel, J. *White Racism: A Psychohistory*. London: Free Association Books, 1988, p. 60.

78. Miles, R. and Phizacklea, A. op. cit., p. 10.

79. See Yeboah, S.K. op. cit.

80. Miles, R. and Phizacklea, A. *White Man's Country*. London: Pluto Press, 1987. p. 9.

81. ibid., p. 5.

82. Orakwue, S. *Pitch Invaders: The Modern Black Football Revolution*, London: Victor Gollancz, 1998, p. 7.

83. Miles, R. op. cit., p. 84.

84. Gilroy, P. *There Ain't No Black in the Union Jack*. London: Unwin Hyman, 1987, pp. 72–111.

85. MacPherson, William. *The Stephen Lawrence Inquiry*. London: The Stationery Office, 1999, 6.34.

86. Smith, A. *New Right Discourse on Race and Sexuality*. Cambridge: Cambridge University Press, 1994, pp. 130–80.

87. Barker, M. *The New Racism*. London: Junction Books, 1981, p. 21.

88. Racialized discourse that makes use of concepts of territory and nation as the basis for creating a mythical nation and also excluding the Black settler has been a feature of British history. Rather than thinking solely about immigration as point of contact for the emergence of socio-biological racism, we can also explore the characteristics of socio-biological racism as a feature of British colonial life. In many if not all British colonies geographical boundaries were set to demarcate physical and ontological boundaries between the White elite and Black masses. Transgression of these boundaries was rarely a possibility for Black people except on occasion when they were admitted to serve the social and sexual needs of the White elite. In a similar fashion, the social demarcation of the plantation is mirrored in the patterns of Black settlement in England. That is, Black urban settlement occurred in context where racialized boundaries marked out acceptable places for Black people to settle, buy homes and be a community. Hence, socio-biological racism is not as new as we have been led to believe.

89. Gilroy, P. *Small Acts, Thoughts on the Politics of Black Cultures*. London: Serpent's Tail, 1993, pp. 91–2.

90. Malik, K. op. cit., p. 186.
91. Gilroy, P. 'One Nation Under a Groove: The Cultural Politics of "Race" and Racism in Britain.' In: Goldberg, D.T. (ed.). *Anatomy of Racism*. Minneapolis: University of Minnesota Press, 1990, p. 223.
92. Some Black Nationalist groups and social welfare workers have adopted a similar conception of culture in order to defend themselves against White hegemony in social policy. Here, Black culture is defined as fixed in order to prevent policies and practices that will limit the rights of Black people. In other words, Whites are told that they cannot have control over particular areas of State responsibility because they are unable to understand, empathize or make sense of Black cultures – presented as fixed and impenetrable. Gilroy, P. *There Ain't no Black in the Union Jack*, pp. 114–51.
93. See Solomos, J. op. cit., pp. 52ff.
94. Hiro, D. *Black British, White British: A History of Race Relations in Britain*. London: Paladin, 1992, pp. 96–104.
95. Carr, L.G. *Colour-Blind Racism*. London: Sage, 1997, p. 140.

3 Uprising

A Genealogy of Black Resistance

At secondary school many of us second-generation Black British found ways of resisting the neo-colonial education embedded within the curriculum. Some of us decided that we 'can' tek it no more' and were excluded. But the vast majority found ways of negotiating our resistance. Whether by working hard, playing the joker or being quarrelsome we found ways of signifying our unease with inner-city comprehensive education. Black resistance in the face of oppression is legendary. Black people have found creative, dynamic and even violent ways of responding to oppression. While the previous chapter presented a genealogy of racism, it is now time to explore resistance to racism. I must begin by defining what Black resistance means.

Black resistance is a term well travelled in Black political circles. Here, I want to suggest two things. First, that Black mobilization encompasses Black resistance. Therefore, resistance is a dimension of mobilization. Second, that a useful description of resistance is found in the work of Michel de Certeau.

Certeau makes a distinction between *resistance* and *opposition*. *Resistance* refers to the way a group might tackle or contest a given system from outside using tools developed outside the system. Conversely, opposition works from within the system with tools fashioned from the inside.[1] For example, Black youths inside the Church subvert the clothing conventions as a way of opposing the status quo.[2]

However, in opposition to Certeau, I want to suggest that resistance and opposition are not always mutually exclusive but instead are sometimes intimately intertwined and interrelated. In other words, we might talk about a resistance–opposition syncretism, whereby Black resistance involves a complex interplay between styles of resistance and opposition. For example, opposition may at times involve using tools from outside the system. Consequently, in this study we use the term 'resistance' as a trope for strategies representing interplay between Certeau's resistance and opposition categories. In short, there is not one form of resistance but numerous resistances.[3]

There are several hallmarks of Black resistance that are fundamental to this study. All cannot be outlined here, but there are three points that are pertinent.

First, Black resistance to White racism is historically specific; it takes on a variety of forms in each historical period. Hence, resistance is not fixed but is constantly undergoing change and re-creation. Second, resistance is arranged and organized, it is 'real' and not superfluous. Resistance is a means of contesting domination. Third, and of major significance to this study, resistance ideologies can be articulated through religion. Stuart Hall says of religious ideology:

> Religious ideologies, however 'other worldly' they appear, inform social practices and have a mobilising 'practical' impact on society. They organize men and women into action, win 'hearts and minds'. They form the 'common sense' in which the everyday practicalities of life are calculated and expressed. Ideologies draw groupings together; they help to constitute and unify congregations, supporters, and participants; they cement social alliances.[4]

There is not enough time or space in such a study to explore every aspect of Black resistance. Therefore, here, I want to explore a genealogy of Black resistance. As was the case with the exploration of racism in the previous chapter, I want to construct a relational framework for interpreting Black resistance. This genealogy has a particular focus. While other studies have attempted to focus on aspects of Black resistance such as culture, politics and ideology, I am concerned with the role of religion as a mobilizing force and with religious lines of connection and influence.

There are, however, dangers of misrepresenting Black experience and history when approaching Black resistance through a genealogy which reflects radical resistance narratives. Victor Anderson warns against this form of historiography. For Anderson, Black theology is often a 'cult of heroic genius' whereby Black scholars look only at what is good within Black experience. This process misrepresents the various ways in which Black people organize resistance.[5] Hence, in this study, when exploring resistance I shall, where possible, note traditions of collaboration, indifference and unresolved tensions. In other words, I will point to what Victor Anderson calls the 'grotesque' in Black life.[6]

Another issue is the role of women in resistance. As Barbara Bush shows, women's contribution to Black resistance is generally ignored.[7] There are two reasons for this phenomenon. These are sexism in the reporting and sexism in the transmission of traditions. Since most revolts or major acts of resistance occur in and through the work of men and women, the contribution of women must also be acknowledged and analysed.

Resistance is not alien to the Bible or Christian experience. Black and liberation theologians have argued that the Bible contains acts of resistance particularly in the form of socio-political liberation. That is to say, central to salvation history is God's concern to free people from social and political oppression. A classic text is the Exodus narrative. Gustavo Gutiérrez was arguably the first theologian to expound Exodus for oppressive socio-political situations.[8] Similarly, James Cone compared the Exodus event with freedom from racialized oppression for African Americans.[9] The basic premise of Gutiérrez and Cone is that the oppressed person today can identify with the oppressed Israelites. Therefore, the Exodus event becomes a case study or paradigm for resistance in the present. It reveals a God who legitimates resistance against oppression and it informs us that God intervenes in human history and sides with the oppressed.

At present many liberation theologians are reviewing their use of the Exodus paradigm of resistance. The American Indian scholar Robert Warrior has led the way by showing that the Exodus cannot be separated from the conquest of Canaan. That is, God's work of freedom from oppression must be placed alongside the exploitation and extermination of the Canaanites.[10] A similar theme has also emerged in the work of Black South Africans.[11] The main argument here is that the same God who liberates also legitimates the conquest of indigenous people. What is clear from the studies of the Exodus is that God is concerned with resistance to oppression. However, resistance must occur in such a way that it does not result in further oppression. This requires further explanation.

First, that resistance must be holistic. It cannot result in the freeing of one group and the oppression of another. In other words, as Miroslav Volf has argued, reconciliation must be the central focus of resistance so that the ultimate work of God in the world might be fulfilled.[12] A central plank in Volf's thought is the idea that the traditional contrast between oppressor and oppressed is not useful because it does not describe the complex interweaving of suffering on both sides. I affirm

Volf's analysis, because the quest of liberation by oppressed people must ultimately result in reconciliation.

The second point that I want to state is related to the first. Because reconciliation provides an antidote to cycles of oppression and liberation, resistance as a theological category must be seen as a temporary state or phase. That is to say, resistance must lead to reconciliation. Therefore, the act of liberation itself must ultimately result in the embracing of the Other who has been your oppressor. This is truly the ultimate goal of the One who dies at Calvary. Hence, when I explore the themes of resistance within this chapter, I recognize both its limitations and dangers.

Armed with this understanding of resistance I shall now explore a genealogy of Black resistance. There are four areas of concern: African shores, slavery, colonialism and the post-war context. The section on African shores identifies resistance on the journey to slavery in the New World; slavery is concerned with physical and psycho-social resistance during this period; colonialism explores the resistance movements within Bedwardism and Garveyism. The post-war period covers the rise of Black political action in Britain, cultural resistance and the rise of Rastafari.

FROM THE SHORES OF AFRICA

Africans' opposition to their capture began on the shores of Africa and continued during the 'middle passage' that took slaves from Africa to the Caribbean and the Americas.[13] It would be inaccurate and unfair to say that all Africans resisted their entry into slavery. As James Walvin has demonstrated, there is evidence of Africans of all statures and ranks who assisted the enslavement of their fellow Africans. There are also traditions of collusion that sit beside resistance narratives.[14] Enslaved people waiting in transport ships, in the primary eight regions from which slaves were shipped,[15] plotted, arose and liberated themselves from their captors. These first 'Pan-African' actions showed the slavers that Africans did not accept such dehumanization.[16]

Resistance also occurred during the middle passage, the wretched journey from Africa to the New World. The confrontations between captured Africans and the slavers were ferocious and ingenious. It is clear that despite their bondage Africans found a variety of ways to resist their captors. Some chose suicide by throwing themselves overboard; mothers killed their babies; some refused food, preferring starvation, and others chose the bloody path of revolt. For some, death meant reunification with Africa and its peoples; for others it was the only possible response to enslavement and the unspeakable trauma caused by enslavement, rape and brutality on the slave ships.

Vincent Harding highlights the role of African women as central to many quests for freedom aboard slave ships. The greater freedom accorded to women made them ideal spies, lookouts and assistants.[17] Furthermore, brutality, including the ubiquitous sexual assaults and rape, would have given them an additional incentive for resisting capture. Despite the punishment for revolt being death, some African women viewed it as the only alternative.[18]

Regarding the role of religion, Vincent Harding's *There is a River* suggests that if those responsible for illuminating African religion, its priests or musicians were present, struggle would have been inevitable.[19] Gayraud Wilmore argues that African religions enabled captured Africans to resist because capture and enslavement was spiritual, social and political bondage all at once for many of the Africans.[20] In other words, African religion's holistic response associated physical bondage with spiritual bondage. I therefore want to affirm the belief that African resistance to slavery was inherent within its religious and cultural systems. This is a central reason for resistance in the middle passage.

RESISTANCE IN SLAVERY (JAMAICA)

While focusing on African experience in Jamaica, it is important to note that resistance to European enslavement began with the Arawak people of Jamaica.[21] The archives tell of a range of resistance activities ranging from suicide to warfare among the Arawak as a means of resisting the unbearable demands of the Spanish invaders.[22]

There are various forms of slave resistance among the early African arrivals and their Creole descendants. Here, I shall explore physical resistance (armed rebellion and insurrection) and psycho-social resistance (such as culture and religion). However, these traditions are not exclusive but interwoven. The former may lead to the latter and the latter is dependent upon the former.

Physical Resistance

African physical resistance begins with the arrival of the Spanish colonizers and their importation of slaves from West Africa around

1517.[23] Physical resistance had a variety of purposes ranging from the removal of enslavement to outright rejection of White economic, political and ideological power. In Jamaica, physical resistance was frequent: over 400 revolts, with three major confrontations (1729–39, 1760 and 1831–2). Here I want to explore two types of physical resistance, Maroonage and armed insurrection.

By the time the British won Jamaica from the Spanish, there existed communities of escaped Coromante slaves, known to the Spanish as *Cimarron* meaning 'wild', untamed. The British corruption of *Cimarron*, was the term '*Maroon*'. Over the course of 76 years, irregular warfare raged between Maroon settlements and the British colonizers. Events intensified in the 1730s when the British Assembly made its most determined effort to quash the rebels.[24] The first Maroon War consisted of British military attempts to defeat Maroon communities in the East and West of the islands during the first sixty years of British occupation (1660s–1730s).[25] Not all White colonizers were in favour of war and some frontier people concluded their own treaties with the Maroons. The second Maroon War was to result in the breaking of the 1738 treaty by the British in 1795.[26]

Maroonage by African men and women[27] was limited resistance because once peace treaties were signed and land allocated to the Maroons, the colonial system was left unaltered. Hence, Maroonage is often colloquially analysed as a selfish/limited form of resistance because of its inability to eradicate slavery.[28] I agree with Ernest Cashmore's suggestion that it was the Myal-Obeah religious system that limited Maroonage in Jamaica. Maroonage viewed evil as in the 'immediate idiom', not in the White man – in the environment rather than the system.[29] Therefore, Maroonage only challenged slavery in so far as it offered space for an alternative form of existence – in the Jamaican case, autonomy for a few. In contrast, other slave revolts, such as the Tacky Rebellion of 1760, were concerned with island-wide insurrection.[30] To a degree, the limitations suggested by Cashmore of the Myal-Obeah complex live on in African Caribbean religious traditions, including Christianity. That is the traditional Church. Also, my analysis of Maroonage reaffirms the importance of a holistic resistance which opposes injustice in all its forms.

The emergence of Creole or West Indian-born Jamaicans in the middle of the eighteenth century resulted in the development of traditions of armed uprisings occurring outside the confines of Maroon autonomy. The Baptist War and the Morant Bay Rebellion are significant because here Christianity rather than the Myal-Obeah complex was the primary religious resource for resistance.

Christianity among the slaves was due to Black and White missionary activity in Jamaica. Of particular significance is the Black American inspired Baptist missionary activity that produced a more militant Black church leadership before the arrival of the British Baptists.[31] These slave Baptists practised a syncretistic Christianity in the period before emancipation; they were known as the 'Spirit Baptists' because of their emphasis upon spirit possession.[32] Furthermore, as Mary Turner has shown,[33] the success of slave Baptists lay in their training of Black ministers. Many of these trained Baptists became local leaders and potential revolutionaries.

One product of the Baptist mission was the Baptist War of 1831 initiated by Sam Sharpe. It was fuelled by a belief that the slaves had been set free in England through the work of the Anti-Slavery movement. Therefore, in Sharpe's mind, the British planters in Jamaica were denying freedom. Beginning as a general strike after Christmas in 1831, the Baptist rebellion developed into armed insurrection. Sharpe, a Baptist lay preacher, used his freedom of movement and church meetings to organize slaves. As Stella Dadzie has shown, women played an active part as go-betweens, spies and guides.[34] The Baptist rebellion was the largest uprising in Jamaican slave history and arguably the most important one.[35] What interests me about Sharpe is that the ideological basis for his action was his faith in the Bible and its sense of justice for the oppressed. Sharpe believed that all men were equal and that the Bible prohibited slavery. This resistance was eventually quashed in 1832 by the British troops on the islands and severe retribution was dispensed upon those involved. On a trip to the Public Record Office in London, I discovered that one of the slaves from Westmoreland involved in the rebellion received 300 lashes and life imprisonment. His name was Robert Beckford!

Despite the Baptist missionary efforts to secure confessions from the leaders of the rebellion, in hope of saving their souls, many, including Sharpe, refused to condemn what they had done.

Several important issues emerge. First, instead of the Myal-Obeah tradition of the Maroons, it was the Bible that was used to legitimize resistance to slavery. For Sharpe, freedom in Christ (Colossians 3.11) was a vindication for rebellion against the English planters. However, the level of syncretism between Myal (a survival of African religion) and Black Baptists at the time of Sharpe would suggest that Sharpe's Christianity, as Abigail Bakan suggests, was intertwined with African religious traditions.[36] Consequently, the 'Baptist War' of 1821–2 was also a 'Myal War'.[37]

Second, as with the resistance of the Maroons, the Baptish War was limited because Sharpe's Christian beliefs did not envision a utopian dream of social transformation. He wanted freedom from bondage, but society would otherwise be left relatively intact. Once more there was no holistic model of emancipation. Nonetheless, it is important to note that his uprising hastened emancipation by ensuring that the economics of sugar production was dealt a major blow through increased labour costs.[38]

The second example of Creole physical resistance that deserves a mention is the Morant Bay Rebellion. Physical resistance did not end with emancipation. Neither did the involvement of Black church leaders schooled in the Myal-influenced Baptist Church. In 1865, the Morant Bay rebellion was instigated by Baptist lay preacher Paul Bogle with the assistance of George William Gordon, a Baptist deacon and a wealthy, coloured lawyer. However, despite the male leadership, as Barbara Bush has demonstrated, there is evidence of a major female contribution to the struggle.[39] Like Sharpe, Myalism and other forms of African religious retention influenced Bogle's theology and praxis. In short, Christian belief in justice, freedom and equality provided the moral basis for Bogle's quest for better working conditions for the Jamaican poor.[40] Despite taking control of the Morant Bay area, Bogle was unable to gain the support of the Maroons and mulattos. His movement was eventually crushed and Bogle was captured by the Maroons and was hanged for treasonable offences.[41]

What I find most significant here is that the Christian moorings provided a critique of class as well as of race. Morant Bay was a class struggle because of its concern with poor working conditions, the closeness of starvation and the pressure of taxation.[42] However, it was also a racial struggle because Bogle called upon his followers to 'cleave to the Black', that is, to engage in racial solidarity for the sake of racial liberation. Hence, at a time of racial subordination based on dubious nineteenth-century concepts of 'race', Bogle used racial identity as a focus of resistance. Indirectly, Bogle's faith enabled him to overturn a sign of Otherness (Black skin) into a symbol of liberation.

Bogle represents both a break and continuity with the past. It was a break in that evil was now located in the White man's system as opposed to solely the spiritual realm.[43] However, it was continuity in that, like the Maroons, Tacky and Sharpe, Bogle had no plan for social reconstruction beyond the removal of the immediate oppression.

What then can be concluded about physical resistance in Jamaican history? There are several issues. First, despite the commentators focusing on the actions of great men, African and later Creole women played an integral role in these resistance movements. Second, religion was a significant legitimizing force for insurrection; Christian leaders constructed a proto-Christian liberation theology as both Sharpe and Bogle believed that their quest for freedom and dignity was grounded in the Bible's recognition of the universality of humankind. Third, resistance was limited in that it did not contend for or visualize a society beyond the immediate concerns.

Psycho-social Resistance

The absence of revolt and uprising did not mean that slaves accepted their lot. Scholars have shown that slaves developed cultural, psychological and non-violent forms of resistance.[44] Psycho-social resistance represents forms of resistance which while not resulting in revolt, indicated non-acceptance of the system as well as providing psychological support for coping with the system. Not all slaves chose freedom as a means of coping with the terrors of enslavement; others chose to survive as best as they could.

Women also played an important role in psycho-social resistance. Black women in Jamaica were actively involved. Stella Dadzie outlines areas of plantation life where Black women concentrated their psycho-social resistance.[45] The following is a summary of several of her key points.

As women were not protected against the brutalities of slavery, they were expected to work as hard as their men-folk. For instance, until 1826 no distinction was made between a man and a woman on the number of lashes received for insubordination. Production was also an area of psycho-social resistance. Black women engaged in a 'petticoat resistance' by engaging in uncooperative practices such as down tooling (strikes), insubordination, physical strikes and malingering. Considering Black women also had to contend with pregnancy, child-care and domestic chores for their partners, their resistance is even more daring.

Reproduction was one area where African and Creole women were best able to subvert the prevailing economic system. Dadzie argues that African and Creole women were consciously involved in controlling their fertility. Such was their effectiveness that despite pro-natal legislation in the eighteenth and nineteenth centuries to encourage

Black women's fertility and ensure the economic survival of the
planters, there was still a natural decrease in the Black population.[46]
Black women's resistance in the past provides a rich source of
inspiration for Black men and women in the Black Church today.

I will now briefly mention three forms of psycho-social resistance
that also have relevance to this study of contemporary Black
Pentecostalism. These are the persona, culture and religion.

One of the most obvious forms of slave resistance was the development of a complex personality, masking real motives and feelings and
thereby creating space for an alternative mode of being and security:

> The majority of the slaves never accepted the system of slavery, contrary to
> the historical accounts which referred to the slaves as docile, lazy and
> childlike in character ... But what the chroniclers of slavery did not
> understand was that the peculiar personality trait of the slave was in itself
> a response to and a form of resistance to slavery.[47]

This statement suggests that slaves would act in a subversive manner in
order to oppose and subvert the system without getting caught.
According to Cranton, these acts of sabotage were endemic on the
Jamaican plantations.[48] Carolyn Cooper uses the Jamaican patois word
'(h)ideology' for the process of subversion.[49] (H)ideology was predicated upon the dual consciousness of the slave. A good way of
explaining dual consciousness is by deconstructing the mythical
Anansi stories which travelled with African slaves from West African
societies.[50] This consciousness transcended the personality and became
a part of slave culture.[51] In my opinion, the problem with this
personality is that while many of the gestures, attitudes and other
behavioural traits remain today, they are not necessarily associated
with resistance.

The second form of psycho-social resistance I want to explore is
culture – a signifying system that communicates meaning. Culture is a
part of all institutions. Moreover, culture is both created and reproduced by humans. Because we create it, culture is not just 'out there' to
be internalized. This way, culture becomes an aspect of every part of
life.[52] Culture was also an important form of resistance. Despite the
varieties of African cultures represented in Jamaica, there is evidence to
suggest that slaves fused their traditions with those of the Europeans.
This African–European cultural syncretism ensured that slaves retained
values consistent with overtones from Africa, where most of the slaves
in Jamaica originated.[53] Successive generations of African slaves were
able to pass on worldviews based upon a muted African cosmology,

language and culture. According to E.K. Braithwaite, despite its heterogeneous nature, African culture was able to survive and not be destroyed because of its essential form and nature: it was 'immanent: carried within the individual/community, not existentially externalised in buildings, monuments books, "the artefacts of civilisation" ... dance was African architecture ... history was not printed but recited.'[54] Therefore, Africans were able to reconstruct a complex religious, cultural and philosophical system. However, there is a great debate about how much African culture was retained. Consequently, the degree of persistence and maintenance of African retention in Jamaican history is subject to scrutiny.[55]

Finally, religion, as well as being part of a complex of ideas underpinning Christian-led revolt, was also a form of psycho-social resistance. Missionary activity did not begin in earnest in Jamaica until 1774 with the arrival of evangelicals. First Moravian missionaries came from Saxony, Germany; they were followed by the Methodists and Baptists. Slaves were left to their own practices and deities for over 100 years. Consequently, indigenous African religious systems were retained by slaves and helped to inspire the early acts of rebellion. However, what has become clearer in Caribbean studies is the depth to which African retention became embedded in and indistinguishable from Christian religion among the Creole slave community and their post-emancipation offspring. There was a complex interplay between Myalism and the Christian Baptist tradition. According to Robert Hood, native Baptists retained African elements in their beliefs and practices:

> These Native Baptists practised baptism by immersion in the name of the Father, Son, and Holy Spirit, a practice similar to rites long known among traditionalists in Africa, who baptised in lakes and streams. The Native Baptists also connected the interpretation of dreams with the Holy Spirit. In fact, for them dreams and visions quickly became prerequisites for baptism rather than 'right' doctrine ... The Holy Spirit and possession by the Spirit also play major roles in the Native Baptist ritual, since it is the Spirit that gives life, knowledge, and healing.[56]

Myalism (the term is from the Akan language of Central Africa) was a complex amalgam of African religion. There is no scholarly agreement on its precise nature – whether it was devotion to a particular spirit, or involved the use of some plant. But it seems that slaves used Myalism as a form of protection against their British oppressors as well as against the opposing powers of Obeah.

The Myal–Christian syncretism meant that Myal leaders were able to go about their business under the cloak of Christian leadership.[57] Herbert De Lisser claims that many Myalists became Obeah priests and priestesses for the purpose of moving from defensive to offensive religious practice.[58] Similarly, Barry Chevannes suggests that many Myalists and Christians belonged to both traditions.[59] The most successful missionaries were in fact Black American Baptists such as George Liele, Moses Baker and George Gibb who arrived in Jamaica in the early 1780s to begin missionary work among slaves. These Baptists retained a highly syncretized Christian religion that had resonance for the Jamaican slaves.

Christian religion as a form of psycho-social resistance received a mixed response. On the one hand, in its strongest form Myalized Christian religion provided a powerful pneumatology and a leadership base. Sam Sharpe and Paul Bogle prove this point. In a weaker form, Myalized Christianity enabled a sacred space to emerge, in which Black bodies and minds could be free from the dictates of slavery and colonialism and thereby envisage an alternative worldview.[60]

On the other hand Christian religion as psycho-social resistance was not oppositional for all Creole/Black church-goers. For example, there is evidence of freed slaves and mulattos (a mixed race having African and European parentage) identifying with the religious dictates of the ruling British colonials. For example, John Wilkinson infers that Anglicanism in Jamaica, as the oppressors' church, sought collaboration with the plantation owners and willing Creoles.[61]

In summary, psycho-social resistance reveals the intensity and universality of resistance. The majority of the slaves did not accept the legitimacy of slavery and sought covert means to destroy it. Despite evidence of collusion, there was resistance through personality, culture and religion. I turn now to colonialism as part of the resistance genealogy.

RESISTANCE TO COLONIALISM

At this point I want to move beyond the context of slavery to explore the traditions of resistance in the post-slavery colonial context of the Caribbean in general and Jamaica in particular. As revealed in the last chapter, the latter part of the nineteenth century in Europe was marked by the development of a new stage of ideological legitimization of Black inferiority. Pseudo-sciences were mobilized to justify a negative evaluation of Black Africans and Blacks in the Caribbean. Through government and education (where available), English White supremacy informed and maintained the myth of Black inferiority. In the Caribbean context, White supremacist ideas were played out in the form of European colonialism. Colonialism as a form of social and economic exploitation ensured the continued subordination of the Black masses. In response, Jamaica, riddled with race and class inequality, became the focus for new forms of Black resistance. These new forms of mobilization reconfigured previous systems as well as drawing on new motifs to make sense of the new, post-emancipation context of Jamaica, the Caribbean and the diaspora. Here I shall explore Bedwardism and Garveyism. However, I shall ground both of these movements in the philosophical developments known as Ethiopianism.

Undergirding the ideas of figures such as Bedward, Blyden and Garvey is the doctrine of Ethiopianism. Put simply, Ethiopianism is a complex and varied doctrine that idealizes Africa. Although never a systematic movement or coherent ideology, it provided a reservoir of ideas from which many resistance traditions drew in the early part of the twentieth century. Some scholars locate the origins of the concept with the secessionist Church in Southern Africa in the early 1890s.[62] However, in each context, whether South Africa, North America or the Caribbean, Ethiopianism had its own particularities and resonance. For example, in Jamaica, Ethiopianism has been viewed as an evolving ideology with distinct phases.[63]

Ethiopianism can be analysed from numerous standpoints, for example, its attack on White supremacy,[64] the idealization of Africa[65] or the emergence of the concept and practice of repatriation.[66] However, here I want to look briefly at the role of the Church and the Bible in the movement.

Jamaican Ethiopianism had its roots in the first Black Baptist church of George Liele, called the Ethiopian Baptist Church (1784). Obviously, Liele had understood from his Black American past the significance of Ethiopia in the Bible and made it a trope for Black Christian identity in the diaspora. The founding of the African Methodist Episcopalian Church in the USA showed a similar tendency. The emergence of Black Christian leaders as the standard bearers of Ethiopianism is also important. In each context – Africa, the Caribbean and North America – Black church leaders played a central role in developing the movement.

One of the first Carribbean intellectuals to document African contributions to biblican theology was Edward Wilmot Blyden, an early Pan-Africanist.[67] In his writings he reclaims the pyramids, Egypt and the contribution of African theologians (Tertullian, Cyprian and Augustine) to biblical interpretation.[68] Controversially, Blyden also believed that Islam was preferable to Christianity as a religion for Black advancement. His reasoning was based on his observation of African Muslims and Christians: the conversion to Islam in Africa had disrupted the dignity and self-worth of the African less than was the case with Christianity. Consequently, Islam provided a better vehicle for self-sufficiency.[69] Blyden's concern for acknowledging Black participation in ancient history is still relevant today.

Another interesting case is the writings of Marcus Garvey. For Garvey, there was an inevitable link between Black pride and *rediscovering* a Black deity. He wanted to decolonize God as a means of freeing the minds of Black people. He understood Christianity to be a vehicle of White supremacy which therefore did little to enhance the self-identity of Black people. In response, Garvey, although not the first,[70] recontextualized the Christian God for the sake of Black liberation. Garvey saw something intrinsically wrong with Black people following a religion designed for and articulated by White people. I will later show that the ideas of Garvey are not 'dead and buried' but live on in muted forms in the work of Black theologians and Afrocentrists today.

To show how Ethiopianism led to the development of more comprehensive systems of resistance, I will explore the significance of two post-colonial activists. While not representing all views during this period, Bedwardism and Garveyism outline central issues for this genealogy of resistance.

Bedwardism

Alexander Bedward was a Native Baptist leader who developed a millenarian movement in Jamaica at the beginning of the twentieth century. Bedwards exceptional Baptist church in August Town, Jamaica was the setting for his criticism of the colonial rulers.

In my opinion, Bedward is significant because he focused the 'resistance potential' within revival Christianity, by providing a socio-political critique of the Jamaican situation. For example, in January 1895 he was quoted in a national newspaper as saying:

> We are the true people; the White men are hypocrites ... The Government pass laws which oppress the Black people. They take their money out of

their pockets, they rob them of their bread and they do nothing for it. Let them remember the Morant War.[71]

His solution to the situation was an apocalyptic end to White rule and the emergence of a new Earth where Black people would reign. However, Bedward believed that the Whites were too powerful to defeat militarily and therefore it was necessary to mobilize supernatural forces to ensure their defeat. To this end Bedward believed that he and his followers would ascend to heaven on a specific date in 1920. They would return to earth after it had been ravaged by fire destroying the White man. Interestingly, he thought that a new Earth was required for Black freedom. Inevitably, after Bedward failed to ascend, his movement lost credibility.

Bedwardism, while not an island-wide mass movement, does provide insight into the reconfiguration of resistance. Unlike Sharpe and Bogle, Bedward had a utopian vision of a 'new world' in which the present order would be totally transformed so that the marginalized and oppressed were free. He replaced the quest for physical space found in Maroonage with an apocalyptic vision of a 'new Earth' found in Christian apocalyptic scriptures. I suggest that Bedward rooted evil squarely in the midst of the colonial system and believed supernatural powers were necessary for their defeat. Hence, according to my analysis Bedward had the vision, but not the necessary plan of action to transform Jamaica. Even, so with Bedward begins a more complex analysis of oppression where religion, ideology and political action are woven together as part of a strategy for change. However, the beginnings of a modern analysis of oppression and a complex Black response start in earnest with the work of Marcus Garvey.

Garveyism

Marcus Mosiah Garvey (1887–1940) was raised in a Wesleyan Methodist home in Jamaica. After becoming involved in union and anti-colonial activity in Jamaica, like many he sought better employment prospects abroad. It was during his time in Costa Rica, Panama, Ecuador, Nicaragua and other countries as a migrant worker that Garvey became convinced of the need for a movement to secure Black uplift and racial pride.[72] (While in London, he was greatly influenced by Booker T. Washington's classic text, *Up from Slavery*.) He returned to Jamaica in 1914 to establish the Universal Negro Improvement Association (UNIA).

There have been numerous scholarly texts that study the meaning and significance of Garvey's movement. For example, Tony Martin has attempted to place Garveyism as a potent Pan-African racial ideology.[73] In a similar vein Horace Campbell has explored Garvey and Garveyism as part of a continuum of Jamaican resistance to colonialism in the twentieth century.[74] On a different level, Barry Chevannes has explored the personal impact of Garvey on ordinary, everyday Jamaicans who later became Rastafarians.[75] However, in recent years there has been an attempt to explore the religious dimensions of the Garvey movement, particularly Garvey's reinterpretation of the Christian religion.[76]

I want to take this last point seriously. Garvey reworked the Christian religion as an integral dimension of his movement. He went beyond Christianity by attempting to unite all religious traditions under the non-sectarian banners of UNIA and the African Orthodox Church. In essence, Garvey attempted to reform Christianity for the benefit of Black people.

In order to understand Garveyism in a way that is consistent with my concern for identifying Black resistance and its interaction with religion, I will outline in brief Garvey's theological ideas of God, Christ and religion.

Garvey believed in the centrality of God in his liberation struggle. With greater intellectual honesty than White theological contemporaries, Garvey realized that God was understood through 'racial lenses'. He encouraged Black people to imagine God as Black, even though he knew God was Spirit and without form. Garvey was concerned with ensuring that Black people might better respect themselves as created beings.[77]

> If the White man has the idea of a White God, let him worship his God as he desires ... We as Negroes, have found a new ideal. While our God has no colour, yet it is human to see everything through one's own spectacles, and since the White people have seen their God through White spectacles ... [we] Negroes believe in the God of Ethiopia, the everlasting God – God the Father, God the Son and God the Holy Ghost, the one God of all ages. That is the God in whom we believe, but we shall worship Him through the spectacles of Ethiopia.[78]

Forty years before the work of James Cone, Garvey's Black God was a God of Black liberation 'of oppressed people'.[79] Moreover, Garvey's God was intimately related to Africa. Garvey's God was 'a God of Ethiopia'.[80] Such a God was fundamentally concerned with racial uplift and self-reliance. Although at times he adopted traditional language about God,[81] he related the being of God to his liberation programme. Hence, in Garveyism, a Black God and Negro uplift were concomitant.[82]

A similar process occurs in Garvey's Christology. Garvey understood Christ's ethnicity as having political importance for Black people. Because Christ was a person of colour, Garvey believed that Christ has additional resonance with the Black masses; he could understand, participate and side with their racial struggle. Hence, at one UNIA conference (1924), Garvey called Christ 'a Black Man of Sorrows'.[83]

Garvey made a distinction between the White Christ exposed in Euro-American Christianity and his Black Christ. Writing in the UNIA newspaper, *The Negro World*, (1923) Garvey states:

> The Negro is now accepting the religion of the real Christ, not the property-robbing, gold-stealing, diamond-exploiting Christ, but the Christ of love, justice and mercy.[84]

What I am suggesting here is that Garvey, prefiguring the work of Black and other liberation theologians, argued that Jesus assisted Black people in their struggle for justice. Christ was not exclusively for Blacks however, as this Christ was accessible to all.[85] At times Garvey compared himself to Christ as both were leaders of mass movements geared towards the liberation of oppressed people; both suffered persecution and rejection; both would die for their cause.[86] Hence it should be no surprise that after Garvey's death his followers introduced creeds that elevated him to the status of a prophet.[87]

Finally, Garvey understood religion as a vehicle for Black emancipation. Religion was primarily functional – a tool for a more general protracted struggle against racial subordination.[88] To this end Garvey established a 'denomination', the African Orthodox Church, to serve the religious needs of UNIA. As with Blyden, Garvey did not subscribe exclusively to Christianity. He believed that all religions had the capacity to express the meaning of God, including Islam. Even so, he was critical of remnants of African religions in Jamaica such as Pucommina. This was primarily because of his general critique of otherworldly religious movements such as Bedwardism.[89] He did not believe that religion by itself had the ability to liberate Black people. Instead, only combined with concrete material force would religion enhance Black struggle.

Garveyism as a political movement failed. Repatriation to Africa did not take place on any meaningful scale. Moreover Garvey died alone and broken. What then is significant about Garveyism? First, it should be mentioned that although based around the cult of one man, Garveyism was indeed a movement followed by both Black men and Black women. For example, Garvey's wife, Amy, became an enthusiastic spokesperson for his cause after his death.[90] Second, Garvey deals with the immediate situation by demanding a radical transformation of the Black psyche. Like the Maroons, Bogle, Sharpe and Bedward, Garvey has a vision of a new beginning for Black people – the promised land on this occasion is Africa. But he was not totally committed to destroying White power through protracted struggle. Garvey went beyond his predecessors by offering a systematic programme for Black regeneration based on pride, racial uplift and self-reliance. Most important to this study, Garvey presents a comprehensive critique and reinterpretation of White Christian religion, offering an alternative religious ideology based on Black emancipation. Garveyism countered the most central elements of White racism within his experience and context. UNIA offered land, religion, ideology and pride as the primary solutions to the psychological, ideological and physical brutality central to White racisms.

POST-WAR RESISTANCE

When referring to post-war resistance focusing on the role of religion as the mobilizing force, I am primarily concerned with Rastafari. Why Rastafari? Because no other religious system within African Caribbean British history has attempted to undermine the influence of European Christianity and develop an alternative theological system for Black people. Although Islam has re-emerged as a force in the UK, it has yet to provide the comprehensive popularist critique found in Rastafari.

Rastafari

Over the last two decades there have been numerous studies of Rastafari. Some have attempted to highlight the millenarian aspects of the movement.[91] Others have focused on the socio-political dimensions of the movement.[92] In contrast, new approaches have focused on the evolutionary relationship between Myal, Native Baptists, Revivalism and Rastafari.[93] While recognizing the various dimensions of the movement, this study is concerned with Rastafari as a system of resistance.

Numerous factors account for the development of Rastafari in colonial Jamaica: economic depression in Jamaica,[94] the teachings of Marcus Garvey, the rise of Haile Selassie in Ethiopia and the emergence of the Ethiopian World Federation during the Italian invasion of Ethiopia.[95] All assisted the development of this movement and require further investigation. Of particular significance to the theological concerns of this study are the results of the teachings of Marcus Garvey.

As mentioned above, Marcus Garvey presented a vision of eschatological redemption located in Ethiopia as a solution to the concerns of Black people in the African diaspora. Garvey's prediction that Ethiopia would be the centre of Black redemption became clearer to some when in 1930 Prince Ras Tafari (1891–1975) was crowned Emperor Haile Selassie. Black Nationalists throughout the world celebrated Selassie's coronation and much was expected from this new African king. Furthermore, the titles and attributes claimed by Selassie – King of Kings, Lord of Lords and Conquering Lion of the Tribe of Judah – corresponded for some with New Testament messianic texts, such as Revelation 19.11, 16. In short, Selassie's titles were those ascribed to the returning Messiah. The 'prophecies' of Marcus Garvey led several Black ministers to preach that 'Black redemption was at hand'.[96] They looked to the Bible for acknowledgement and certitude of their conviction that Selassie was divine and the God of Ethiopia of whom Marcus Garvey spoke. Revelation 5.2–3, 19; Daniel 7.3; Psalm 68.31 gave them the Biblical endorsement that Selassie would lead the Black 'race' out of Babylonian captivity.

After establishing a community of followers in Kingston, they set about preaching to the masses in Jamaica. The early missionary activity of Leonard Percival Howell in 1933–4 introduces us to the initial ideas of these early Rastafarians. Howell advocated six principles:

> (1) hatred for the White 'race'; (2) the complete superiority of the Black 'race'; (3) revenge on Whites for their wickedness; (4) the negation, persecution, and humiliation of the government and legal bodies of Jamaica; (5) preparation to go back to Africa; and (6) acknowledging Emperor Haile Selassie as the Supreme Being and only ruler of Black people.[97]

Naturally, the authorities did not take kindly to the elevation of Selassie over the King of England, nor to the revolutionary doctrine of the Rastafarians, particularly its appeal to the poor and disaffected – the majority of its adherents and supporters. Consequently, Rastafari's founding patriarchs were all given prison sentences in 1934. Upon the release of Howell two years later, the movement established a community of followers in the hills of St Catherine. Here, through communal living, they were able to work out some of the beliefs and practices of the movement.

How was Rastafari in Jamaica part of Black resistance? I want to describe four areas: epistemology, theology, culture and politics.

Epistemology is concerned with how we know what we know as truth. Rastafari provided an alternative basis upon which to determine truth. As Chevannes has shown, Rasta epistemology can be traced back to Myalism and Revivalist Christianity in nineteenth-century Jamaica.[98] Through 'reasoning' or what the Rastafarian intellectual Walter Rodney would call 'groundings', intuition and experience discern truth. This process is threefold. First, either individually or communally, truth is the product of reasoning with 'Jah'. Second, the truth provides insights into life and reality. Finally, the Bible can verify truths that emerge from an encounter with the Rastafarian reality or *Dread*, although, ultimately, authority is located within. As shown above through my analysis of studies of the Black Church, the hermeneutical processes of Black Pentecostalism make use of experience as a means of determining truth. The alternative epistemology enabled an opposing and empowering process of locating truth outside traditional centres such as education or the Church.

As for *theology*, through reasoning, Rastafarians in the 1950s developed several ideas that became 'truths' within the movement. But as there was no central authority or creed, these truths vary and have historically undergone revision. Clarke states:

> By 1960 scholars were suggesting that the central teachings could be reduced to four: (1) Rastafari (Haile Selassie) is the living God; (2) Ethiopia is the home of the Black person; (3) redemption, which will soon occur, is by repatriation; (4) the ways of White people are Evil. Shortly afterwards another observer maintained that there were only two essential truths; (1) Ras Tafari is the living God; (2) salvation for Black people is through repatriation to Africa.[99]

I want to explore these latter two points in more depth. We have seen that Garvey advocated the worship of a Black god as part of a reconstructed Black Self. Rastas developed this theme further by uncovering a 'living' God. The process of elevating man to God/God to man has theological implications – Rastafari's immanent theology places the locus of divine presence within the individual. God is the inner power that enables the individual to live righteously. As I have shown above, Pentecostal pneumatology also focuses on the divine empowerment of the individual. Also the location of spiritual power within the individual emerges in Myalism – the coming together of the Spirit and the human. Furthermore Satan, the opponent of God, is also ever present and active:

> Simple man is not completely divine, in the Rastafarian view, because he is still partly under the sway of Satan, the embodiment of all that is in opposition to God in Man. Just as the God of the Rastas is not allowed to be an other-worldly, intangible being estranged from the ways of man, so also Satan is conceived by the brethren as being immediately present to the working of history.[100]

I want to argue that in terms of resistance, by emphasizing the divine as a Black person, this hallmark of Rastafari uplifts the Black Self. In a context of colonialism/neo-colonialism such activity encourages self-worth and self-reliance and agitates against Europeanized Christianity, particularly its overemphasis on the view that God is far away.

Second, Ethiopia as the land of liberation/salvation is of theological significance because it corresponds with the theme of the promised land in Old Testament theology. That is, like the Children of Israel, Rastas must be rescued from their captivity in Babylon – in this case Jamaica and the Western world. Interestingly, exile in Babylon is viewed by some as the result of Black people not being true to Jah in the past.[101] In this theological-historical system, Africa is akin to Eden, without evil or suffering. It has long been thought that Rastas in Jamaica identify with repatriation; it is now generally acknowledged that not all Rastas subscribe to this belief. Instead, return to Africa has become a metaphor for a spiritual and mental return to one's African identity and heritage.

The third arena in which resistance occurs in Rastafari is *cultural* resistance. Campbell identifies food preparation, language, music and politics.[102] Of major significance to this study is the use of language.

I want to argue that language was also a form of cultural resistance. Common language in Jamaica was the product of slavery. It was a fusion of African and European language systems. Even so, common language was and is considered inferior to Standard English – the requirement for advancement in Jamaican society. By emphasizing common 'patois' (Jamaica Creole), Rastas reaffirmed the language of the common people, that is 'Jamaican' language, showing that it was not necessary to speak the Queen's English in Jamaica. Instead, they developed 'Rasta talk' which used patois as the vehicle for expressing the historical memory of oppression and the quest for total emancipation.[103] Probably the most significant linguistic development was the transformation of the personal pronoun 'I'. I quote Chevannes at length:

> Certain words and phrases have become popular modes of speech ... Indeed, the most important of them carry religious and moral implications. The most important is 'I', the personal pronoun. To the Rastafari this is the same as the Roman numeral *I*, which follows the name Selassie. 'I' substitutes for 'me' and for 'mine.' The religious meaning behind this substitution is that the Rastafari is also part of God, and if God is a visible, living man, it must mean that the Rastafari is another Selassie, another 'I'. Because everyone is an 'I' one does not say 'we' for plurality, but says 'I and I'. As the most central word in Rastafari speech, 'I' transforms other words as well. 'Brethren' pronounced in the dialect as 'Bredrin' becomes 'Idrin'; 'eternal,' 'Iternal'; 'hour,' 'Iowa'; 'times,' 'Itimes'; 'creator,' 'Ireator'; and so forth.[104]

Later in this study, I will make use of the language tradition of Rastafari to find a tool for politicizing Black Pentecostalism.

Finally, the last area in which Rastafari represented resistance is in *politics*. When considering Rasta politics it is important to note the gender critique of the movement. Numerous studies have identified the sexism and gender bias within its practices and history.[105] Any analysis of the movement must acknowledge this shortcoming.

Given the history of male domination, it is no surprise that it is a man who was the most influential force in shaping the Rastafari political agenda. Walter Rodney was born in Guyana in 1942, and educated in Jamaica between 1960 and 1963. After post-graduate study in England, he returned to the Caribbean to share his expertise in African history and the Atlantic slave trade. While teaching in Jamaica, Walter Rodney gave Rastafari intellectual credibility, and as a consequence, many middle-class Jamaicans became Rastas.[106]

Rodney, as a Black intellectual, understood the importance of focusing upon African history and its role in Black liberation. Historical knowledge was a weapon against White cultural imperialism:

> One of the major dilemmas inherent in the attempt by Black people to break through the cultural aspects of White imperialism is posed by the use of historical knowledge as a weapon in our struggle. Firstly, the effort must be directed solely towards freeing and mobilising Black minds ... Secondly, the

acquired knowledge of African history must be seen as directly relevant but secondary to the concrete tactics and strategy which are necessary for our liberation.[107]

However, what I find of vital importance is that Rodney did not stand for a romanticized picture of Africa and was quick to counter the misunderstandings of Ethiopian history in Rastafari. He added socialism to his Africa-centred approach to history. This was to show how the exploitation of Africans by mulattos and Whites was the product of capitalism in colonialism and imperialism. In short he demanded that Blacks in Jamaica should identify with the African workers in the past and not necessarily their rulers, kings and queens:

> Even in those kingdoms the historical accounts often concentrate narrowly on the behaviour of elite groups and dynasties; we need to portray the elements of Africa everyday life and to comprehend the culture of Africa irrespective of whether they were resident in the Empire of Mali or an Ibo village ... With the same criteria in mind, it is worth noting the following aspects of African social behaviour: hospitality, the role and treatment of the aged, law and public order and social tolerance.[108]

Rodney saw Rastafari as a movement through which an Africa-centred personality could be achieved. Like Garvey, Rodney thought evil lay in the colonized minds of Black men and women as well as the social and economic system that ensured their subjugation and exploitation. His influence was such that after he was banned and exiled from Jamaica in 1968, many Rastas began to focus on the need for domestic emancipation and a people's government in Jamaica, rather than focusing on repatriation and the deity of Haile Selassie.[109] Rodney's legacy lives on amongst Rastas who linked nationalism with communism and a scientific assessment of the liberation struggle. Rodney built upon Garvey's holistic analysis but was subject to similar sexist presuppositions.

In summary, I have attempted to show that in Rastafari we see a new reconfiguration of Black resistance. Rastafari made use of the Jamaican nationalist heritage; its critique of Whiteness, Black pride, the focus on religion as a vehicle for emancipation and the quest for self-sufficient space/land. Here, the critique of Whiteness, inspired by Garvey, took seriously the effects of Whiteness on the Black mind. Hence, White systems of thought are contested. The solution was not just learning Black history or challenging the political hegemony, but also a commitment to psychological change – becoming a new Black (being). Rastafari's analysis of the Black condition is very important. It suggests that liberation is both a *spiritual* and *social* matter. Both realities must be seen as a whole and not separate. This means that Rastafari as the Caribbean's first liberation theology sets an important tone for the development of a Black political theology.

Rastafari in Britain

Rastafari travelled beyond Jamaica, becoming a significant cultural and political force for the Caribbean diaspora in Britain, especially among second-generation Black British youths, making its most visible show in Britain in the early 1970s. However, it is important to note that before the emergence of Rastafari, it was the Black Muslims who set a platform for post-war religio-political movement amongst the Caribbean diaspora in Britain.[110]

By the late 1970s Rastafari was the subject of numerous academic studies attempting to find conceptual frameworks for understanding the phenomenal spread of the movement among Britain's Black working-class youths in London, Birmingham, Manchester, Bristol, Leeds and Liverpool. Rastafari's religious appeal was of considerable interest.

Studies both from inside[111] and outside[112] the Black community have analysed Rastafari in Britain in terms of its religious viability. Both sets of studies make use of concepts of 'cult' and 'sect' to analyse the movement's appeal among Britain's Black youths in the 1970s.

Such an approach viewed Rastafari only as a response to the social and economic crisis faced by Black youths – a form of withdrawal from a hostile world.[113] This approach does not take seriously the inherent religio-cultural heritage found in Rastafari and noted above.

From the perspectives of this study, a better analysis of the movement in Britain is found in Paul Gilroy's analysis of 'interpretative community'.[114] As an interpretative community Rastafari provided symbols, language and identity that signified resistance to Black oppression in Britain. I would suggest that the influence of this 'interpretative community' was felt within the Black-led churches.

Rastafari is often viewed in diametric opposition to Pentecostalism. This was because Rastafari was viewed as the religion of the conscious Black youths, and Christianity as the slave master's religion deceiving the older Black generation of migrants in Britain.[115] Consequently,

Rastafari became the bane of Black Pentecostalism, taking its young people and offering them a more militant ideology.[116] Politically, Rastafari became associated with assertion and Black Pentecostals with evasion. Moreover, several studies attempted to view both as 'withdrawal' from the socio-political world. For example, both religious traditions were interpreted as escapism, failing to engage in British social life.[117] However, such studies fail to grasp the complexity and influence of both movements in Britain, a realization that would be later acknowledged by some.[118]

What can be concluded about Rastafari in the British context? First, we must acknowledge that while tackling the issue of racialized oppression, Rastafari failed to take seriously oppression within its own ranks. Much has been written regarding sexism in Rastafari,[119] in particular its reproduction of sexist norms. In this respect, Rastafari was limited resistance. Second, Rastafari located evil both in the immediate situation and also within evil people. Rastafari eventually opted for a vision of a new Earth, looking to repatriation and domestic political struggle to rid the economic and social systems of evil. Evil also had profound effects upon the Black psyche; therefore, mental decolonization was integral to the liberation project – holistic spiritual and social transformation of the Black person.

MacRobert's study mentions radicals within the Black Pentecostal Church who were influenced by Black Nationalist ideologies. To date, however, there has been no attempt to show how Rastafari as an 'interpretative community' influenced Black Pentecostal youth who chose to articulate a political philosophy. If we accept the widespread influence of Rastafari beyond Rasta communities, then it is vitally important to explore how Rastafari affected those Black Pentecostals who chose to stay within the confines of the Church. This issue will be explored later in this study. However, for now it is necessary to point out that Black Pentecostalism has a radical history that provides resources for a political theology.

The Pentecostal movement born at Azusa Street in Los Angeles in 1906 was led by a Black minister called William Seymour (1870–1922). Seymour's approach to Christianity was Black resistance for three reasons. First, he developed a theology of the Holy Spirit (pneumatology) that was counter-hegemonic. For the Azusa church the gift of speaking in tongues, a defining hallmark of the movement, was not just an initial sign of receiving the Holy Spirit, but also a sign of a commitment to radical social transformation. The early Black Pentecostal movement came to regard tongues as a continuation of a just order established by God.[120] Therefore one could not have tongues and continue with forms of social discrimination.

Second, Seymour developed an anti-oppressive Christian practice. His church was anti-racist, anti-sexist and anti-classist in a context of race, gender and class oppression in America at beginning of the twentieth century. This egalitarian theme was represented in the seating arrangements, which:

> reflected the oneness in equality Seymour envisioned. Worshippers gathered in a new way completely equal in the house of God, the body of Christ not a collection of individuals looking over the back of many heads simply to the clergy or choir but an intimate whole serving one another. This unconventional seating plan revealed Seymour's conviction that events transpiring at Azusa Mission were different, unique and revolutionary.[121]

The fact that a Black minister in a racist context was able to develop and maintain such a theological orientation was truly revolutionary in its time.

Third, Seymour utilized Black cultural resources in order to develop the holistic ministry at Azusa. For example, the Pentecostal movement made use of the Black music tradition:

> He affirmed his Black heritage by introducing Negro spirituals and Negro music into his liturgy at a time when this music was considered inferior and unfit for Christian worship.[122]

However, Seymour's cultural contribution was more than the intro- duction of music. As MacRobert demonstrates, Seymour brought to Azusa the Black religious heritage. This was a religious tradition that utilized story, song, dance, polyrhythmic clapping and the swaying of bodies.[123]

This third point is important to this study because (as will be shown in Chapter 5) cultural resources in the form of the concept of 'dread' were to be merged with aspects of Black Pentecostalism. I will demonstrate that it is possible to make use of aspects of the theological framework found at Azusa (radical pneumatology, praxis and African retention) to form a political theology today.

CONCLUSION

This chapter has explored the genealogy of religious-influenced resistance from the shores of Africa to the streets of Britain. I have shown that Black resistance is historically specific, multiple and expressed through religious ideologies worked out differently in each historical moment. It has been shown that as well as traditions of survival, there are also traditions of liberation concerned with physical and structural transformation of the status quo. It is the latter tradition that offers the best hope for a holistic political theology because it is concerned with removing what are perceived as the real causes of distress. The next task is to develop a methodological framework from the resistance genealogy that can be the basis for a political theology.

NOTES

1. For a fuller discussion see Burton, R.D.E. *Afro-Creole: Power, Opposition and Play in the Caribbean.* New York: Cornell University Press, 1997, pp. 6–7.
2. Certeau, M. 'On the Oppositional Practices of Everyday Life.' *Social Text*, 1980, 3:3–43.
3. For example, armed insurrection and religious devotion are both forms of resistance found within Jamaican history. The former displays a greater commitment to Certeau's concept of resistance while the latter is more akin to opposition. However, at times resistance/opposition types are combined. For example, religious-inspired insurrection, such as the Baptist rebellion of 1831–2, combined elements of *resistance* (uprising) and *opposition* (Christian religious inspiration).
4. See Hall, S. 'Religious Ideologies and Social Movements in Jamaica.' In: Bocock, R. and Thompson, K. (eds). *Religion and Ideology.* Manchester: Manchester University Press, 1985, pp. 269–7.
5. Anderson, V. *Beyond Ontological Blackness: An Essay on African American Religious and Cultural Criticism.* New York: Continuum, 1995, p. 80.
6. ibid., p. 129.
7. Bush, B. *Slave Women in Caribbean Society 1650–1880.* Bloomington and Indianapolis: Indiana University Press, 1990, p. 1.
8. Gutiérrez, G. *A Theology of Liberation.* Maryknoll, New York: Orbis, 1973, pp. 87–92.
9. Cone, J. *God of the Oppressed.* San Francisco: HarperCollins, 1975, pp. 62–6.

10. Warrior, R.A. 'Canaanites, Cowboys and Indians: Deliverance, Conquest and Liberation Theology Today.' *Christianity and Crisis* 1989, 49, 261–5.

11. For a useful review see Prior, M. *The Bible and Colonialism: A Moral Critique*. Sheffield: Sheffield Academic Press, 1997.

12. Volf, M. *Exclusion and Embrace: A Theological Exploration of Identity, Otherness and Reconciliation*. Nashville: Abingdon Press, 1996, pp. 99ff.

13. See Williams, C. *The Destruction of the African Diaspora Civilisation: Great Issues of a 'Race' from 4500 B.C. to 2000 A.D.* Chicago: Third World Press, 1987, pp. 243–72.

14. Walvin, J. *Black Ivory: A History of British Slavery*. London: Fontana Press, 1992, pp. 25ff.

15. Simpson, G. *Black Religions in the New World*. New York: Columbia University Press, 1978, p. 3.

16. Here is one such example. Near the end of the seventeenth century a Dutch slave ship on the coast of Guinea (Gold Coast) was overpowered by its cargo of slaves. The slaves, using a hammer, converted an old anchor left in their quarters into several weapons, which they used to good effect against their captors. See Harding, V. *There is a River: The African Diaspora Struggle for Freedom in America*. New York: HJB, 1981, p. 10.

17. ibid., pp. 12–13.

18. For example, one failed attempt at liberation in 1721 off the coast of Sierra Leone bears testimony to the cost of freedom for one of the female protagonists of a failed revolt. Commenting on her punishment Harding asks, 'And what of the woman who chose the struggle for Black freedom over her privileged bondage among White men? We are told that "the woman he hoisted up by the Thumbs, whipp'd and slashed her with Knives, before the other Slaves till she died". And so, not far from the shores of the homeland, the swaying, bleeding body of a sister in struggle bore terrifying witness to the cost of the decision for freedom. Yet perhaps she would have considered this lonely vigil above the sea a better use of her body than any that the crew members had had in mind'. (ibid., p. 13)

19. ibid., p. 5.

20. Wilmore, G. *Black Religion and Black Radicalism*. New York: Orbis, 1998.

21. The Arawak were the original inhabitors and first discoverers of Jamaica. Arawak Indians may have settled in Jamaica in two

waves, first around AD 650 and second between AD 850 and 900. 'They called their land', meaning Xaymaca 'the land of wood and water'. Jamaica and the Arawak were first stumbled upon by Columbus during his second voyage in 1494. Spanish colonization of the island, which began in earnest in 1509, brought torture, enslavement and near total extermination of the Arawaks. As forebears of European enslavement in Jamaica, the Arawaks resisted Spanish rule. Clinton, B. *History of Jamaica.* Harlow: Longman Group, 1983, p. 10.

22. Such was the viciousness of the Spanish, the Arawaks' unwillingness to comply and their inability to resist European disease, that by the time the British came to rule in 1655 the Arawak were almost completely wiped out: their population had been reduced from 60,000 to less than one hundred. (ibid., p. 27)

23. The first African slaves were brought to Jamaica by Spanish colonizers. They were predominantly slaves, although some manumitted freepersons were also present.

24. The leader of this first rebel army that merited British military efforts in the 1730s was Cudjoe. Accompanied by his brothers, Accompong and Johnny in the West and the sub-chiefs Quao and Cuffee in the East, and with the assistance of his inspirational 'Obehwoman' and 'Sister' Nanny, Cudjoe began a battle against the British colonizers in the 1730s which is known in Jamaican history as the first Maroon war.

25. See Hart, R. *Blacks in Rebellion.* Jamaica: Institute of Social and Economic Research, 1985, p. 126.

26. After the unfair treatment of two Maroons from the Jamaican parish of Trelawny, the British authorities, rather than listening to the Maroon grievance, and fearful of a repeat of the Haitian revolution, acted swiftly and illegally by imprisoning several Maroon leaders. Furthermore, after offering unrealistic and unfavourable terms of surrender, they attacked the Maroon settlement at Trelawny. The Maroons were able to hold out for five months against superior numbers and firepower in the hill country of that region. Eventually, attacked and chased by other Maroon settlements, the Trelawny Maroons surrendered and were deported to Nova Scotia in 1796 and then to Sierra Leone in 1800, where their descendants can be found in Free Town to this day.

27. One of the most famous Maroon leaders was Nanny, a female Coromante. See Bush, B. op. cit., pp. 69ff.

28. Campbell, H. *Rasta and Resistance: From Marcus Garvey to Walter Rodney.* London: Hansib, 1985, p. 13.
29. Cashmore, E. *Rastaman: The Rastafarian Movement in England.* London: George Allen and Unwin, 1979, p. 13.
30. Black, C. *History of Jamaica.* London: Longman, 1983, p. 64.
31. Simpson, G. op. cit., p. 42.
32. ibid., p. 53.
33. Turner, M. *Slaves and Missionaries: The Disintegration of Jamaican Slave Society, 1787–1834.* Urbana: University of Illinois Press, 1982, p. 12.
34. See Dadzie, S. 'Searching for the Invisible Woman; Slavery and Resistance in Jamaica.' *Race and Class,* 32:2 (1990), pp. 21–38.
35. Significantly, Sharpe destroyed property thereby undermining the economic stability of the island. In total over £1.5 million worth of damage was caused. At its height, Sam Sharpe's resistance involved some 20,000 slaves in rebellion.
36. Bakan, A. *Ideology and Class Conflict in Jamaica: The Politics of Rebellion.* Montreal: McGill-Queen's University Press, 1990, p. 53.
37. Chevannes, B. *Rastafari: Roots and Ideology.* Syracuse: Syracuse University Press, 1994, p. 20.
38. The higher cost of production and the loss of political sympathy among the British public assisted the abolition of slavery by the British Parliament in August 1833. Unfortunately, as the British government set the terms of freedom, there was no significant change in the ownership of property or the means of production.
39. Bush, B. op. cit., pp. 65–77.
40. See Burton, R. *Afro-Creole: Power, Opposition and Play in the Caribbean.* New York and London: Cornell University Press, 1997, p. 109.
41. Campbell, H. op. cit., pp. 37–8.
42. See Robotham, D. '"The Notorious Riot:" The Socio-economic and Political Bases of Paul Bogle's Revolt.' Mona: University of the West Indies, Working Paper no 28, Institute of Social and Economic Research, 1981.
43. ibid., p. 15.
44. Geggus, D. *Slave Resistance Studies and the Saint Domingue Slave Revolt: Some Preliminary Considerations.* Miami, Latin American and Caribbean Center: Florida International University, 1983, pp. 2–3.
45. Dadzie, S. op. cit., pp. 21–38.
46. ibid.

47. ibid., p. 22.

48. Cranton, M. *Testing the Chains: Resistance to Slavery in the British West Indies*. New York: Cornell University Press, 1982, p. 25.

49. Cooper, C. *Noises in the Blood: Gender, Orality and the Vulgar Body in Jamaican Popular Culture*. Durham, USA: Duke University Press, 1993, p. 141.

50. Burton, R. op. cit., p. 62.

51. First, in the form of the 'Quashie phenomenon', who behind an exterior of smiling compliance masked a desire for freedom and a commitment to agitation. Second in the Jonkonnu Christmas celebrations, and third in the dual-consciousness tradition of the Negro spiritual. The spiritual gave an outward expression of a future eschatological hope that was really a grounded existential desire for freedom. As I have shown elsewhere, sometimes this sentiment still lives in the traditions of contemporary Black Christianity.

52. Williams, R. *Culture*. Glasgow: Fontana, 1981, p. 13.

53. Patterson, O. *The Sociology of Slavery: An Analysis of the Origins, Development and Structure of Negro Slavery in Jamaica*. New Jersey: Fairleigh Dickinson University Press, 1967, p. 106.

54. Braithwaite, E.K. *The Folk Culture of the Slaves in Jamaica*. London: New Beacon, 1974, p. 13.

55. On the one hand, there are Caribbean scholars who argue that African cultural retentions, stories, rites of passage and world-views ensured the maintenance of an implicit African identity among slaves. On the other hand, there are those who argue that slave culture transformed African retentions so that they became a totally new form. These scholars argue that it is also important to acknowledge that for African retentions to be maintained in the New World they became fixed to a new social order in order to maintain and contain them. Cf. the debate between Frazier and Herskovits: Frazier, F. *The Negro Church in America*. New York: Schocken Books, 1963. Herskovits, M.J. *The Myth of the Negro Past*. New York: Harper and Brothers, 1941.

56. Hood, R. *Must God Remain Greek? Afro Cultures and God Talk*. Minneapolis: Fortress Press, 1990, pp. 65–6.

57. Obeah men and women were brokers who were able to do injury to a person. Whereas Myalism deals with good spirits, Obeah deals with the bad. Even so, Caribbean theologian Noel Erskine contends that Obeah was used positively among slave communities in bondage. For instance, as we have seen, Nanny of the

Maroons was considered to be a powerful Obeah woman. Furthermore, Obeah provided the existential 'courage to be' against slavery, giving protection and assurance. Erskine, N. *Decolonizing Theology: A Caribbean Perspective.* New York: Orbis, 1981, p. 29.

58. Quoted in Barrett, L.E. *The Rastafarians: The Dreadlocks of Jamaica.* Jamaica: Sangster's Book Stores Ltd, 1977, p. 22.

59. Chevannes, B. op. cit., p. 20.

60. Curtain, P.D. *Two Jamaicans: The Role of Ideas in a Tropical Colony.* Cambridge: Harvard University Press, 1955, p. 68.

61. Wilkinson, J. *The Church in Black and White.* Edinburgh: St Andrew Press, 1993, pp. 23–35.

62. Sundkler, B. *Bantu Prophets in South Africa,* 2nd edn. London; New York; Toronto: Oxford University Press, 1961.

63. Chevannes, B. op. cit., p. 34.

64. Ethiopianism was a response to White supremacy. As noted in the previous chapter, the nineteenth century in Europe heralded the emergence of pseudo-scientific racisms that were evident in colonial and imperial policies in England. Hence, in the midst of White worldwide domination Ethiopianism emerged as a catalyst for a global Black response to White supremacy. Through the writings of learned Black scholars, such as Edward Wilmot Blyden and Martin Delaney, Black communities began to focus on their African heritage and identity. The Church was a primary vehicle for expressing Ethiopianism. For example in both the Caribbean and North America, Black denominations took the name 'African' or 'Ethiopian' as a component in the title of their denominations. This was a most remarkable affirmation of Black identity in contexts where Africa was synonymous with barbarity and incivility in the White psyche.

65. Ethiopianism placed an emphasis upon the glories of the African past in order to affirm Black identity and dignity among continental and diasporan Africans. For example, the Caribbean intellectual and traveller Edward Wilmot Blyden wrote in 1887 of the ways in which Ethiopia historically served the world. Similarly, Marcus Garvey's Universal Negro Improvement Association (UNIA) emphasized the glories of the African past. It was with Garvey that Ethiopianism reached unprecedented heights.

66. Ethiopianism focused on repatriation. The idea of Africa as the homeland of Black people was stimulated by missionaries found-

ing Sierra Leone in the 1780s; White Christian missionaries hoped that freed Blacks would return to Africa, spreading trade, education and 'civilization'. Some Black Americans took seriously the opportunity to return to Africa for missionary work. For example, Paul Cuffe, a New England trader, advocated repatriation and began transporting Black Americans in 1815. Not all of the early returnees were positive about Black Africans. Some internalized the pejorative perspectives of White missionaries. The concept of repatriation reached a high point in the writings of Blyden and Garvey. Blyden argued that Africans abroad had the opportunity to enhance development in Africa.

67. Blyden, E.W. *Christianity, Islam and the Negro.* Baltimore: Black Classic Press, 1994, pp. 130–50.
68. Lynch, H.R. *Edward Wilmot Blyden: Pan-Negro Patriot, 1832–1912.* London: Oxford University Press, 1967, p. 55.
69. ibid., p. 12.
70. Clarke, P.B. *Black Paradise: The Rastafarian Movement.* Wellingborough: Aquarian Press, 1986. p. 39.
71. Quote from Cashmore, E. op. cit., p. 19.
72. Hood, R.E. op. cit., p. 88.
73. Martin, T. *Race First: The Ideological and Organizational Struggles of Marcus Garvey and the Universal Negro Improvement Association.* Dover, Mass.: The Majority Press, 1986.
74. Campbell, H. op. cit.
75. According to eyewitness accounts, there were at least four themes in Garvey's message to the Black Jamaicans during his activism in the late 1920s. These were Africa as the natural home of Black people, Black Unity, self-reliance and confronting the White oppressors. Chevannes, B. op. cit., pp. 94–7.
76. For example, Hood, R.E. op. cit., pp. 87–91.
77. See Wilmore, G. *Black Religion and Black Radicalism: An Interpretation of the Religious History of African Americans.* 3rd edn. New York: Orbis, 1988, p. 178.
78. Cited in Hood, R.E. op. cit., p. 89.
79. Martin, T. op. cit., p. 69.
80. ibid.
81. Martin, T. (ed.). *Marcus Garvey, Message to the People, The Course of African Philosophy.* Dover, Mass.: The Majority Press, 1986, pp. 45–9.
82. ibid., p. 73.
83. ibid., p. 70.

84. ibid., p. 71.
85. ibid., p. 71.
86. ibid., p. 68.
87. ibid., p. 69.
88. ibid., p. 71.
89. ibid., p. 74.
90. See Martin, T. *Amy Ashwood Garvey, Pan Africanist, Feminist and Wife No. 1*. Dover, Mass.: The Majority Press, 1985.
91. Barrett, L.E. *The Rastafarians: The Dreadlocks of Jamaica*, Jamaica: Sangster's Book Stores, 1977.
92. See Campbell, H. 'Rastafari: Culture of Resistance'. *Race and Class*, 22:1 (1980), pp. 1–22.
93. Chevannes, B. (ed.). *Rastafari and Other African-Caribbean Worldviews*. London: Macmillan Press, 1998.
94. Jamaica was involved in a class and 'caste' struggle in the 1930s. The economic depression in the US and Europe drifted southward and resulted in mass unemployment of Black workers and misery for the poor. Campbell, H. *Rasta and Resistance*, p. 78.
95. The third foundational factor influencing the emergence of Rastafari is the Italian invasion of Ethiopian in 1936. This event helped to focus attention towards Ethiopia as a symbol of Black pride and redemption. Selassie established the Ethiopian World Federation in 1936 to gain support for Ethiopia and her cause. In Jamaica a branch was established in 1938. The EWF's goal of uniting Black people in the struggle against White imperialism did much to advance the cause of the Rastas in Jamaica. However, it was not until the 1950s that the movement began to spread rapidly across colonial Jamaica, especially among the underclass of Kingston. Rastafari in Jamaica had no central body or organization, no codified creed or core beliefs adopted by all adherents. Ironically, the movement was able to flourish by permitting a number of variant doctrines and teachings to be valid at the same time, and by having no central authority or structure.
96. Leonard Howell, Robert Hinds, Archibald Dunkley and Nathaniel Hibbert were prominent among them. All four were originally Garveyites, and aware of the cultural and political needs and aspirations of Black people in the Americas. Barrett, L. op. cit., pp. 81–2.
97. ibid., p. 85.
98. Chevannes, B. *Rastafari: Roots and Ideology*, pp. 22–6.

99. ibid., p. 65.

100. Owens, J. *Dread: The Rastafarians of Jamaica.* Jamaica: Sangster's Book Stores, 1989, p. 132.

101. Clarke, P. *Black Paradise: The Rastafarian Movement*, p. 69.

102. Campbell, H. *Rasta and Resistance*, pp. 121–50.

103. ibid., p. 124.

104. Chevannes, B. op. cit., p. 167.

105. cf. Austin-Broos, D.J. 'Pentecostals and Rastafarians: Cultural, Political and Gender Relations of Two Religious Movements.' *Social Economic Studies* 36:4 (1987), pp. 1–39.

106. Campbell, H. *Rasta and Resistance*, p. 132.

107. Rodney, W. *Groundings with My Brothers.* London: Bogle-L'Ouverture, 1969, p. 51.

108. ibid., p. 53.

109. ibid., p. 132.

110. The arrival of Black Muslims in Britain is directly related to the emergence of Black Muslims in the United States of America and the perceived failure of liberal Black political organizations. The initial impetus for the emergence of Black power was the visit of Malcolm X to Britain in 1964. Meeting Malcolm X inspired Trinidadian-born Michael de Freitas (Michael X) to set up a British version of the Black Muslims. Through the agency of the Racial Adjustment Action Society (RAAS), Black Muslims endeavoured to provide a Black Nationalist spearhead in Britain. According to RAAS it was time for a more militant approach to dealing with racial dis-crimination; it was time for Blacks to 'hit back'. The religious dimensions and influence of RAAS is generally overlooked by most commentators. For example, neither Ramdin or Hiro men-tion the influence of Islam upon the thinking of RAAS. Instead what is mentioned as being significant is RAAS's public display of strength and purpose in 1965 when RAAS supported striking Asian workers in Preston. By November 1967 RAAS had become a spent force; the imprisonment of Michael X and his eventual deportation robbed the movement of its charismatic leadership.

111. See Lee, B.M. *Rastafari: The New Creation.* Jamaica: Media Productions, 1982.

112. Miles, R. *Between Two Cultures? The Case of Rastafarianism.* SSRC Working Papers in Ethnic Relations no. 10, 1978.

113. For a useful study of these issues, see Centre for Contemporary

Cultural Studies *The Empire Strikes Back: Race and Racism in the 70's*, London: Routledge, 1982, pp. 182–230.

114. Gilroy, P. *There Ain't No Black in the Union Jack*. London: Unwin Hyman, 1987, p. 187.

115. Cashmore, E. op. cit., p. 73.

116. Clarke, *Black Paradise*, p. 54.

117. Rex, J. and Tomlinson, S. *Colonial Immigrants in a British City*. London: Routledge & Kegan Paul, 1979, pp. 247ff.

118. Rex, J. *Ethnic identity and Ethnic Mobilization in Britain*. Warwick University: Centre for Research in Ethnic Relations, 1991, pp. 80, 85.

119. See for example, Yawney, C.D. 'To Grow a Daughter: Cultural Liberation and the Dynamics of Oppression in Jamaica.' In: Miller, A. and Finn, G. (eds). *Feminism in Canada*. Montreal: Black Rose Books, 1983.

120. Gerloff, R. *A Plea for British Black Theologies: The Black Church Movement in Britain in its Transatlantic Cultural and Theological Interaction*. Vol. 1. Frankfurt: Peter Lang, 1992, p. 102.

121. Nelson, D.J. *For Such a Time as This: The Story of Bishop William J. Seymour and the Azusa Street Revival*. Unpublished PhD dissertation, University of Birmingham, May 1981, p. 120.

122. Hollenweger, W.J. *Pentecostalism: Origins and Developments Worldwide*. Massachusetts; Hendrickson Publishers, 1997, p. 20.

123. MacRobert, I. *The Black Roots and White Racism of Early Pentecostalism in the USA*. London: Macmillan Press, 1988, p. 35.

4 Overstanding

Tools for a Black Political Theology

How do we make use of the genealogy of resistance? What I would like to do in this chapter is provide a theological method or framework that can be used to develop a political theology by identifying analytical tools that emerge from the previous discussion in the historical sections. These tools are concerned with developing a resistance tradition within the Black Church in Britain. This study breaks new ground by providing a broad framework for a Black British political theology.

'Overstanding' is a word used in Black communities to describe a process of gaining insight into a situation. It represents a revelation of hidden knowledge not disclosed in traditional forms of 'understanding'. The inversion of the term 'understanding' to form 'overstanding' has roots in Rastafarian culture in Jamaica. This chapter is about a form of overstanding: Black Christians drawing on the history of Black resistance to find new tools to help make sense of the present situation.

In order to guide the development of these tools, I want to revisit in more detail Valentina Alexander's analysis of active radicalism. In short, I will use active radicalism as a trope or unifying principle to draw out analytical tools from the genealogy of Black resistance, the purpose being the development of a theological praxis based on active radicalism.

This chapter has three sections. First, I will outline tools that emerge from the correlation of active radicalism with the genealogy of resistance. Second, I will construct a framework from a development of these tools. Third, I will illustrate the efficacy of the framework by exploring the closest attempt at its articulation in Britain, that is, the Black Theology Support Group (BTSG) in Birmingham.

In recent years, Valentina Alexander has attempted to codify Black resistance within the context of the Black Church tradition. In terms of resistance motifs, Alexander, like Gayraud Wilmore, draws a distinction between survival and liberation in Black faith.[1] She refers to the tradition of liberation as 'active radicalism'. I quote Valentina Alexander's description of active radicalism at length:

> An actively radical approach to liberation would involve building on the foundations of liberational spirituality, which lies at the heart of passive radicalism. Whilst retaining an African epistemological centre, an actively radical impetus would, nonetheless, broaden the scope of social analysis, providing it with a multi-dimensional insight into social transformation and allowing for the possibility of an historic-analytical element to be added to its method of interpreting the social world. Above all, active radicalism is uncompromised radicalism. To borrow from sociological analysis, it turns what might be described as the latent functions of the BLC [Black Led Church] into manifest functions. However, with a twist to traditional structural-functionalist readings, it means that, in becoming manifest, it is now able to more effectively undermine the oppressive hegemonic practices of society, which in its latent state it could only attempt to *cope with* and *survive* under. Believers are able to recognise therefore that liberation must address structures of oppression as well as provide personal empowerment for individual advancement. To this extent, the cognitive appropriation of liberation is represented as something of a journey. It begins with the personal conviction that the individual is made in the image of God and therefore of worth and value. It continues through the exploration of Biblical hermeneutics in which believers are able to understand that God is 'no respecter of persons.' It then comes to fruition with a conscious theological understanding of God's alignment with the struggles of the oppressed and the conviction, therefore, that the Church has both a divine calling and a social responsibility to speak out against oppression in the Church and in society. As a personal conviction which leads to the pursuit of a life long journey, active radicalism serves to heighten both spiritual and theological consciousness, allowing it to incorporate the entirety of the human experience, both metaphysical and material . . . This means that an explicit theology need not lose touch with its eschatological convictions; it need only include them within a wider, multi-dimensional understanding of societal transformation.[2]

The technical detail mentioned by Alexander can be distilled into three themes. These are epistemology, analysis and theology.

It begins with a commitment to African-centred *epistemology*. Above I outlined an epistemology emerging from the African Caribbean resistance. In particular, Garveyism and Rastafari crystallized earlier traditions of resistance that emerged from Black experience in the Caribbean (Jamaica).

Her second point is a commitment to *analysis,* particularly historical-social analysis that pinpoints social and political issues so that the ministry of the Church is geared towards a multi-dimensional analysis rather than just personal and spiritual fufilment. Above I identified the move towards a growing awareness of multi-dimensional analysis in Black resistance, particularly through my examination of Garveyism and Rastafari.

Alexander's third concern is *theological,* namely God's alignment with the struggles of the oppressed. As noted in the previous chapter, the mobilization of Christian religion for the alleviation of oppression has precedence in African Caribbean Christian experience.

These three themes will be further developed to provide tools for a Black political theology. In other words, this chapter will seek to build on Alexander's programme of active radicalism by providing a more complex theo-political framework for understanding.

AFRICAN-CENTRED EPISTEMOLOGY

In the previous chapter I demonstrated that Africa was a central idea in Ethiopianism, Garveyism and Rastafari. What I would like to suggest here is that the emergence of an African-centred epistemology provides us with an important continuation of those schools of thought.

The contemporary home of African-centred epistemology lies in Afrocentricity, which is the latest reconfiguration of Black Nationalism in Black North Atlantic cultures. As was shown in the genealogy of resistance, varieties of Black Nationalist thought have been around for a long time in African Caribbean experience. Afrocentricity or African-centred analysis is not a unified or homogeneous subject. The subject has been advanced by the work of numerous scholars. While Molefi Kete Asante has given the subject the greatest treatment in Black North Atlantic cultures, Kariamu Welsh-Asante, Maulanu Karenga, the late Cheikh Anta Diop, Theophile Obenga and many others have been at the forefront of developing African-centred analysis. Because of the African American domination of Afrocentric criticism some have argued that Afrocentrism would be better termed 'Americocentrism'.[3] This criticism suggests that Afrocentrism must be understood primarily, but not exclusively, as an African diasporan gaze or perspective on the African continent. In contrast, the Afrocentric tradition in Britain is relatively new. The International Institute for Black Research (Reading), Kemet Educational Guidance (Manchester) and the magazine *The Alarm* have been at the forefront of the movement in Britain in the 1990s.

There is no consensus concerning the definition of Afrocentrism. One of its leading architects, Molefi Kete Asante, describes it as an intellectual approach that draws from a particular history for a particular purpose – it is:

> the belief in the centrality of Africans in post modern history. It is our history, our mythology, our creative motif, and our ethos exemplifying our collective will. On the basis of our story, we build upon the work of our ancestors who gave signs towards our humanising function.[4]

This definition suggests that Afrocentricity focuses on the achievements of African people which takes seriously history, culture and social transformation, that is, its humanizing function.

A second definition, by Maulana Karenga, claims that Afrocentricity is fundamentally an academic discipline and must be distinguished from *Afrocentrism*, a form of popular Black Nationalism rooted in popular cultures.[5] Like Asante, Karenga sees Afrocentricity as a 'quality of thought and practice rooted in the cultural image and human interests of African people'.[6] However, while grounded in the particularity of African experience, it is also concerned with issues and concerns common also to non-African peoples.

However, such ideas must not be allowed to demean non-Africans, or indeed Black women. Hence, when exploring Afrocentrism here, I am concerned with what Stephen Howe describes as 'loose' Afrocentrism:

> An emphasis on shared African origins among all 'Black' people, taking pride in those origins and an interest in African history and culture – or those aspects of New World cultures seen as representing African 'survivals' – and a belief that Eurocentric bias has blocked or distorted knowledge of Africans and their cultures.[7]

Movements such as Ethiopianism and Garveyism reinterpreted the Bible from a Black perspective, and this has implications for understanding salvation or soteriology. In a context of Black subjugation and marginalization, Ethiopianism recast the Black subject at the centre of God's plan for the world. In recent years Black North Atlantic cultures, faced with continued racialized subordination have made critical use of African-centred thought.

Arguably the most concise theological articulation of African-centred thought is Cain Hope Felder's (ed.) *Stony the Road We Trod: African*

American Biblical Interpretation (1991), in which there are two hermeneutical concerns. First, it is important to take experience into account when analysing the biblical text. Therefore, theological analysis is reconstructed so as to serve the socio-political concerns of the Black community. Second, Africa is prioritized in the analysis of the text so as to produce a distinctive gaze or perspective on the Bible. This gaze is exemplified in Dr Randall Bailey's analysis of Africans and African nations in this volume.[8] Consider Bailey's reading of the narrative of the Queen of Sheba (1 Kings 10). Here, he attempts to identify the role of the Queen and assess what Africa meant in the mind of the ancient writer:

> As one looks at the narrative it appears that there are several keys to the question of valuation. First the fact that the writer is trying to establish, or further ground, Solomon as the one who is wise. The vehicle used is that of having him pass the test of African riddles and wisdom. The assumption, therefore, of the narrator is that this is the most difficult test to be posed. The African Queen states: 'The report was true which I heard in my own land of your affairs and of your wisdom, but I did not believe the reports until I came and my own eyes had seen it; and behold, the half was not told to me; your wisdom and prosperity surpass the report which I heard' (vv. 6–7).[9]

What is of theological importance here is that Afrocentrism has influenced the development of Black theology and it reinterprets history, and indirectly theology, from Black perspectives. However, a more critical analysis is necessary to evaluate the use of Afrocentric heuristics.

Aims

The African American theologian Cheryl Sanders has summarized the aims of Afrocentric scholarship as: (1) to celebrate the achievements of African people and cultures; (2) to analyse critically the hegemony of the Eurocentric worldview and ways of knowing that have served the interests of racial oppression; (3) to construct an alternative framework for understanding and evaluating human experience.[10] What I want to suggest from these points is that Afrocentrism's project is primarily a philosophical and cultural one. Its aims focus on the Black political and social well-being. From Sanders' analysis it is not necessarily concerned with economic analysis and economic development. I will now provide a fuller exploration of Afrocentrism's aims based on Sanders' first two points.

First, the celebration of African people and cultures assumes that African history and culture is worthy of study and crucial for a fuller understanding of contemporary African diasporan experience. As we have seen above, this was a view popularized in both Pan-African and Rastafarian circles. In practice Afrocentricity attempts to utilize theories, concepts and ideas from African civilizations as a resource for Black diasporan communities today. In order to construct a picture of pre-colonial Africa, Afrocentrists focus on key civilizations and histories as a basis for understanding and developing African essentials. I want to affirm Afrocentricity's celebration of Black achievement as a positive development, because as a form of Black Nationalism it places the history of Black people at its centre rather than on the margins. Decentring Europe and White history creates an intellectual space for an articulation of the achievements of disempowered peoples.

However, there are several problems with this celebration of African achievements and history. First, it risks the homogenizing of the ancient African continent so that its history, thought and culture become a unitary system rather than a dynamic and contradictory one. For example, many Afrocentric texts such as *Stony the Road We Trod* fail to consider the great differences between African peoples and their histories. Second, it is also important that the celebration does not ignore that which is tragic in African history. This is because much can also be learned from exploring the grotesque in Black life. Also a critical question not addressed is the inherent patriarchal focus in the Afrocentric project. Asante includes no women in his historical analysis of Afrocentrism.[11] Finally, the celebration does not necessarily have a praxis that is political mobilization. Instead it provides individual psychological empowerment. As I noted in my critique of the Black Church in Chapter 1, and in the genealogy of resistance also, mobilization must be holistic, contesting inequality in the political as well as the personal sphere.

I want to suggest that a critical approach to 'celebration' is useful for the aims of this study, that is, the development of a Black political theology. It encourages a critical investigation of African and African diasporan history. This means viewing Black history as a dynamic process – how African values have been reconfigured in the Caribbean, in the Americas and also in Britain. We need a perspective which will prevent us romanticizing pre-colonial African history; therefore, we should nurture a critical dialogue between continental and diasporan concerns so that we may better understand Black Christian experience in contemporary society. Later I will employ this focus in the analysis of the concept of 'dread'.

The second task of Afrocentricity concerns epistemology. It is necessary to analyse the hegemony of the Eurocentric worldview and ways of knowing because, from our Afrocentric viewpoint, Eurocentric thought with its attendant cultural values is destructive. This is uncompromisingly expressed in Marimba Ani's critique of European cultural thought and behaviour:

> Europe's political domination of African and much of the 'non-European' world has been accompanied by a relentless cultural and psychological rape and by devastating economic exploitation ... beneath this deadly onslaught lies a stultifying intellectual mystification that prevents Europe's political victims from thinking in a manner that would lead to authentic self-determination. Intellectual decolonisation is a prerequisite for the creation of successful political decolonisation and cultural reconstruction strategies. Europe's political imperialistic success can be accredited not so much to superior military might, as to the weapon of culture: The former ensures more immediate control but requires continual physical force for the maintenance of power, while the latter succeeds in long-lasting dominance that enlists the co-operation of its victims (i.e. pacification of the will). The secret Europeans discovered early in their history is that culture carries rules for thinking, and that if you could impose your culture on your victims you could limit the creativity of their vision, destroying their ability to act with will and intent and in their own interests.[12]

In order to counter the harmful effects of European thought, people of African descent must construct an alternative way of thinking, being and doing. In other words, Afrocentricity advocates that the best way of empowering Black people is by developing their own epistemologies for analysis of the social and political world. This was also a theme within the resistance genealogy.

An example of Afrocentric epistemology is Patricia Hill Collins. Collins has attempted to construct a counter-hegemonic Afrocentric feminist epistemology. Using the analytical knowledge from the contexts of African American women's discourse, Collins suggests an alternative system utilizing experience as the criterion for evaluating truth,[13] dialogue as a means of assessing knowledge claims,[14] the ethic of caring,[15] and the ethic of personal accountability.[16] In a similar manner, but without the sensitivity towards gender issues, Asante makes several suggestions to the Afrocentric scholar in order to counter traditional Western epistemologies.[17] In addition, as I demonstrated briefly above, Rastafari nurtured an alternative epistemology through its focus on 'reasoning' and 'grounding'. Hence, alternative epistemology is a part of African Caribbean experience and history.

Epistemology has implications for African Caribbean Christianity, especially because Asante rejects Christianity and Islam as options for Afrocentric people,[18] because anything not in Afrocentric history is problematic.[19] Therefore, Christianity can only be responsible for limiting and confusing people of African descent:

> The most crippling effect of Islam as well as Christianity for us may well be the adoption of non-African customs and behaviours, some of which are in direct conflict with our traditional values. We out-Arab the Arabs, we have out-Europeanised the Europeans from time to time. This is not so with the Afrocentrist ... We have a formidable history, replete with the voice of God, the ancestors, and the prophets. Our manner of dress, behaviour, walk, talk and values are intact and workable when we are Afrocentric. Our problems come when we lose sight of ourselves, accept false doctrines, false Gods, mistaken notions of what is truly in our history, and assume an individualistic and autocratic posture ... The dispensing with symbols and scriptures which stand outside of us is a move towards national recovery.[20]

There are several constructive issues that emerge from Asante's critique. First, Asante encourages Black Christians to ask if it is possible to accept uncritically the thought, action or behaviour that emerges outside Black history. This is a very important question for Black Pentecostals, many of whom have worshipping traditions that display remnants of African religion but subscribe to theological ideas from Euro-American traditions. This dialectical tension has led to a re-evaluation of Blackness and Christianity in many of these churches. For example, several Black Pentecostal churches have introduced Black iconography into their places of worship.[21] These churches are suggesting that some aspects of Eurocentric Christian thought must be rejected. However, these churches are the exception. For many Black Pentecostals, the dialectical tension between African Caribbean retentions and European society is resolved through assimilation.[22] What is clear is that Asante asks us to evaluate the psychological and sociological effects of adopting uncritically aspects of European religious traditions.

However, there are aspects of Asante's analysis of Christianity that are problematic. First, Asante does not seem to be aware of the African contribution to Christianity's historical and theological development[23] as identified by Black biblical scholars. Therefore it is wrong to assume that Christianity is a 'White person's religion'. Christianity is not alien to Black people – it contains the history of many Black people.[24] Hence, Asante has not fully deconstructed Eurocentric interpretation-hegemony of the Bible.

Second, Asante does not realize the significance of syncretism in Black Christianity. As shown above in my limited study, Black Christianity as represented in Black Pentecostalism is a mixture of several religious traditions, but primarily African religious traditions with European Christianity. Therefore, African Caribbean Christianity occupies a contradictory space, both 'inside and outside' African history. How African does a religious system have to be to be taken seriously by Black people? Furthermore, Asante does not consider the complex relationship between Christianity and African identity – that Black Christians in African Caribbean history have been responsible for maintaining a view of Africa as a symbol of Black pride and Black liberation. For example, Ethiopianism placed Black people within the biblical narrative and within the divine purposes of God. Through an inversion of colonial soteriology, Black people became central rather than marginal to the purposes of God in the world.

It is clear that the strength of Afrocentricity is its attempt to value African achievements and provide intellectual resources that emerge out of Black experience and thought, in order to make sense of Black existence today. These tools are useful for this study. That is, Afrocentricity challenges us to find intellectual tools and methodological approaches to Black Pentecostalism that emerge from Black perspectives and take them seriously. In terms of the analysis of Black Pentecostalism, African-centred analysis encourages an excavation of the Black roots and routes in Pentecostalism. However, while Afrocentrism reminds Black Pentecostals of thinking about Black experience as a collective narrative of struggle and resistance, we must hold Afrocentrism in tension with post-modern Blackness. Post-modern Blackness, as we shall see later, nurtures diversity and multiplicity.

THEOLOGICAL OR THEO-CULTURAL ANALYSIS

I demonstrated in the previous chapter how various forms of social analysis were evident in all aspects of Black resistance. Hence, social analysis is not alien but integral to Black resistance.

Here, I am concerned with developing a methodological approach to interpreting aspects of the social and political world. A useful starting point is with the social analysis of Black Britain, much of which has used the concept of 'race' as a trope for exploring issues of Black politics and Black identity. As we shall see, in recent years 'culture' has also emerged as an important focus for analysis. I shall briefly survey three recent trends in the analysis of the socio-political context of the Black community in Britain, and then explore the role of 'culture' in this framework. However, it is first necessary to provide a theological justification for the emphasis on analysis.

I want to suggest two theological presuppositions that legitimate social analysis. First, analysis is necessary because of the 'earthly' focus of Jesus' ministry. Jesus' care for the marginalized and disenfranchized in the first century was built upon an understanding that the Kingdom of God had arrived. The arrival of the Kingdom of God in Black theological thought has led to the development of historicized eschatologies – a view of God's future as a concrete reality in the present. For example, Garth Baker Fletcher, a second-generation Black theologian, has argued that the arrival of the Kingdom provides revolutionary hope in the present. Revolutionary hope ensures that the socio-political reversals witnessed in the time of Jesus are possible today. Therefore, it is of fundamental importance for Christians to engage in social analysis in order to contextualize revolutionary hope.[25]

Second, analysis is necessary because of the importance of the social location of divine revelation. As mentioned in my introductory chapter, all theological thought occurs within a social context. Therefore in order to interpret the meaning of God in the world, it is also necessary to understand social location. This is not a new idea. Historical and biblical criticism was founded upon the need to understand the historical and social world of the reception and transmission of biblical traditions. However, what is different here is the central importance of contemporary issues of race, class and culture.

In the British context, both Black and White scholars have constructed a variety of theoretical models for understanding Black social and political life. Debates, arguments and perspectives have been articulated through the discourses of *class* and *race*. John Solomos and Les Back identify three trends.[26]

The first trend is found in the work of John Rex. John Rex conducted empirical work on immigrant communities from the Caribbean and Asia in Birmingham in the 1960s and 70s. By what he termed a 'loose

Marxism' based on Weberian notions of class, he set out to define racial discrimination in Birmingham.[27] Rex described the position of Black communities, their families and workers as primarily an 'underclass' experiencing discrimination in housing, education and employment.[28] In short, Black workers did not benefit from gains made by working-class struggle. In response, African Caribbean people focused on various forms of 'defensive confrontation' to safeguard resources.

In his earlier works, in order to explain Black social and political action Rex developed a four-cornered, ideal type model with four categories of action. The categories were withdrawal, confrontation and aggression, integration and allying to revolutionary groups.[29] The Black Church and Rastafari were assigned to the category of withdrawal, where no part was played in the social and political world. Solace was sought in revivalist forms of Christianity with an explicit otherworldly emphasis.[30] Rex would later revise his understanding of Rastafari but not that of Black Christianity.[31] I suggest that while Rex's analysis allows us to evaluate the role of the Church as a part of a separate class faction and part of the development of a class-for-itself, his conclusions about the Church are unsatisfactory. This is because Rex has failed to understand the passive/active radical dimensions of Black faith, which, as we have seen above, contains at least an inherent and implicit mobilization. Therefore the actions of the Church cannot be dismissed as simple withdrawal.

A second trend appears in the scholarship of Robert Miles. Working from a neo-Marxist perspective, Miles (in opposition to Rex) argues that 'race' is false consciousness. In other words, 'race' is simply a way of obscuring the real relations that lie behind inequality. In other words 'race' is illusory.[32] The process by which the economic is obscured by race Miles calls 'racialization'. Because 'race' is ideological, Miles suggests that the only valid form of Black political action is class action – participation in the struggles of the British working class. Hence, Miles would not support 'race'-driven politics. The major problem with Miles is that his class reductionism does not account for forms of discrimination which occur before and outside concepts of class or capitalism. As we have seen in the previous chapter, racialized oppression exists in a variety of forms and crosses boundaries of ideology and politics. Therefore, class reductionism fails to evaluate the complex nature of racism effectively.

Finally, a third trend is found in the work of the Centre for Contemporary Cultural Studies (CCCS). Whereas Rex understood 'race' as class, and Miles as an ideology, the Black scholars of the

CCCS recaptured 'race' as a basis for social and political action. Here, 'race' was declared distinct from class, politics and economics and therefore a legitimate basis for action. In other words, Black communities in Britain constitute a new development in class dynamics – a separate class faction. By emphasizing 'race' CCCS implied that Black oppression constituted more than economic exploitation and related to other spheres of politics ideology. Here, 'race' is a socio-political construction that can 'accommodate a variety of meanings'[33] that are related to the struggles of Black people.

This approach to the politics of 'race' appears in the work of Black British writers such as Paul Gilroy. In *There Ain't No Black in the Union Jack*, Gilroy shows that racialized oppression occurs in more than just the socio-economic sphere and that Black resistance uses a variety of strategies in order to resist. For Gilroy, 'race' is a fluid concept, which is constantly changing, and being reconfigured. This process he calls *race formation*.[34] Because 'race' is a political and social construction, Gilroy has demonstrated that Black people, particularly Black cultures, have responded to racialized oppression by constructing Black identities to counter racism.[35]

How does the work of the CCCS effect the construction of an analytical framework? I suggest that, bearing in mind that 'race' is a dynamic construct, it is important for African Caribbean Christians to be aware of race formation and the role of the Church as a vehicle of resistance. As shown above, the most recent study of Black Pentecostals in Britain, Nicole Toulis' *Believing Identity*, reveals a 'limited' identity politics of a Black church in Birmingham. However, Gilroy encourages us to go a step further by evaluating the way in which race formation occurs so that Black Christians can develop effective strategies of resistance to racisms. For example, because racisms are expressed through culture, then it is important for the Black Church to offer cultural resources and training to encounter racialized stereotypes. In short, as demonstrated in the introduction to this study the third trend implies that in order to evaluate the social-political world, the Black Church must evaluate itself as part of the African Caribbean community's struggle for justice, and must engage in cultural analysis as a means of countering cultural forms of racialized oppression. This last point requires further explanation.

Social analysis means taking cultural analysis seriously. Cultural analysis *of* and *for* the Black Church in Britain must consider the theological dimensions of cultural analysis. This is so that the perspectives of the Church as a religious institution are incorporated into its cultural analysis. Such a focus moves us into the area of religious reflection and cultural analysis or 'theological/theo-cultural criticism'.

In order to explain my understanding of theo-cultural criticism I will first say something about cultural criticism, and then outline theo-cultural criticism as part of this analytical framework. I shall begin by reiterating my understanding of culture found in the work of Raymond Williams, and then define what is meant by criticism.

Williams' working-class background led to his insistence of a more global understanding of culture. For Williams culture represents 'a whole way of life, material, intellectual and spiritual'.[36] More specifically, culture is 'the signifying system through which . . . a social order is communicated, reproduced, experienced and explored'.[37] Culture as a signifying system prescribes culture as a dimension of all institutions. What I am most interested in is the relationship between human subjects and cultural creation, that is to say, culture has a *material force*. We have seen that Ani shows that culture has a political force in the world. When assessing culture, I recognize that Church culture and theology are related wider processes of production and political power. That is, church culture has the power to transform.

Regarding the second component, 'criticism', I affirm Victor Anderson's use of Raymond Geuss.[38] Geuss identifies three tendencies within cultural criticism: *descriptive, pejorative* and *positive*. The *descriptive* mode focuses on concepts, attitudes and psychological dispositions exhibited in culture.[39] The *pejorative* mode is concerned with debunking reality. That is, looking for illusions and falsifications within cultural activity that mask real interests. This mode is linked to the Marxist notion of false consciousness. Finally, the *positive* mode focuses on the transformatory interests of the critic. In short, the critic engages in ideological warfare arguing the case for an ideology that will make culture serve particular interests. The ideological dimension is therefore a fruitful attempt to challenge, transform and make known new possibilities for culture. The positive mode requests that ideological criticism change power relationships for the better. Therefore when analysing culture I will suggest ways in which culture can act as an ideological force. This tendency will become evident in the use of the concept of 'dread'.

Theo-cultural criticism is concerned with asking theological questions about Black expressive cultures including those of Black Christians. This form of cultural criticism is informed by Theophus Smith's analysis of Black expressive culture in the African American context, where he describes Black expressive cultures as having the ability to heal and also do harm. To express these concerns Smith describes Black cultures as a *pharmacopoeia*.[40] The pharmacopoeial nature of culture encourages us to ask theological and ethical questions about Black Church cultures. This is because not all of Black culture is sustaining or uplifting. Such an analysis of culture must also acknowledge the relationships between expressive cultures and other social arenas such as issues of power, domination and resistance. One purpose for this analysis is to identify those aspects of Black expressive cultures that enable the sustenance, uplift and liberation of Black people in Britain.

So, both social analysis and cultural analysis are integral tools within the analysis framework. I have focused primarily upon a theo-cultural analysis in order to interrogate the context of the Black Church in Britain, because theo-cultural analysis enables 'race' and 'culture' and theology to be addressed in the struggle against oppression.

LIBERATION THEOLOGICAL PRAXIS (THEOLOGY)

Alexander's definition also requires an evaluation of theology that takes seriously God's alignment with the struggles of the oppressed, so that it is able to 'speak out against oppression in the Church and in society'. Here, in order to respond to Alexander's concerns and also to the development of tools for analysis, I will focus on how a theological method can make contemporaneous the struggles of marginalized Black people and the biblical text. I will draw upon the work of Black Atlantic scholars to develop a *liberation theological praxis* (LTP).

This process has four parts. First, I will describe in brief two ideological presuppositions. These are the concepts of *liberation* and *praxis*. Next, I will critically outline the theological presuppositions necessary for a LTP. Third, I will describe the theological method necessary for LTP. Finally, I will end by illustrating the efficacy of LTP by critiquing the work of the Black Theology Support Group in Birmingham, England.

Before going any further, it is necessary to define liberation and praxis. LTP represents particular ideological concerns that are expressed in the concepts of *liberation* and *praxis*.

Liberation has two implications. First it describes a theology from the margins. In this case, it is a theology that emerges from the context of Black people in Britain. Above I noted the history of marginalization and oppression of Black people within the racism genealogy.

However, because Black people are diverse (heterogeneous), not all Black people face or are affected by racism in the same way. For example, as an educated Black theologian with post-graduate qualifications, despite living in the inner city, I experience racism in a very different way from the other men and women on my street. Liberation differs because class location within the Black community affects how liberation is articulated.

Second, as a theology from the Black context, the purpose of liberation is emancipation for all, both within and outside the Black community. As shown in the previous chapter, the quest for liberation is a theme within African Caribbean experience. But now I want to take this theme further. Hence, here, liberation is what womanist theologian Kelly Brown Douglas calls multi-dimensional and bifocal analysis.[41] Multi-dimensional analysis means being concerned with liberation at all levels of human existence. Bifocality means being concerned with liberation both inside and outside Black communities. By making its starting point the concrete experience, this approach sidesteps the ahistoricism and abstract principles of theology found in some, but not all, European theologies. However, the concept of liberation as understood here, also embraces *reconciliation* as a dimension of liberation. This means that the end-goal of liberation does not produce new oppressors but creates a new society based on justice and reconciliation. Hence, the importance of *praxis*.

The word 'praxis' comes from the Frankfurt school of sociology and denotes a method or model of thinking where rational thought must be accompanied by action. In short, as the Marxist maxim states, to transform the world one must not only interpret it but also change it. Praxis is transforming activity that is undergirded by theory.[42] It follows that 'praxis theology' refers to a way of doing theology where the commitment to transforming a situation is the central purpose.

Praxis is not unproblematic. By presupposing that humans are responsible for the transformation of structures, there is a risk of 'sidelining' God. In response, here I contend that it is vital that the role of theological reflection be seen as an integral dimension of praxis. Such a process enables the shortcomings (sin) of humans not to be neglected as human subjects act and reflect. As Daniel Schipani has suggested, praxis must not neglect biblical revelation, or else objective Christian 'truth' collapses into relativity.[43] While Schipani does not clarify his understanding of 'truth', what is important for me is that praxis must be driven by the Spirit. This means that praxis must have certain safeguards such as being worked out in community and being in dialogue with other traditions. Later I will outline an understanding of the Spirit that takes seriously the practicality of praxis.

What I want to do here is combine *liberation* and *praxis* into a *theological* method where the prime task of theology is to express the meaning of God in the world. In this case, the Black worlds in which Black men and women live in Britain. Here theology must ensure that the message of the gospel enables the marginalized and oppressed to participate in God's work of liberation in the world.[44] This is the central meaning of what I want to call 'liberation theological praxis' (LTP). In the rest of this chapter I will show that LTP is based upon theological presuppositions which emerge from the concepts of revelation, history and culture. I will also outline a theological method for LTP.

Theological presuppositions

I begin with revelation, because the central task of Christian people is making sense of God's self-disclosure to us. Revelation in the LTP is concerned with the nature of God's self-disclosure in the world. In the tradition of Wolfhart Pannenberg, rather than focusing solely upon an internal, subjective understanding of revelation, I am more concerned with public, accessible acts of God's revelation that occur in events and history.[45] In other words, I am concerned with God's self-disclosure in history among the Black disaffected and disenfranchised. Here I will continue to work with this perspective by focusing on how God is revealed in the social, economic and political worlds in which we live. This presupposition suggests that social location or social context is intimately related to revelation. On this premise African American Black liberation theologian James Cone argued that divine revelation expresses partiality towards the poor:

> The social context of theology is not only evident in our language as human beings with certain political and social interests; it is also implied in the nature of divine revelation ... the God of history, the God of the Bible is involved in history, and his revelation is inseparable from the social and political affairs of Israel. He is the political God, the protector of the poor and the establisher of the right for those who are oppressed. To know him is to experience his acts in the concrete affairs and relationships of people, liberating the weak and helpless from pain and humiliation.[46]

Cone understands God's partiality towards the poor in terms of divine freedom. Because oppression denies divine freedom, God sides with those who are oppressed in order to secure their liberation.[47] In a similar manner, Gustavo Gutiérrez states that God's 'preferential option for the poor' is not a statement about the moral superiority of the poor. Instead, this statement points to who God is and only secondarily the condition of the poor. That is, God's preferential option for the poor tells of God's love.[48] Hence, like Gutiérrez, Cone focuses upon God's action rather than the moral superiority of the oppressed. This is an important point because it prevents the romanticization of poverty and marginality as concrete realities.

I would suggest that the main difficulties with this view of revelation are, firstly that it is not always easy to discern who are the marginalized. For example, in South African history both the Afrikaaners and Black South Africans have claimed to be the oppressed seeking divine favour. Secondly, as mentioned in the presuppositions, liberation must also include love as a central goal alongside freedom. This is so that freedom for one group does not lead to the oppression of another.

The second presupposition concerns history. God's presence in history is found in the concrete issues and concerns of everyday life. This means that experience is a valid means of assessing what God is doing in the world. What I want to suggest here is that God's work in history, like the nature of revelation, pays particular attention to the historical needs of the marginalized. Liberation theologians have attempted to demonstrate this view through a social analysis of the historical contexts within the Bible. James Cone argues that his emphasis on the oppressed in history arises out of the biblical tradition itself.[49] That is to say, the Bible not only emphasizes the liberation of the oppressed, but also identifies God and Jesus as siding with oppressed communities in history.

In terms of the Hebrew scriptures, Cone focuses upon the Exodus narrative and God's concern about the oppressed within the Israelite community as examples of God's concerns for the oppressed in history. Furthermore God's election of Israel has implications for doing theology:

God's election of oppressed Israelites has unavoidable implications for the doing of theology. If God had chosen as his 'holy' nation the Egyptian slave masters instead of the Israelite slaves, then a completely different kind of god would have been revealed . . . Here God discloses that he is the God of history whose will is identical with the liberation of the oppressed from social and political bondage.[50]

In the Greek scriptures Cone argues that Jesus reaffirms the theme of liberation in history:

> The conflict with Satan and the powers of this world, the condemnation of the rich the insistence that the kingdom of God is for the poor, and the locating of his ministry among the poor – these and other features of the career of Jesus show that his work was directed to the oppressed for the purpose of their liberation.[51]

Of particular significance to Cone is Christology – making sense of who Jesus Christ is for us today. Jesus, in Cone's thinking, represents God's rule of justice upon the earth. Therefore, Jesus fulfils the Old Testament's concept of the Messiah as one who would bring 'justice to the nations'.[52] Therefore every aspect of Jesus' life is directly related to the theme of God's liberation of the poor. Therefore, from his reading in Nazareth at the beginning of his ministry (Luke 4.18–19) to his death on the cross and his resurrection, Jesus personifies the divine freedom in action. That is, God breaking into history in order to liberate the oppressed. For Cone the resurrection signifies how:

> God becomes the victim in their [oppressed] place and thus transforms the condition of slavery into the battleground for the struggle of freedom. This is what Christ's resurrection means. The oppressed are freed for struggle, for battle in the pursuit of humanity.[53]

Cone concludes, with the contemporaneous resonance of the biblical theme of liberation, that because the biblical text is concerned with liberation, it is natural that the Christian community today should continue the work of Christ in the world.

However, Cone does not totally subscribe to historical liberation. He also suggests that liberation is often ahistorical as God cannot be limited to history. Consequently, the 'otherworldly' liberation found in Black Christian history can also be read as an announcement or proclamation of historical liberation to come.[54]

In recent years Cone's conclusions about God in history has been challenged by Black theologians who have a less optimistic view of God's liberating role in human history. An important criticism comes from the womanist theologian Delores Williams, who in *Sisters in the Wilderness* argues that liberation is not always promised to or experienced by the oppressed in history. After demonstrating her thesis through a study of Hagar, Williams broadens her argument to include others:

God is clearly partial to Sarah. Regardless of the way one interprets God's Command to Hagar to submit herself to Sarah, God does not liberate her. In Exodus God does not outlaw slavery. Rather, the male slave can be Part of Israel's rituals, possibly because he has no control over his body as Hagar had no control over her body. Thus the Lord said to Moses and Aaron, 'this is the ordinance of the Passover: no foreigner shall eat of it; but every slave that is bought for money may eat of it after you have circumcised him' (Exodus 12:43–44) but 'no sojourner or hired servant may eat of it' (12:45). The sojourner and hired servant can refuse to be circumcised, but the slave cannot because the slave master owns the slave's body.[55]

This leads Williams to suggest that:

when non-Jewish people ... read the entire Hebrew testament from the point of view of the non-Hebrew slave, there is no clear indication that God is against their perpetual enslavement.[56]

Williams also disputes the argument that the New Testament is also concerned with historical liberation. Williams has been critical of atonement theology found in Black and womanist theology. Unlike Cone, here, the cross is problematic because of its association with systems of domination:

For Black women, there is also the question of whether Jesus on the cross represents coerced surrogacy (willed by the Father) or voluntary surrogacy (chosen by the son) or both. At any rate, a major theological problem here is the place of the cross in any theology significantly informed by African American women's experience with surrogacy. Even if one buys into the notion of the cross as the meeting place of the will of God to give up the Son (coerced surrogacy?) and the will of the Son to give up himself (voluntary surrogacy?) so that 'the spirit of abandonment and self-giving love' proceeds from the cross 'to raise up abandoned men,' African-American women are still left with the question: Can there be salvific power for Black women in Christian images of oppression (for example, Jesus on the cross) meant to teach something about redemption?[57]

In short, Black women's negative experiences of exploitation are legitimated by traditional views of redemption and atonement.[58] For Delores Williams, a response to the situation is to articulate a theology based on the life of Jesus. Jesus' life arguably has more significance than his death on the cross, in particular, his empowerment of people whose existence was under threat: 'humankind is then redeemed through Jesus' *ministerial* vision of life and not through his death'.

Williams suggest that a more adequate representation of Christ is that of healer and sustainer.[59]

In response to the questions raised by Williams, it is clear that the unequivocal belief that the biblical history is one of unquestionable liberation is not the case. Therefore, any meaningful analysis of history must be multi-dimensional, addressing the structural issues that lie behind and within history to identify conflicts and contradictions.

A Theological Method for LTP

LTP requires a particular theological method that takes into serious consideration liberation, praxis, revelation and history. In terms of theological methodology the action–reflection dynamic best expresses the central thrust of this model (Figure 1).

The action–reflection model prioritizes creative transformation of the social context through action. By bringing together the action–reflection model with my earlier discussions on epistemology, analysis and theology, it would be consistent to suggest that action must be reflected upon through theo-cultural analysis and through theological reflection – what the Bible has to say about a given situation. This is a dynamic process that results in more action.[60] Here, I will conflate the action–reflection model in LTP into three distinct phases for LTP theological method. These are *experience, analysis* and *action* (Figure 2). These elements require a brief explanation.

Taking the concrete experience seriously is a starting point. Whereas for Cone the primary concern was the elimination of racism, other Black theologians have suggested alternative starting points. For example, womanist theologians, as we noted with the example of Delores Williams above, start with the experiences of Black women. Similarly, other theologians have made class and sexuality other existential starting points.[61] What this means for me is that the experience of being Black in England is a legitimate starting point for theological inquiry. Because Blackness is multiple, this multi-dimensional approach

Figure 1.   Action–reflection model

Experience

Action   Analysis

Analysis of scripture

Figure 2

to experience means that the liberation strategies will not all be the same because experience is not singular.

My focus on analysis as theo-cultural provides a greater understanding of oppression, particularly race, class and gender concerns within the British context. Furthermore, the theological dimensions of analysis ensure that a holistic approach is normative.

Analysis also involves biblical reflection, that is, what the Bible has to say about our analysis of a situation. As demonstrated above, Cone and Williams have shown that there are ideological issues of justice, oppression and resistance within the biblical text that must be explored. Hence, as well as asking what the Bible has to say about a particular experience, I must also enable a dialogue between analysis and scripture in order to discern African-centred and theo-cultural themes within scripture. Hence, there is a two-way action between analysis and analysis of scripture represented with two arrows in Figure 2.

Finally, these new insights must result in action which transforms the experience that began the first movement. For example, if the starting point or experience is responding to a racist attack then the final movement must be action that makes sense of and deals with the attack. Transformation must be related to the theo-cultural analysis and theological reflection so that praxis is holistic, challenging and changing the social world as well as the hearts and minds of the individuals within it.

The strength of this method is that it ensures that theology takes seriously Black experience and also the Black Church's centralization of the Bible. In essence, experience is held as equally valid a tool for theology as scripture. However, the danger with this method is whether it can ensure that radical praxis is the regular outcome of theological analysis or an illusion to be pursued but never arrived at. Bearing this in mind, I want to end this chapter by exploring the utility of LTP through an analysis of the Black Theology Support Group (BTSG) in Birmingham.

The Black Theology Support Group

In my opinion the BTSG represents the most advanced Black theological centre in the UK context. Nowhere else do Black theologians 'do theology'. Therefore, applying the method found within LTP provides insight into BTSG and also the theological content for LTP. As stated in the introduction, illustrative material is used to ground theory. In this case the material is derived from my participation within the BTSG over a two-year period. During this time, as a member of the BTSG, I was able to address and explore the issue of praxis raised above.

In addition, a search for a LTP should also include an exploration outside the confines of traditional worship and church services to locate evidence of a LTP. This is possible because defining the Church as an expressive, urban social movement enables a search for similar patterns of organization outside the perimeters of the 'Black Church'. The idea of 'church' outside Church is not a new concept in Black African Caribbean Christian circles. Black Pentecostals often say that they have 'had church' when the presence and the power of the Spirit are experienced. Such a panlocation pneumatology enables 'church' to occur in any space: 'wherever the twos or threes are gathered'.

The BTSG was established in 1995 by a group of Black theologians and Black church leaders in Birmingham. Meetings occur roughly every six weeks at the Centre for Black and White Christian Partnership in Selly Oak, Birmingham. Although based in Birmingham, it has a national perspective: its participants come from the Southeast and the North of England as well as the Midlands area. Initially, the group was concerned with providing mutual support and encouragement. Hence, each session begins with greetings, sharing of information, a presentation and fellowship. However the need for analysis of the social context and the intellectual prowess of the group resulted in the writing of papers, essays and the emergence of a *Journal of Black British Theology*.

My task here is to make a brief assessment of the BTSG in light of my previous discussion on LTP. There are two areas of concern. First I will explore the 'experience' of the BTSG through an evaluation of it as an ecumenical group. This is because its Black ecumenism encompasses several features that constitute and shape the self-understanding of the group. Second, I will assess its approach to analysis and action. These categories are important because they are central to LTP.

In analysing the BTSG from the perspective of LTP, it is important to unlock its central concerns. While not being a worshipping community, the BTSG provides an important theological and experiential function for its participants as an ecumenical group. As an ecumenical group of Black Christians, the BTSG represents a paradigm of Black ecumenism. There are three points of importance.

First, it encourages participation from Black men and women. The group has nurtured the emergence of a second generation of womanist theologians[62] by providing a space for the development and articulation of a British womanist theology. However, despite the participation of women, the 'unofficial' leadership of the group continues to be male-dominated. Hence, while there is an inclusive thrust, male leadership still prevails.

Second, the BTSG experiences a particular understanding of ethnicity and identity. Regarding the former, the mode of Blackness present at the group incorporates African Caribbean, African and Asian identities. In other words, while 'Black' is used as a signifier of non-White interests and experiences within the group, there is also recognition of Black diversity and multiplicity. For example, Pradip Sudhra, an Asian church leader said on one occasion to the author that 'it is important to remember that "Black" includes Asian Christians as well – and that Asian Christians engage in and develop Black Theology'. This view of Blackness is not true for all Asians. However here it suggests that Blackness is organically related to Christian identities. In contrast to the analysis of Toulis, Black identities are here held in a diunital (both/and) and dialogical (relational) coalition with Christian identities (Figure 3), rather than Christian identity overwhelming ethnicity.

Ideologically, the group are explicit about the need to undermine the influence of White hegemony, in particular its effects upon Christian and ethnic identity. For example, in one paper Anthony Reddie, a PhD student at Birmingham University, argues for the use of Black oral history as a tool for developing an alternative epistemology. Hence, in contrast to Black churches, the BTSG articulates an explicit Black identity and Black politics as part of its commitment to transformation.

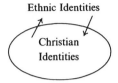

Figure 3. Ethnic identities and Christian identities

Finally, as an ecumenical group, the BTSG articulates a new relationship between spirituality and political engagement. The BTSG makes political analysis an integral dimension of their spirituality. For example, Lorraine Dixon, a BD student and Anglican priest in training, stated in an analysis of the praxis of gospel singer Mahalia Jackson that it is impossible to ignore the political dimensions of Black faith in a context of racial subordination.[63]

However, as the BTSG is not a worshipping community, it has greater freedom to explore and be explicit about political liturgy as an integral function of the support group. A critical question however, is to what extent is spirituality ignored or undervalued at the expense of political prowess. I want to suggest that the implicit spirituality in the explicit politics of the BTSG is an inversion of the implicit politics within the explicit spirituality of Black churches. Neither approach creates a healthy relationship between spirituality and political action. This is because neither approach allows a creative and explicit spirituality of liberation.

The BTSG has developed expertise in analysing Black British experience of gender, ethnicity and politics. Numerous papers have been presented that analyse the experiences of Black People. For example, themes have included womanist theology, Black male education, the Black Christ, Blacks in White-majority churches, the death of Diana and Black people, Black oral history and methods for a Black British theology. These papers and discussions have revealed a willingness to engage with socio-cultural and theological analysis of Black British experience. However, during my visits and participation in the group there was an under-representation of theological analysis. As a consequence, although there is an awareness of the socio-cultural issues within the Bible, most explorations made little reference to scripture. Instead the emphasis was upon the socio-political analysis of Black experience. Such an imbalance fails to address the centrality of the Bible in the Black Church.

There are two possible reasons for this situation. First, there is a structural issue. There are few Black British theologians. Furthermore most are still in the process of gaining higher degrees. Second, very few, if any, participants in the group are engaged in biblical studies; instead, there is a bias towards pastoral and systematic theology. This situation mirrors the professional development among first- and second-generation Black British who tended to enter professions that most readily helped to meet the social needs of Black people. Hence, pastoral studies and systematic theology provide bridgeheads into the White-dominated world of academic theology. From the perspective of LTP, the BTSG needs to mobilize the Bible in order to avoid the danger of developing a socio-cultural gospel that lacks theological reflection. A similar concern emerges over the issue of action.

The theological method employed at the BTSG is primarily intellectual – the production of texts and journals. As we have seen above from my analysis of culture, the creation of intellectual ideas has material force in the world and can challenge the status quo. In this sense, the collective praxis of the BTSG is that of 'organic intellectuals'. Organic intellectuals express the interests of a class without necessarily belonging to that class. Their task is to produce ideas that challenge received knowledge and systems of understanding. Organic intellectuals contrast with traditional intellectuals who maintain continuity.[64]

However, while organic intellectualism offers a cognitive challenge it must be accompanied by a structural challenge. Structural challenge is concerned with making concrete the principles of justice and equality envisioned within the social context and integral to 'action' within LTP. While the intellectual challenge will ensure the development of a class of Black theological intellectuals, without structural challenge the group will have a weakened affect on the academic and social life in Birmingham. Therefore, in terms of LTP, the BTSG offers limited liberation praxis. Whereas Mile End represented *passive active radicalism* and Ruach, *reactive active radicalism*, from my perspective the BTSG represents a *cognitive active radicalism*. That is to say, its focus is primarily intellectual radicalism. However, intellectual development by itself is only limited challenge. I argue that *cognitive active radicalism* is synonymous with the survival tradition in Black faith. Survival nurtures full-blown liberation from oppression, similarly, *cognitive active radicalism* nurtures full *active radicalism*. Hence, in many ways the BTSG has not moved beyond the limitations of passive radicalism within the Black Church. Instead it has reconfigured the weaknesses of passive radicalism in academic clothes.

CONCLUSION

In this chapter I have outlined three tools that emerge from the genealogy of Black resistance when placed in dialogue with Alexander's construct of active radicalism: African-centred analysis, theo-cultural analysis and liberation theological praxis (LTP). LTP was shown to have its own theological method that utilized experience, analysis, theological reflection and action. Finally, the utility of LTP was illustrated through a brief analysis of the Black Theology Support Group in Birmingham to identify weaknesses within the BTSG and provide insight into the articulation of LTP.

In sum, the weaknesses of the BTSG necessitate the development of a political theological content that takes seriously the dictates of LTP. This is the task of the next chapter.

NOTES

1. See Wilmore, G. *Black Religion and Black Radicalism*. New York: Orbis, 1998.

2. Alexander, V. *'Breaking Every Fetter'? To What Extent Has the Black Led Church in Britain Developed a Theology of Liberation?* PhD thesis, University of Warwick, 1997, p. 252.

3. Gilroy, P. *Small Acts*. London: Serpent's Tale, 1993, p. 197.

4. Asante, M.K. *Afrocentricity*. New Jersey: Africa World Press, 1988, p. 6.

5. Karenga, M. *Introduction to Black Studies*. 2nd edn, California: The University of Sankore Press, 1993, p. 34.

6. ibid., p. 36.

7. Howe, S. *Afrocentrism: Mythical Pasts and Imagined Homes*. London: Verso, 1998, p. 1.

8. Bailey, R. 'Beyond Identification: The Use of Africans in Old Testament Poetry and Narratives'. In: Felder, C.H. (ed.). *Stony the Road We Trod: African American Biblical Interpretation*. Minneapolis: Fortress Press, 1991.

9. ibid., p. 181, quoting from RSV.

10. Sanders, C. (ed.). *Living the Intersection: Womanism and Afrocentrism in Theology*. Minneapolis: Fortress Press, 1995, p. 158.

11. Asante, M.K. op. cit. See Chapter 1.

12. Ani, M. *Yurugu: An African-Centred Critique of European*

Cultural Thought and Behaviour. New Jersey: African World Press, 1994, p. 1.

13. Collins, P.H. *Black Feminist Thought: Knowledge, Consciousness and the Politics of Empowerment.* London: Routledge, 1990, pp. 203ff.

14. The communication between two subjects is a means of humanizing and countering domination, according to Collins. This method of assessment is related to the call and response genre in the African diasporan communities and is diametrically opposed to the adversarial method found in European epistemology.

15. This presupposes that emotions and empathy play a central role in the process of knowledge validation. Collins introduces three elements: the importance of individual uniqueness to encourage individual expression as a positive process; emotional involvement with the subject at hand (in contrast to the Western model of emotional detachment in the process of analysis) because being in touch with one's feelings is a part of the mind–body integration necessary for sound, accurate evaluation; empathy with the community that one is engaged with. ibid., p. 212.

16. Here, individuals must have a praxis that reveals their commitment to the issues. This perspective is not dissimilar to the feminist argument that the 'personal is political'. ibid., p. 218.

17. First, that the researcher sees no separation in the cultural environment and instead searches for a holistic impulse in reality. Second, because there is no objectivity, the researcher is rooted in a 'particularistic view of the universe'. Third, an approach to research that seeks a humanizing function, that is to say research geared towards a better human understanding of humanity and social transformation. Asante, M. Kemet, *Afrocentricity and Knowledge.* Trenton, NJ: Africa World Press, 1992. p. 27.

18. Asante, M.K. *Afrocentricity*, p. 71.

19. ibid., pp. 5–6.

20. ibid., pp. 5–7.

21. For example, The Pilgrim Holiness Church in Nottingham and Trinity Fellowship Pentecostal in Birmingham.

22. Brooks, I. *Another Gentleman to the Ministry* Compeer Press: England, 1986.

23. See Felder, C.H. *Troubling Biblical Waters: Race, Class and Family.* New York: Orbis, 1989, pp. 12–17.

24. See Felder, C.H. *Stony the Road We Trod.*

25. Baker-Fletcher, K. and Baker-Fletcher, G.K. *My Brother, My Sister: Xodus and Womanist God Talk*, New York: Orbis, 1997, pp. 270ff.
26. Solomos, J. and Back, L. *Race, Politics and Social Change*. London: Routledge, 1995, p. 17.
27. See Rex, J. 'Some Notes on the Development of the Theory of "Race" and Ethnic Relations in Britain.' Unpublished discussion document, University of Warwick: Centre for Research in Ethnic Relations, 1989.
28. Rex, J. and Tomlinson, S. *Colonial Immigrants in a British City*. London: Routledge and Kegan Paul, 1979, p. 275.
29. ibid.
30. Rex, J. *Ethnic Identity and Ethnic Mobilisation in Britain*. Warwick: CRER, 1991, pp. 82–6.
31. ibid.
32. Miles, R. *Racism*. London: Routledge, 1989, p. 9.
33. Solomos, J. and Back, L. op. cit., pp. 33–40.
34. Gilroy, P. *There Ain't No Black in the Union Jack*. London: Unwin Hyman, 1987, pp. 38–40.
35. Gilroy, P. op. cit., pp. 49ff.
36. Williams, R. *Culture*. Glasgow: Fontana, 1981, p. 13.
37. ibid.
38. Geuss, R. *The Idea of a Critical Theory: Habermas and the Frankfurt School*. Cambridge: Cambridge University Press, 1981, pp. 5–26.
39. ibid., p. 5.
40. Smith, T.H. *Conjuring Culture: Biblical Formations of Black America*. Oxford: Oxford University Press, 1994, pp. 5–6.
41. Brown-Douglas, K. *The Black Christ*. New York: Orbis, 1994, p. 109.
42. See Gutiérrez, G. *A Theology of Liberation*. New York: Orbis, 1988, p. xxx.
43. Schipani, D. *Conscientization and Creativity: Paulo Freire and Christian Education*. Lanham; London: University Press of America, 1984. pp. 25–8.
44. Cone, J. *A Black Theology of Liberation*. New York: Orbis, 1970, p. 1.
45. See McGrath, A. *Christian Theology*. 2nd edn. Oxford: Blackwell, 1997. p. 187.
46. Cone, J. *God of the Oppressed*. San Francisco: HarperCollins, 1975, p. 62.

47. Cone, J. *A Black Theology*, p. 94.
48. Gutiérrez, G. 'Liberation and the Poor: The Puebla Perspective'. In: *The Power of the Poor in History*. New York: Orbis, 1983, pp. 138–40.
49. Cone, J. *A Black Theology*, p. 2.
50. Cone, J. *God of the Oppressed*, p. 65.
51. ibid., p. 3.
52. ibid., p. 75.
53. ibid., p. 81.
54. ibid., pp. 160–1.
55. Williams, D. *Sisters in the Wilderness: Womanist Theology and God-Talk*. New York: Orbis, 1993, p. 145.
56. ibid., p. 147.
57. ibid., p. 162.
58. ibid., p. 162.
59. ibid., p. 167.
60. Bevans, S. *Models of Contextual Theology: Faith and Culture*. New York: Orbis, 1992, p. 69.
61. See Cone, J. and Wilmore, G. *Black Theology: A Documentary History*, 1979–1992. New York: Orbis, 1992, pp. 1–11.
62. Beckford, R., *Jesus is Dread*, op. cit., pp. 153–65, where I have outlined the emergence of womanist theology in Britain.
63. Dixon, L. *Mahalia Jackson: Neo-African Gospel Singer, Preacher and Theologian*. BD dissertation, University of Birmingham, 1998.
64. See Gramsci, A. *Selections from the Prison Notebooks*. London: Lawrence and Wishart, 1971.

5 Mobilization

Dread and Pentecostalism

So far in this study I have identified the limited political acumen of the
Black Church. Also, that there is an alternative radical religious
genealogy that contains resources for a political theology. These
elements were distilled into a liberating theological praxis (LTP). I
have also attempted to construct a liberation theology in and through
African Caribbean history. Furthermore, LTP revealed weaknesses in
attempts to develop liberation theologies within the Black British
context (BTSG). In response, in this chapter, my task is to utilize the
insights gained from LTP, so as to outline the content for a political
theology that resonates with African Caribbean Christian experience in
general, and Black Pentecostalism in particular.

I will begin by revisiting Rastafari in order to examine the concept of
'dread'. I will then examine aspects of Black Pentecostalism in Britain in
order to define how 'dread' refocuses Black Pentecostalism so that it
provides political inspiration and ignition. I will end by exploring how
this last theme can be further illustrated through the worship contexts
of Ruach and Mile End.

One dimension of LTP was theo-cultural analysis, in particular, the
mobilization of cultural forms within African Caribbean history. Here, I
want make use of this tradition in the development of a political
theology, beginning with Rastafari. Rastafari represents the first attempt
to construct a liberation theology in African Caribbean history.[1] For
African Caribbean people it is an important resource, because there is
no other contemporary African Caribbean religious tradition in Britain
that embraces Black identity, politics and struggle. Second, some
aspects of Rastafari's theological method resonate with Black
Pentecostalism. As shown above, they both share epistemological
roots in the Myal-Obeah complex. This relationship is seen in the
similarities between their hermeneutical processes outlined above.
Also, a primary resource for both traditions is the Christian scriptures.

Hence, there are sufficient grounds for turning to Rastafari to find a theo-cultural focus for politicizing African Caribbean Christianity as found in Black Pentecostal Churches.

However, I am not suggesting that the Black Church accept Rastafari uncritically. There are numerous difficulties for Black Christians. The use of the 'holy herb' and the idea of the deity of Selassie are but two of many social and theological objections for Black Christians in Britain. But a critical appropriation of aspects of Rastafari can provide a theo-political catalyst for Black Pentecostals in Britain.

DREAD

Language represents an important arena for cultural resistance and it is to this tradition that I appeal now. The concept of 'dread' has been re-worked in Rastafari, so that its meaning moves beyond that found in European theological discourse. Whereas European philosopher Søren Kierkegaard viewed '*dread*' as a form of remorse and despair,[2] within Rastafari the concept is given alternative meanings. What I would like to offer here is three definitions on a continuum of meaning. These are the *religious-philosophical, socio-political* and *word-symbol*. Whereas the religious-philosophical meaning is concerned with the 'internal' or psyche, the socio-political is more concerned with the 'external' or structural. In contrast, the word-symbol concerns the way the term has gained a greater sense of ambiguity. None of these three aspects of the term is exclusive – they overlap and interplay in a complex manner.

Religious-philosophical

While there is no consensus of its meaning among Rastas, Joseph Owens states that 'the well-spring in Rastafarian theology, the centre around which everything revolves and from which all moves outwards, is the experience of *dread*. *Dread* is an experience: it is the awesome, fearful confrontation of a person with a primordial but historically denied racial selfhood'.[3]

Owens' religious-philosophical usage consists of two features. First, dread is an experience. It is a relationship between the individual and God (Jah). This means that dread cannot be simply reduced to an ideology or system (ism) – it is a living existential reality. Dread is the encounter with Rastafari, its theology and orientations. Dread emerges through a particular process that begins with acknowledging the truth of one's existence: the concrete nature of being Black.[4] This leads to the second feature of Owens' definition, which emerges from engagement with 'racial selfhood'. In other words, dread is the Black experience of finding one's 'true' identity, consciousness and place in the world. Elsewhere, I have demonstrated that in the lyrics of Bob Marley there are numerous examples of confronting racial selfhood. For example, the title song from the *Natty Dread* album reveals one of many examples of the awakening of Black consciousness.[5]

In sum, in this usage dread is an experience that requires a particular praxis – coming to terms with one's Blackness in an explicit way so that one's African identity is reclaimed. This kind of essentialist reasoning is accompanied by a rejection of oppressive psychological and social dictates of colonial and post-colonial societies. Hence, dread is the spirit and essence behind Black enlightenment.[6]

The strength of this definition of the term is that it provides room for a 'strategic essentialism', a particular understanding of what it means to experience dread. However, the weakness of this definition is that it cannot incorporate all Black experience.

Socio-political

Whereas the religious-philosophical motif is concerned with the internal – the mind and psyche – the *socio-political* concerns the external world, the working-out of the religious-philosophical (internal). The movement from internal to external is a holistic rather than a dualistic concept. For example, within Rastafari the external manifestation of wearing of dreadlocks represents the internal conversion to the philosophy of dread.[7] Dread in its socio-political manifestation is concerned with a particular type of activity and behaviour: 'to the Rastafarians it signifies power, freedom, and defiance. *Dread* means rebellion or a certain behaviour pattern outside of society.'[8] This suggests that to be 'dread' is about resisting oppressive practices. Another way of talking about this activity is to say that 'dread' is prophetic.

The emergence of 'dreadlocks' among the forerunners of modern Rastafari in the early 1950s introduced a more critical focus to the movement and also the concept of 'dread'.[9] The defiant attitude and judgemental proclamations about Jamaica brought a new rendering of dread as prophetic and sometimes war-like judgement.[10] The idea of Rastafari and prophetic judgement is also witnessed in some traditions of reggae music. However, according to cultural critic Carolyn Cooper, judgement is never mobilized without the possibility of hope.[11] There are several eschatological issues that emerge from this viewpoint which will be explored in the next chapter when Dread Pentecostalism is viewed as a theological system.

In recent years scholars have attempted to identify how the prophetic dimensions of Rastafari emerge from its socio-political critique. Two studies highlight the socio-political dimensions of 'dread' in the Caribbean and Britain.

First, Horace Campbell and Leonard Barrett have highlighted the working-out of the socio-political aspects of dread in Jamaica and the rest of the Caribbean. Campbell concludes that the main socio-political thrust of dread is cultural resistance. Cultural resistance in the Caribbean is a complex critique of neo-colonialism.[12] Although Rastafari was an inconsistent critique,[13] Campbell argues that Rastafari offered the Caribbean a source of inspiration (but not the social apparatus) for cultural liberation: social and economic autonomy and self-determination.[14] Hence, for Campbell dread is best understood as a social movement with wider cultural influence. While not achieving its aim to rid the Caribbean of the various dimensions of neo-colonialism, it has provided the ideological basis for a radical critique that went beyond the boundaries of the movement. In some Caribbean countries, dread was a more potent political force than it was in others.

In a similar fashion, Paul Gilroy has identified the socio-political mobilization of dread among Caribbean and English youth in Britain. Gilroy shows that the concept of dread moved beyond Rastafari and was incorporated into a wider cultural framework.[15] In Britain, dread culture provided an 'interpretive community' for a radical and militant Black critique of racial subordination and capitalist exploitation in the West. Through music and culture, dread provided practical ideologies that enabled both Black and White youths to contest oppressive forces and make connections between Pan-African liberation and the anti-racist struggle; and an arena was thus provided for a creative celebration of Black British identities.[16]

Weak and Strong 'Dread' Analysis

Drawing on the themes of multi-dimensional and bifocal analysis found in LTP, I want to suggest two themes that emerge from these studies in Jamaica and Britain. First, that the socio-political outworking of dread has been primarily 'weak'. Weak dread analysis is primarily concerned with providing a counter-ideology – a socio-political space for a critique of oppression. The analysis is weak for two reasons. First, it fails to produce a social movement geared towards social transformation. As Campbell, Barrett and Gilroy show, dread was primarily ideological and therefore made only limited gestures in the struggle for social transformation.[17] In this sense, weak dread analysis exhibits some of the negative characteristics of resistance shown above in aspects of Black resistance and the Black Church tradition and the BTSG. Second, dread analysis is weak when it fails to engage in internal critique of it's own inadequacies. For example, various studies have shown that in both the Caribbean and Britain, dread culture exhibited an inability to overcome masculine and heterosexual presuppositions of its male adherents.[18]

Theoretically speaking, a 'strong' dread analysis, while emerging from the space provided by weak dread analysis, would go further by relating ideology to social movements. For example, regarding Rasta, Walter Rodney adopted aspects of Marxism to show that cultural liberation must be combined with an ideology of change for effective social transformation.[19] In other words, to be truly effective, dread must combine socio-political critique with meaningful praxis – a transforming action articulated in LTP. (Later I will address the importance of including theolological reflection in strong dread analysis.) In addition, strong dread analysis is self-critical. That is, it is aware of the need for liberative ideologies that go beyond the critique of racial and classist subordination and addresses issues of gender and sexuality. Strong dread analysis functions as a theoretical model of good practice. Later I will attempt to analyse an aspect of Black Pentecostalism from the viewpoint of strong dread analysis.

The evidence above suggests that, despite its deficiencies, the socio-political dimension of dread in Jamaica and Britain has provided an important framework for an alternative vision of social relations. The socio-political use of dread functions as a powerful, if limited, counter-ideology. The final usage of dread is the word-symbolic.

Word-Symbolic

As a word-symbol 'dread' moves beyond its religious and political resonance and gains a mobile quality. Barrett illustrates this transition:

> In recent years it [dread] has become an established word among the youth; for example, if a teacher is severe; that teacher is known as 'dread'. Subjects such as mathematics and science are 'dread'. If a man is good at sport he is 'dread'.[20]

Barrett's analysis of the Jamaican context is mirrored by similar developments in Britain. Gilroy argues that by the early 1980s the cultural hegemony that associated 'dread' with Rasta became increasingly tenuous. Dread moved 'beyond Afro-Caribbean young people who wear locks, colours, and wraps, or smoke herb, to old people, soul boys and girls, some Whites and Asians'.[21] Hence, the term, once recontextualized, became a common expression among Black, White and Asian people in Britain.[22] For example, in Handsworth where I live, I have experienced Black, White and Asian people using the word 'dread' in everyday life. One morning I went to buy a magazine at an Asian newspaper shop. The manager said to me that the magazine I was buying was 'a dread read'. Here, at the newspaper shop, 'dread' signified to the Asian man and myself something that was good, interesting, stimulating and dynamic. However, the term still has a range of meanings charged with implicit socio-political significance. For the purposes of this study, I want to suggest that in contemporary Britain the term has a range of meanings, two of which are important to this study, namely 'progress' and 'insight'.

'Dread' as Progress
First, the term 'dread' can symbolize progress. For example, Jazzy B, the leader of Black British Soul group Soul II Soul uses the term 'funky dread' to express Black music and community initiative and achievement.[23] In short, funky dread expresses a form of Black progress. First, it relates to identity formation in Britain, because 'funky dread' is concerned with wearing dreadlocks in a well-groomed and highly stylized manner, with smaller, thinner and smarter dreadlocks. The style is important because hair in Black British communities is a form of identity politics, particularly, how we aspire and place ourselves within a situation of repression and dispossession.[24] For Jazzy B and other second-generation African Caribbean men, this style combined aspects of the cultural heritage of Rastafari and the African American 'funk' genre. In short, 'funky dread' was a construction of a Black British identity from cultural resources from the Caribbean and America.

Second, the concept of 'funky dread' relates dread to Black ambition and the realization of dreams. The concept was also concerned with what Jazzy B termed 'positivity'. Positivity was a way of describing a psychological conversion that placed self-initiative, self-pride and self-belief at the centre of the Black British psyche. In short, positivity was about making the impossible a concrete reality. The origins of funky dread in the late-1980s can be interpreted as a statement on how to strive and thrive despite the forces of non-being in Margaret Thatcher's and John Major's Britain. This second theme suggests that Jazzy B and the Soul II Soul following realized the importance of psychological transformation to Black advancement. Hence, in this second rendering 'dread' was closely associated with psychological emancipation.

Third, within the funky dread motif dread is associated with a sense of community and collective action. Jazzy B's business enterprises were built through a close network of family and friends. Although it was not a co-operative in business terms, it was presented to the Black public as a family business. For example, at one concert I attended in early 1992, Jazzy B introduced every member of his band as his family. In short the *funky dreads* were a collective. What I am suggesting is that in this context the concept of *funky dread* related *dread* to a sense of collective action and collective will. Because of the success of the funky dreads in the music business, the concept became closely related to Black progress in Britain.

'Dread' as Insight

In contemporary Black British youth cultures 'dread' is used to describe a complex mixture of danger and cunning as well as insight. In general conversation with Black British friends, I might use the term 'dread' to express a range of meanings. For example, as Barrett points out, depending upon context the phrase 'that man is dread' can describe a person who is good, bad, or clever. Similarly, to describe a particular situation as 'dread' also carries a range of meanings depending on the context. For example, to say that 'university is dread' can refer to a good or bad description of university life.

Sometimes the meaning of 'dread' in one context is multiple. For example, dub poet Linton Kwesi Johnson, in a poem about false imprisonment, uses the term in one poem to describe danger and racial terror in England: 'It *dread* inna Inglan ...'[25]

On the one hand Johnson's use of 'dread' describes a negative situation: life in England is dread because of bad things that happen to Black people. Hence, 'dread' points to what Victor Anderson calls the *grotesque* in Black life.[26] 'Dread' as danger is important because it is not just about positivity; it is also concerned with the results and consequences of living with racial terror.

However, 'dread' as used by Johnson can also imply insight. Because England is 'dread', Black people must acquire knowledge and education for their survival. In this sense, dread represents the insight necessary to survive by out-manoeuvring the oppressive forces in education and employment or racist practices from the police and government. In this sense having great insight and awareness is to have what the Caribbean diaspora term 'overstanding' – the ability to exhibit wisdom and knowledge in relation to Black struggle.[27]

'Dread', then, is a word-symbol that moves beyond its religious Rastafarian meanings. It has become a common expression transcending race and class to express a range of meanings including progress and insight. Most importantly, the word-symbol category informs us that 'dread', while losing its religious significance, can in some contexts be connected to Black resistance and overcoming. The significance that the word-symbol has to this study is that it introduces the importance of language as it reveals how socio-political concerns are encoded in word meanings.

'Dread' as Theological Construct

In this study I want to use several features of 'dread' from its range of meanings in order to develop a theological construct – a heuristic device that reveals theological characteristics and relationships.

First, 'dread' is understood as having a religious-philosophical dimension. It is a way of describing the encounter between Black experience and the divine. However, it does not necessarily lead to a belief in Rastafari. Instead, to encounter dread is to gain insight into the being of God and the depths of Black experience. It is to interpret Black experience based on the theological method found in LTP. Naturally, theological presuppositions will shape the religious orientation of dread.

Second, dread combines elements of the religious with the socio-political. It is a religious experience concerned with social improvement in general and Black emancipation in particular. To be 'dread' is to be concerned with a sophisticated analysis of experience that is married to social transformation. This is what I termed 'strong' dread analysis. Relationally, strong dread analysis makes use of the analytical foci found within LTP.

Third, dread also draws from the word-symbolic usage. The word-symbolic as a theological concern identifies a *prophetic orality*. Prophetic orality is concerned with the power of words to speak critically into the social world for the sake of transformation. Transformation is achieved by 'dread talk' offering an alternative vision of human relationships. The prophetic orality of dread is related to the concept of ontological symbols. (The term 'dread' as an ontological symbol will be discussed in detail in the next chapter.)

The word 'dread' as a form of prophetic orality has several characteristics. First, because the word-symbol displays a transcendent quality I want to describe 'dread' as also being more than just interested in resistance to oppression or Black struggle. As shown above it also symbolizes Black progress and insight. Dread as progress is concerned with Black thriving, striving and accomplishment. Furthermore, dread is also concerned with the insight gained from engagement with the tragic and grotesque in Black life. Furthermore, while being concerned with Black experience, the word-symbolic focus demands that dread have a universal dimension; I want to suggest that 'dread' as a theological construct, while emerging from Black space, is not confined or limited by it. It also transcends the Black moorings in which I have placed it. In this sense 'dread' is naturally inter-subjective, engaging with other contexts.

These dimensions together form a theological construct which we can think of as *emancipation-fulfilment*. This is what I mean by 'dread' in this study.

However, this use of *dread* is selective, that is, it is a subjective interpretation of the concept and cannot encompass all meanings. It represents a strategic essentialism – a deliberate attempt to draw upon set meanings of the notion of 'dread' for political and ideological motivations.

PENTECOSTAL

So far in this study, I have focused on African Caribbean Christianity. However, at this point I would like to turn more specifically to one aspect of African Caribbean Christianity, that is, Black Pentecostalism in Britain. Above, I defined Black Pentecostalism as a movement consisting of many congregations – the common feature of all Black Pentecostal churches being the baptism in the Spirit.[28] However, Black Pentecostalism is not a unitary system or homogeneous practice. Instead it is a dynamic tradition consisting of a legion of denominations and congregations.[29] Therefore no description can encompass all perspectives or traditions.

In this section I want to define what I understand by the term 'Black Pentecostal' within the British context. In the introduction, I identified some of the differences among Black Pentecostals. Here, I want to look at what is common among them. Second, I want to explore the *dread* dimensions of Black Pentecostalism. That is to show how 'strong d-read' analysis permits a politicized orientation for Black Pentecostalism.

Despite the differences outlined in the introductory chapter, several features are common to most Black Pentecostal churches in Britain. In the introduction, I described the historical dimensions of African Caribbean Christianity, including how the waves of missionary activity shaped this tradition before its replanting in England. These waves of activity were the African slave religious heritage, eighteenth-century European missionary activity and twentieth-century Pentecostal mission from North America. Here I want to explore Black Pentecostalism's theological characteristics, and then its function, as a means of further defining Black Pentecostalism.

Theological Characteristics

Pentecostalism begins with the experience at Azusa Street in 1906. Elsewhere, I have attempted to outline the theological-political significance of the birth of the movement which are central to its history:

> For many students of Pentecostalism, such as myself, the birth of Pentecostalism is a Black event beginning with the Black Holiness preacher William J. Seymour. Seymour was born in the American South in 1870. His initial Christian orientation was that of the Black American Church in the South. However, Seymour was keen to be a part of inter-racial reconciliation and saw the power of the Spirit as a means to transform segregated American society. Seymour found an acceptable doctrine for reconciliation in the Holiness teaching of speaking in tongues. For Seymour evidence of the Spirit would break down barriers of race, class and gender because all would become 'One in Christ'. Combined with his Black American spirituality, the dynamism of speaking in tongues as evidence of Spirit baptism culminated in the birth of the Pentecostal movement in Azusa Street, Los Angeles in 1906.
>
> Seymour built a multi-cultural church at Azusa Street where for several years the outpouring of the Spirit brought heaven to earth, God to humanity and Spirit to body. Women were encouraged to preach, inter-racial worship was practised and missionaries were sent to over fifty nations worldwide in a period of two years. Many Pentecostal scholars argue that Seymour's spirituality was a combination of African retentions in Negro spirituality in America, combined with new ideas about the manifestation of the Spirit in tongues. Hence, for some, Seymour was simply doing what his

ancestors had taught him: using every aspect of his being to praise and
worship God through interaction with the Spirit world.

Unfortunately, White racist Holiness preachers who could not stomach
inter-racial worship eventually split Seymour's church. Further racial division
by White leaders in the Pentecostal movement in the US before 1920 led to
a distancing from the Black roots. Both Black and White American
Pentecostal traditions, born at Azusa Street, grew rapidly among
Caribbean people in the post-war period, especially poor rural folk, with
their highly syncretised Christianity. It is this faith tradition that many
migrants from the Caribbean brought with them to Britain. Given the
'travelling power' of Black Christianity, it was inevitable that it would be
established once migrant workers from the Caribbean travelled to Britain.[30]

As well as sharing a history born at Azusa Street, Black Pentecostal
churches in Britain share theological hallmarks of the Pentecostal
movement.

The earliest Pentecostals at Azusa attempted to define themselves in
terms of doctrine in order to explain their experience of the 'full
gospel'. As Steven Land shows, this full gospel consisted of five
theological motifs: justification by faith, sanctification by faith, healing
of the body, the pre-millennial return of Christ and baptism in the Holy
Spirit.[31] These early Pentecostals believed that they were restoring the
authentic New Testament Christianity that had been lost through
centuries of formal, detached, hierarchical and scholarly Christianity.
In contrast their literal hermeneutic fostered a theology that took
seriously the need to experience God through a radical conversion
experience and the necessity of spiritual growth. The power of the
Spirit was experienced through the vehicle of worship. The 'miraculous,' including speaking in tongues, was an authenticating motif of the
movement.

But the emphasis Pentecostals placed upon experiencing God
through the power of the Spirit in worship was more than just an
attempt to restore the New Testament Church. For example, Harvey
Cox's study of Pentecostal spirituality views these early formulations as
an unconscious attempt to recover a primal spirituality that was lost if
not hidden within Christianity at the beginning of the twentieth century.
Cox uses three qualities to identify primal spiritual recovery. First, the
emphasis upon personal piety (especially through the vehicles of
visions, dreams and healings) represented a recovery of 'primal
piety', that is, a 'universal spiritual syntax' of primal religious experiences.[32] Second, the millennial outlook within Pentecostalism was the

recovery of 'primal hope', that is, the belief that a new age is upon us and that all that we see is not the full picture. Finally, speaking in tongues or glossolalia was a recovery of primal speech – a language of the heart.[33]

From the perspective of emancipation-fulfilment, I want to propose that while Cox's analysis provides an important conceptualization of Pentecostalism as a 'recovery' movement, like many other Pentecostal scholars he fails to analyse the socio-political dimensions of Black faith that fuelled Azusa Street.[34] He does not explore how slavery and oppression gave birth to Black faith in America, enabling a radical re-composition of African elements in Black Christianity.[35] Despite providing an important analysis of the movement, Cox fails to fully contextualize political qualities of the Black Christian tradition of passive and active resistance. For example, a study of Black Pentecostalism found within churches such as the Church of the Living Well and Kingdom of God in Christ would suggest the recovery of faith was not divorced from the recovery of a Black Christian politics of faith.[36]

The spread of Pentecostalism into a variety of contexts and cultures this century has been accompanied by attempts to clarify and systematize Pentecostal theology. Walter Hollenweger has done much to give expression to the theology of Pentecostals in recent years. By exploring the dynamics of Pentecostal faith Hollenweger argues that contemporary Pentecostalism is marked by several theological hallmarks: a fundamentalist understanding of the Bible, orthodox understandings of the Trinity and Christology, a fundamental belief in conversion and regeneration, a dynamic doctrine of the Spirit, a belief in healings and miracles, a belief in the Devil, and finally, conservative ethics.[37] What is clear from Hollenweger's studies is that contemporary Pentecostalism has evolved into a sophisticated theological system with an articulate framework. Even so, Hollenweger's studies show that despite its continuing evolution, in general, contemporary Pentecostalism appears to have remained true to the theological focus of the early Pentecostals.[38]

Black Pentecostalism in Britain is a descendant of Azusa Street in that it has inherited many of its theological characteristics. However, the context of the African Caribbean diaspora in Britain has produced a distinctive expression of Pentecostalism. A useful way of exploring the theology of this British tradition is to consider how its theological hallmarks have been explained in recent studies. These hallmarks can be defined in three distinct theological categories: the experience of God, a dynamic spirituality and empowering worship.

At Sunday school, we were always told that 'to know God is to experience God'. As Gerloff has shown, *the experience of God* refers to an understanding of a living existential God involved in the affairs of Black people. As with the concept of religious experience in Rastafari, therefore, God is not a philosophical proposition but the life-giving source. In other words, in order to understand God, it is necessary to experience God who is among us. On one level within this epistemology, God becomes existentially Black, worked out through the Black cultures within Black Pentecostal churches. On another level, this epistemology is concerned with relationship. Knowing God is impossible without prayer or other forms of divine–human communication, such as the Word of God. Knowing one's Bible is therefore fundamental. One only needs to compare the knowledge of scripture between Black Pentecostals and White Anglicans or Methodists in Britain to see a huge discrepancy in knowledge of biblical stories, events and personalities. Furthermore, to know God is to live in a right relationship with God. This is why for Black Pentecostals sin – separation from God – is also viewed as a lack of knowledge of the divine.

I also want to maintain that this understanding of God makes possible a distinctively Black focus. This is because God is expressed in a particular Black context. Therefore, at least on one level, God is made existentially Black. However, the critical issue for LTP is what dimensions of Black life are brought to bear upon the social context in which divine revelation and social analysis occur. LTP demands a more explicit understanding and analysis of the Black context.

Second, the *dynamic spirituality* of Black Pentecostals is related to a two-fold understanding of the power of the Spirit. These are the ability to reckon with superhuman forces and the ability to be 'possessed by the Spirit'. This means taking seriously the power of the Spirit of God, the supreme spiritual force in the universe. Gerloff explains this phenomenon through anthropology. These spiritual phenomena are the 'revitalisation of the pan-human capacity for supra-rational, ecstatic experience'.[39] This experience is manifest in a variety of ways. Regarding the African Caribbean British experience she states:

In Britain, Black believers encounter that kind of a rapture which takes a human being beyond its narrow confines unto a new plane of existence, or into the 'inner court' of an awareness of the presence of the Divine which opens up a new perception of the life and self.[40]

Therefore:

> Touching and falling, weeping and laughing, dancing and speaking in tongues thus becomes quite natural vehicles of understanding the world, not only with one's intellect but with one's whole self.[41]

This is a significant observation because she makes a link between the power of the Spirit and the ability to transform both the individual and society. This point is of great significance for developing a political theology because a pneumatology of concrete transformation and reconstruction is at the heart of LTP.

Spirit baptism accompanied by glossolalia (speaking in tongues) is the most emphasized aspect of Pentecostal pneumatology. It is viewed as both evidence and gift.[42] In addition, MacRobert suggests that pneumatology is both inclusive and pragmatic. It is inclusive because it stresses the importance of experiencing the power of God in all its fullness. Consequently, Black Pentecostals take seriously all the charismata (supernatural gifts of the spirit). Pneumatology is pragmatic in the sense that spirituality is contextualized so as to make sense of what must change in the status quo. Therefore, according to MacRobert, the power of God is brought to bear on all situations, including those outside the Church and in 'the world'. I would add that Black Pentecostal pneumatology opens a window of opportunity for a 'realized eschatology', that is, making God's future a present reality. This will be explored in more detail in the following chapter.

Finally, the third aspect of Pentecostal theology is *empowering worship*. Worship functions as a communal, life-giving experience. Gerloff views worship in the Black Oneness tradition as healing: both physical and social. 'It is an emotional as well as historical experience, integrating home and family, people and society, God and universe.'[43] Therefore, the music, rhythm and dance are integral ingredients for the descent of the Spirit. MacRobert suggests that worship is related to a theology of restoration. As well as providing affirmation, empowerment and solidarity, it is in worship that community is most vividly expressed. Congregations participate in a worshipping community that is constantly striving for the transformation of the individual and the community. That is, it 'grasps a future and rejoices in experiencing a foretaste of the powers of the coming age'.[44] All levels of the human being are involved in this worshipping community, both conscious and unconscious. The Black Pentecostal experience is fundamentally an experience of community. Therefore, any meaningful political theology for Black Pentecostals in Britain must be a communal theology: it must place the individual firmly within the community of faith as well as the Black community.

The Function of Black Pentecostalism

The second area in which Black Pentecostal denominations reveal similarities to each other is in 'function'. By function I mean the ways in which the Black Church serves the interests of its adherents. Function is not rigid. Therefore, each congregation and church will not provide all of these functions in the same way. Furthermore, the internal differences of age and gender will also affect how the church functions for its adherents.

Elaine Foster has shown how issues of gender shape the practice of Black Pentecostals. She argues that because Black churches have not engaged in social analysis, they have failed to understand gender perspectives within the Church. She argues that for Black women the Church is an inverted pyramid with good and bad consequences for women's ministry.[45] In a similar fashion, Valentina Alexander has shown that issues of gender difference pervade the Black church tradition. However, Alexander suggests that Black women have found ways to maintain a power-base within the Church without gaining 'visible' positions of power. Even so, issues of gender are significant when analysing the power dynamics within 'functionalism'.

Age-perspectives also reveal a range of differences in function within Black Pentecostalism. For example, MacRobert has identified six 'ideal type' adherents within Black Trinitarian Pentecostal churches.[46] He identifies 'conformist' and 'radical' members in the older and younger generations, as well as 'respectables' and 'rebels' among the second generation. An older congregation will have different needs to that of a younger one.

Alexander and MacRobert each suggest areas in which the Church serves its members. I will summarize their analyses under three headings: community, identity and self-actualization.

For Alexander the Black Pentecostal Church is a vibrant cultural *community*. MacRobert identifies the ways in which the community provides opportunity for service[47] and the development of personal skills including leadership and artistry.[48] Because the community is concerned with care and mutuality, it is also a place of psychological security and empowerment. Empowerment often leads to material development.[49] In short, by providing a dynamic community the Church functions as a 'counter culture' for the Black Pentecostal affirming his/her whole being. This is what MacRobert means by the function of the Black Church as a 'counter ideology'.[50] However, neither MacRobert nor Alexander considers the exclusivity of this community. Therefore no serious connection is made between the role of the church community and civil society and the political community. As the radical Black Nationalist theology of Albert Cleage has shown, revolutionary theology weakens traditional distinctions between the Black Church and the Black community. Both are held in a 'diunital' relationship – both/and rather than either/or. This view is affirmed in a LTP.[51]

The second function concerns *identity*. The study by Toulis showed that identity politics can be central to how the Black Church enables its members to negotiate being Black in Britain. Hence, what is at stake here is the affirmation of Black identities within the Church. Alexander shows that the Church provided a Black cultural identity which its respondents placed above their national identity. Sometimes both Christian identity and cultural identity were intertwined.[52] This demonstrated that being Christian and Black did not mean that one had to drop Black identity. MacRobert shows that this process is more complex, because not all adherents have the same outlook.[53] Therefore the Church will not affirm everyone's identity in the same way. For example, those on the periphery, the rebels, will not feel that the Church provides them with a sufficiently political Black identity. Even so, it is clear that the Black Church provides a space of belonging for the majority of its adherents. Also important here is the issue I raised with the illustration of the BTSG in Birmingham, that is to say, a critical issue that confronts Black Pentecostals is holding in creative dialogue the tension between Christian and ethnic identity so that neither is submerged beneath the other.

The third area of function is *self-actualization*. Here, what is of concern is the opportunities for personal development on a variety of levels such as the psychological, intellectual, emotional and cultural. The product of development is self-actualization. This does not mean that all Black Pentecostals will experience self-actualization. On the contrary, for some the experience is a negative and repressive experience.

Even so, for many the Black Pentecostal Church provides its adherents with the opportunity to fulfil their potential despite the odds being against them as Black people. A theological motivation lies behind self-actualization. MacRobert suggests that the 'inaugurated eschatology' of Black Pentecostals 'throws a bridge across the gulf between a negative present and a positive future ... the future is reached out for and brought theologically into the present'.[54]

Inaugurated eschatology is of vital theological importance to LTP. This is because it provides a theological framework for articulating holistic struggle for Black people in Britain. Eschatology, particularly contemporary re-reading of Jesus' Kingdom of God teachings, have provided an important theological-political rationale in Black Atlantic cultures. Regarding the Black British context, I have suggested that eschatology based on the Kingdom of God teachings is one way in which Black rage (that is, Black anger in response to racialized oppression) can be appeased in a society which uses narrow categories of race to define its people:

> The Kingdom of God provides a space of radical transformation where boundaries, insecurities and impossibilities are overcome. Black rage within the Kingdom is refocused and redirected so that it becomes aligned to both spiritual and socio-political renewal and transformation.[55]

In summary, Black Pentecostals in Britain share a common history, theological perspectives and functions. My next concern is to identify what is 'dread' within Black Pentecostalism.

The Dread Within Black Pentecostalism

To provide theological content to the theological method of LTP, it is necessary to identify what 'dread' is within Black Pentecostalism. Dread as a theological construct identifies theological characteristics and relationships, so, to apply 'dread' to Pentecostalism illuminates those elements that are an aspect of dread. Naturally, the dread within Black Pentecostalism is that which displays emancipation-fulfilment. Obviously there are many aspects of Pentecostalism that might be considered dread, but the three areas of commonality within Black British Pentecostalism (history, theology and function) provide us with examples of 'strong dread' analysis.

An aspect of Black Pentecostal *history* that might be considered 'dread' is the rise of Pentecostalism at Azusa Street. Azusa Street exhibits elements of 'strong dread' analysis. Because an ideology of transformation (glossolalia) was translated into a social movement. Pentecostalism provided both emancipation and fulfilment for its followers. Furthermore, the race and gender empowerment that was exhibited at Azusa demonstrates a degree of maturity and self-consciousness within the movement.

What I want to suggest here is that the rise of Black Pentecostalism points us towards a dread praxis. This is concerned with holistic transformation through the power of the Spirit. In effect, dread praxis is consistent with the function of counter-ideology. Counter-ideology is 'dread' when it seeks to provide an alternative counterculture to all adherents based on dread praxis.

Next, there are aspects of Black Pentecostal *theology* that I consider examples of 'strong dread' analysis. I will consider these matters in more detail later when constructing a dread Christology, but for now it is important to sketch an outline.

Particularly important is the concept of inaugurated eschatology. That is, God through the work of the Spirit is able to transform human lives and human situations radically. Inaugurated eschatology makes the impossible possible. Consequently, a life in the Spirit has the potential to exhibit emancipation-fulfilment. Hence dread eschatology is very 'this worldly' and concerned with holistic transformation in the present because of what has been secured in the future.

Also of importance for looking at the dread within Pentecostal theology is the focus upon the dynamic pneumatology. Dynamic pneumatology identifies a conception of the Spirit of God as one that energizes the believer to be transformed and also become a transformer. Hence, the dynamic pneumatology introduces the concept of dread pneumatology, that is, conceiving the Spirit of God and possession by it as a mandate for radical activity consistent with 'strong dread' analysis. Such a conception is prophetic in so much as it challenges the status quo and offers an alternative vision of social relationships.

Finally, I would argue that 'strong dread' analysis is also witnessed in aspects of Black Pentecostalism's *soteriology* (doctrine of salvation). As Valentina Alexander has shown, in some cases the Black Pentecostal Church can offer a Christian identity that is integrated into a Black identity. In terms of counter-ideology, the Black Pentecostal Church has the potential to provide a space where Blackness and faith co-exist in a positive relationship.

The dread within Pentecostalism is therefore witnessed in the construction of dread, pneumatology, eschatology and soteriology. However, in order to test the contemporary efficacy and utility of dread Pentecostalism, I will return to the illustrations of Ruach and Mile End.

Dread Analysis: Pentecostal Churches

Dread analysis of worship is important because worship provides insight into the 'real' and 'hidden' meanings within Black Pentecostalism.[56] As MacRobert shows:

> Once God has been pneumatically encountered and experienced in love and power within the worshipping community, faith and hope have a foundation upon which to rest ... the Spirit produces a new way of interpreting the world and a new perception of self and community.[57]

Hence, worship is a legitimate context for a dread analysis. Obviously in a study of limited size it is not possible to cover every aspect of Pentecostal worship, hence, it is necessary to limit the scope of analysis. Here, I will be concerned with hymnody, that is, the theology of song. Put simply, a dread analysis of song seeks to elucidate the foci that emerge from the dread analysis of Black Pentecostalism.

The worship at Ruach and Mile End is lively, energetic and characterized by congregational participation (through testimonies and prophetic utterances), antiphonal singing, rhythmic clapping and extemporaneous preaching. Song-leaders mobilize cultural and spiritual resources to facilitate well-being and freedom. Musical accompaniment in the form of drums, guitars, organ etc. all collaborate in this process. Musical genres at Ruach and Mile End ranged from soul music to traditional Rhythm and Blues and gospel. Occasionally reggae beats or jazz improvization might accompany a song or chorus.

Two issues emerge from the worship format at each church. First, the collection of genres has implications for identity formation. In terms of dread pneumatology, worship not only engages in a vertical relationship (divine–human), but also explores communal identity as Blacks and a few Whites create new modes of urban ethnicity through worship. In short, the worship format provided a space for a dread praxis. However, this praxis was limited. Let me explain through the second point, gender. It is important to note that at Ruach and Mile End women play a major role in the stewarding and in leading worship. However, during my visits I never witnessed a woman preaching at either church. This was not because of any doctrine, but a structural matter – there are very few women involved in leadership of Pentecostal churches. As mentioned above, Black women have linked their under-representation to issues of sexism and also to a willingness to concede power within areas of church life. Hence, despite the worship format providing a context for dread praxis, it was not fully utilized.

Because of the social location of Ruach and the number of relatively inexperienced Christians within the congregation, the emphasis of its hymnody was upon conversion and affirmation of conversion. The songs enabled people to experience the power of God and to keep them focused and empowered. Two themes dominated the worship: deliverance, and experiencing the power of God through the Spirit.

The theme of individual *deliverance* was prevalent during the introductory session of buoyant 'praise' songs as well as during more intense 'worship songs'. Deliverance songs focus on the act of salvation, in the belief that God in Christ has intervened in human affairs and transformed lives – enacting divine freedom. For example, during one deliverance service on a Wednesday evening, at the beginning of the service the congregation sang:

> He set me free,
> He set me free
> He broke the bars of prison for me
> One day in glory his face I shall see
> Glory be to God he set me free

Deliverance also focused on the ability of God to ensure that the individual escaped particular difficulty, including the forces of non-being, or the Devil:

> No weapon formed against me shall prosper
> All those who rise up against me shall fall
> I will not fear what the Devil will bring me
> I am a servant of God

While deliverance can provide an important motif in a holistic theology, this was not the case at Ruach. Instead, deliverance was described in terms of salvation or physical/psychological healing. For example, on occasion there were special 'deliverance Sundays' where the focus of the ministry would be on salvation and healing. This limited soteriology reduces the potential for relating deliverance to wider socio-political concerns consistent with dread eschatology – concerned with making the gospel message apply to the need for social change.

The second theme was *experiencing the power of God through the Spirit*. Here the songs/choruses focused on the presence of the Spirit:

> Holy Spirit, thou art welcome in this place
> Holy Sprit, thou art welcome in this place . . .
> Omnipotent Father of mercy and grace
> Thou art welcome in this place.

Here the Spirit is perceived as being present in the lives of the individual and the congregated worshippers. However, the presence of the Spirit was not just for comfort but also for radical transformation, hence the Spirit had to come with power. On another occasion the congregation sang:

> Welcome, welcome, welcome
> Blessed Holy Ghost we welcome you
> Come with power and fill this temple
> Blessed Holy Ghost we welcome you

The presence of the Spirit with power resulted in superrational ecstatic phenomena such as glossolalia (speaking in tongues) or prophetic utterances from the congregation. At Ruach the presence of the Spirit with power was the high point of the service. Whether obtained before or after the sermon, 'having a good service' was synonymous with experiencing the Spirit in power. Regarding the dictates of a dread pneumatology, in this case the moving of the Spirit was restricted to the confines of the physical and spiritual Church; that is to say, very few songs explored the wider implications of the Spirit moving over the nation or even the local community. As a consequence, the holistic thrust of dread pnuematology concerned with applying the dynamic power of the Spirit to the issues of the local and national community are not acknowledged within the hymnody at Ruach.

At Mile End, the experiential and relational emphasis of song provided a space where Black people could explore and make sense of their humanity. Because song at Mile End was a mediation of socio-cultural location and identity, the songs were partly concerned with enabling a more affluent congregation come to terms with their existence and identity by focusing upon their relationship with God.

As at Ruach, there was evidence of songs relating to deliverance and to experiencing the power of God. However, from my observations, at Mile End there was a greater emphasis upon songs that focused on intimacy and relationship with God. This observation was confirmed in a conversation with the pastor:

In most Pentecostal churches, the hymns that we sang dealt with going away up to heaven, rather than living lives that made sense in the here and now. Most of the songs that you will find us singing now have actually got a lot more to do with our relationship with Christ ... how we live in the here and now.[58]

As a result, worship at Mile End placed a greater emphasis upon the relationship with God. For example, praise songs emphasized adoration:

Lord I lift your name on high, Lord I love to sing your praises.
I'm so glad you're in my life, I'm so glad you came to save us.
You came from heaven to earth to show the way ... From the cross to the grave from the grave to the sky, Lord I lift your name on high.

Another song stated:

I love you, I love you, I love you Lord today.
Because you care for me in such a special way.
I praise you and I love you and lift you up today.

Furthermore, worship was related to the theme of being 'real' and empowering. As the minister, Davey Johnson stated on one occasion:

The worship is helping people to be real with what they have been facing ... I am coming with all my difficulties and bring them before Christ.

In contradiction to Pastor Davey's claims, the emphasis upon praise and adoration, in my analysis, did not provide a medium for moving beyond the 'other worldly' focus of which he was critical. This is because the emphasis upon transcendence found in the adoration genre, popular at Mile End, paid no attention to the socio-political dimensions of the immanent. For example, at every worship service that I attended members were told to forget about their concerns, and focus on God. While this technique enabled transcendence, it did little to locate the divine among the pressing social and structural concerns that effect the lives of Black people, even those in the 'respectable' Church. As a result, the opportunity for a dread eschatology concerned with a holistic breaking in of the divine into the present was neglected.

The theology of song at Ruach and Mile End, then, is primarily geared towards the subjective needs of the individual. Understandings of divine transformation are expressed through language that is non-gendered and non-racialized, despite the issues of gender, race and class that are operative on a visual and managerial level. Hence, the spiritual Self dominates the Black Self in the format and hymnody at these churches. For example, very few if any songs have a focus on communal transformation outside the church community (God in the world).

For a dread Pentecostalism to occur, it would be necessary to re-write and refocus the theology of songs. This would enable a more socially critical dialogue between song and experience. Elsewhere, I have suggested that this process might encourage a greater degree of engagement with the social world:

> Sunday after Sunday Black Christians sing songs about 'lilies and valleys' and 'deer panting after water'. There is little if any awareness of the political and theological implications of singing about places and spaces that have very little real-life similarities or correspondence with the social spaces and places that many Black and non-Black urban people occupy . . . Another way of looking at this issue is to ask what kind of theology would be communicated if the images that are validated in song emerged from Black life settings.[59]

Without explicit acknowledgement of the implicit gendered, racialized concerns, the theology of song limits the ability of Black Pentecostals at Ruach and Mile End to make connections between deliverance and the power of God in the immediate social world a process necessary for emancipation fulfilment.[60] The net result of such hymnody as mentioned in the introduction, is the fostering of political ignorance and naïvety:

> It is extremely naïve for us Black Christians to believe that we can best serve God, be faithful to the scriptures, and enter heaven by denying the realities that Black people face in today's society.[61]

In summary, in this chapter I have attempted to demonstrate what is meant by the concept of 'dread'. It has been shown that by combining religious, political and symbolic usage we arrived at the concept of emancipation-fulfilment. This chapter also identified what is meant by the term 'Black Pentecostal' in Britain. In this case Pentecostalism informed us of the historical, theological and functional distinctives that influence Black Pentecostalism. Furthermore it was demonstrated how emancipation-fulfilment when imposed upon Black Pentecostalism revealed dread elements. However, analysis of Ruach and Mile End showed the limitations of dread Pentecostalism within these churches. Given the importance of dread Pentecostalism as a heuristic for a political theology, my next task is to formulate a dread Pentecostal political theological system.

NOTES

1. Hood, R. *Must God Remain Greek? Afro Cultures and God Talk.* Minneapolis: Fortress Press, 1990, p. 87.
2. Kierkegaard, S. *The Concept of Dread.* Princeton: Princeton University Press, 1946, pp. 99–104.
3. Owens, J. *Dread: The Rastafarians of Jamaica.* Jamaica: Sangster's Book Stores, 1989, p. 3.
4. ibid., pp. 170–8.
5. Beckford, R. *Jesus is Dread: Black Theology and Black Culture.* London: Darton, Longmann and Todd, 1998, p. 118.
6. Owens, J. op. cit., p. 4. Also Campbell, H. *Rasta and Resistance: From Marcus Garvey to Walter Rodney.* London: Hansib, 1985, p. 154.
7. See Barrett, L.E. *The Rastafarians: The Dreadlocks of Jamaica.* Jamaica: Sangster's Book Stores, 1977, p. 136.
8. ibid., p. 138.
9. Chevannes, B. (ed.) *Rastafari and Other African-Caribbean Worldviews,* London: Macmillan, 1998, p. 83.
10. ibid., p. 94.
11. Cooper, C. *Noises in the Blood: Gender, Orality and the Vulgar Body of Jamaican Popular Culture.* Durham: Duke University Press, 1995, p. 125.
12. Campbell, H. op. cit., pp. 148ff.
13. ibid., pp. 148–9.
14. ibid., p. 150.
15. Gilroy, P. *There Ain't No Black in the Union Jack.* London: Unwin Hyman, 1987, p. 159.
16. Gilroy, P. 'Steppin' out of Babylon – Race, Class and Autonomy.' In: Centre for Contemporary Cultural Studies. *The Empire Strikes Back: Race and Racism in 70s Britain.* London: Routledge, 1982, pp. 292ff.
17. For example, the *dread* analysis within Rastafari, while providing a critique of Western education, failed, within the UK context, to establish an alternative, concrete educational system for Black children. Its response was primarily to provide resources such as bookshops and parent support groups. While useful, these responses are limited.
18. Gilroy, P. 'Steppin' Out of Babylon', p. 291. Also Cooper, C. op. cit., pp. 127ff. Also Mercer, K. *Welcome to the Jungle, New Positions in Black Cultural Studies.* London: Routledge, 1994.

19. Rodney, W. *Grounding with My Brothers*. London: Bogle-L'Ouverture, 1975, pp. 50ff.
20. Barrett, L.E. op. cit., p. 138.
21. Gilroy, P. *There Ain't No Black in the Union Jack*, p. 187.
22. For example, the term *dread* is used in the concept of 'funki *dreads*', a music and cultural movement outside Rasta in the 1980s in Britain. Similarly, there exists a multi-racial pop group called Dread Zone. Dread Zone perform a highly syncretized form of music that draws from European and Afrocentric traditions. p. 109.
23. See *True Magazine*. April 1996, Issue 8, pp. 36ff.
24. See Mercer, K. op. cit., pp. 97ff.
25. Johnson, L.K. 'Free George Lindo.' *Dread Beat and Blood*. London: Race Today Publications, 1978.
26. Anderson, V. *Beyond Ontological Blackness: An Essay on African American Religious and Cultural Criticism*. New York: Continuum, 1995, pp. 143ff.
27. 'Overstanding' is used in this way in many reggae songs by Caribbean and Caribbean diasporan musicians. See for example, 'Prodigal Son' by Steel Pulse. Island Records, 1979.
28. See Hollenweger, W. *The Pentecostals*. Minneapolis: Augsburg Publishing House, 1972.
29. In 1997, it was estimated that there were 4,000 Black churches in Britain. *The Voice*, 12 January 1987.
30. Beckford, R. op. cit., pp. 9–10.
31. Land, S.J. *Pentecostal Spirituality: A Passion for the Kingdom*. Sheffield: Sheffield Academic Press, 1994. p. 18.
32. Cox, H. *Fire from Heaven*. London: Cassell, 1996, p. 82.
33. ibid.
34. See for example, the marginalization of Black faith in Wonsuk, M.A. and Menzies, R.P. *Pentecostalism in Context Essays in Honour of William W. Menzies*. Sheffield: Sheffield Academic Press, 1997.
35. See Riggins, E. *Dark Symbols, Obscure Signs: God, Self and Community in the Slave Mind*. New York: Orbis, 1993.
36. Wilmore, G. *Black Religion and Black Radicalism: An Interpretation of the Religious History of African Americans*. New York: Orbis, 1988, p. 182.
37. See Hollenweger, W. *The Pentecostals*. Minneapolis: Augsburg, 1972. See also Hollenweger, W. *Pentecostalism: Origins and Developments Worldwide*. Massachusetts: Hendrickson Publishers, 1997.

38. See Hollenweger. W. *Pentecost Between Black and White*. Belfast: Christian Journals, 1974.
39. Gerloff, R. *A Plea for British Black Theologies: The Black Church Movement in Britain in its Transatlantic Cultural and Theological Interaction*. Vol. 1. Frankfurt: Peter Lang, 1992, p. 62.
40. ibid.
41. ibid.
42. MacRobert, I. *Black Pentecostalism: Its Origins, Functions and Theology*. PhD thesis, University of Birmingham, 1989, p. 272.
43. Gerloff, R. op. cit., p. 64.
44. MacRobert, I. op. cit., p. 529.
45. Foster, E. 'Women and the Inverted Pyramid of the Black Churches in Britain.' In: Saghal, G. and Yuval-Davis, N. *Refusing Holy Orders: Women and Fundamentalism in Britian*. London: Virago, 1992.
46. MacRobert, I. op. cit., pp. 262–8.
47. Alexander, V. *'Breaking Every Fetter'? To what Extent Has the Black Led Church in Britain Developed a Theology of Liberation?* PhD thesis, University of Warwick, 1997, p. 163.
48. MacRobert, I. op. cit., p. 439.
49. ibid., p. 435.
50. ibid., p. 458.
51. Cleage, A. B. *Black Christian Nationalism: New Directions for the Black Church*. New York: William Morrow, 1972, p. 42. Also see Baker-Fletcher, K. and Baker-Fletcher, G. *My Sister, My Brother: Womanist and Xodus God Talk*. New York: Orbis, 1997, pp. 16–17.
52. Alexander, V. op. cit., pp. 166ff.
53. MacRobert identifies several Black identities. These are the Conformists, Respectables and Rebels. While Conformists are most 'Jamaican' and the Respectables most 'White', the young radicals are seen as attempting syncretism with these two cultural identities. In comparison, the Rebels are more likely to identify with constructions of Blackness outside the Church as found in Rastafari or Black Nationalism.
54. Alexander, V. op. cit., p. 404.
55. Beckford, R. *God of the Rhatid: A Black Theology of Redemptive Vengeance*. Unpublished conference paper, October 1998.
56. MacRobert, I. op. cit., p. 498.
57. ibid., p. 458.
58. Johnson, D. Interview with author, 6 March 1998.

59. Beckford, R. *Jesus is Dread*, p. 127.
60. Cone, J. *The Spiritual and the Blues*. New York: Orbis, 1972, pp. 13–16.
61. Nathan, R. *New Nation*. 2 November 1997, p. 7.

6 Ism and Schism
Dread Pentecostalism as Political Theology

The task here is to construct a theological system that explores more fully the conjunction of dread with Pentecostalism and also with my earlier reflections on liberating theological praxis (LTP). Above, I outlined my theological method in LTP and also theological content in emancipation-fulfilment. Drawing on my central ideas, here I want to outline the theological system consistent with what I want to call *dread* Pentecostal theology (DPT). There is difficulty associated with such a task. African Caribbean cultures have always held a healthy suspicion of theological ideas and systems that emerge from intellectual thought.

In conversations with some of my Black friends about Black Theology there is always a warning against what is colloquially described as 'ism' and 'schism'. The main danger is that complex ideas stay as intellectual construct (ism) to cause division (schism) among Black people. In response, I want to reaffirm that this study is concerned with mobilization. As mentioned before, it is a holistic approach, concerned with internal mental emancipation and social action. Hence, while this chapter is concerned with theological systems, it is not divorced from Black experience. The overriding concern is to produce theological ideas that contribute in a meaningful way to Black liberation in Britain. In short, I aim to recapture the importance of 'ism' without undue schism!

In this chapter I will begin by identifying three central components of DPT, after which I will explore the theological ideas that emerge. This will be articulated through a discussion of hermeneutics and Christology.

The three central components are holism, transformation and eschatology. Holism is important because any meaningful political theology must address every aspect of Black life. Transformation is important because political theology must be geared towards change or alteration. Finally, eschatology is important to this theological system because a Black political theology must be grounded in hope.

HOLISM

The holism of dread Pentecostal theology has internal and external dimensions. Internal dread Pentecostal theology deals with the psyche, the raising of consciousness and the spiritual empowerment of the individual. This is what 'the renewing of the mind' means within DPT. Internal dread Pentecostal theology is the liberation of the mind from oppression. It concerns consciousness. In short, freedom begins with the liberation of the mind.

Internal dread Pentecostal theology presupposes that Black minds are in need of liberation. In *Pedagogy of the Oppressed* Paulo Freire suggests that oppressed people are likely to internalize oppression: 'They are at one and the same time themselves and the oppressor whose consciousness they have internalized.'[1] Internalized oppression is not merely a form of indoctrination but also a coping mechanism. By accepting a given negative stereotype, it is possible for individuals and groups to accept the status quo. Oppression becomes involuntary, natural and internalized by the oppressed. Socio-politically, internal oppression is false consciousness. In terms of Afrocentric thought it is mental colonization, uncritical acceptance of the superiority of Europeans. In religio-cultural thought it would be the acceptance of White supremacy in religion. In terms of Black theology, internal oppression is the internalization of the slavemaster's religion. Black Pentecostals might describe such a process as spiritual oppression – living a life without the emancipating power of the gospel. Internal dread Pentecostal theology is therefore concerned with developing strategies against internal oppression.

In its external manifestation, dread Pentecostal theology is concerned with action. It is the creative response to living in a complex society. Contrary to the suggestion in Chapter 1 that Black Pentecostalism is a religion of the heart and not of the head, DPT is a religion of the head, heart and 'street'. That is, it aims to put into expression theological ideas and practices, governed and inspired by the Spirit that are related to the life-setting of Black people. The nature and content of internal dread Pentecostal theology will determine the nature and content of external dread Pentecostal theology. Jesus makes this connection when he talks about the potential for good or wrongdoing being grounded in one's heart (Matthew 15.19). However, the relationship between internal and external dread Pentecostal theology is not only causal but also dialogic and holistic. It is dialogic because external forces will influence internal and *vice versa*. It is holistic because these two aspects are part of a unified system of being. That is, the internal and external are diunital, a both/and proposition. The diunitality of DTP means that it is also a theology that lives with tensions of both/and rather than the either/or dichotomies that have plagued the social theology of Black Pentecostals, such as Church/world and Black/White.

Internal and external dread Pentecostal theology must be balanced. If internal dread Pentecostal theology dominates then dread Pentecostal theology is reduced to right thinking without action. For example, my analysis above identified the limitations of internal empowerment from the Caribbean plantations to African Caribbean Pentecostal churches in London (Chapter 2). Furthermore, I explored the limitations of the BTSG in Birmingham to show how critical reflection without action within academia also reduces the effectiveness of LTP (Chapter 4). In contrast, if external dread Pentecostal theology dominates then dread Pentecostal theology will lack critical reflection and result in misguided action.

Another dimension of holistic theology is that it is also concerned with every aspect of human life. No limitation is placed upon the areas of life that concern God. Another way of expressing this understanding is to suggest that a DPT is concerned with the liberative work of God in the world. Because it is multi-dimensional it interrogates every aspect of life. Because it is bifocal, it addresses issues of oppression and marginalization both inside and outside Black communities. Hence DPT is a theology that seeks liberation for the entire community.

The central missiological concern of DPT is emancipation-fulfilment for the 'least of these'. As shown above, while racialized oppression is a feature of Black life in Britain then most, but not all, Black people live under the threat of victimization and marginalization and therefore fall in this category. Such a Pentecostal theology places a premium upon the role the Spirit because 'the comforter has come' and will 'lead into all truth' (John 16.13). In other words, it is also important to acknowledge that DPT does not rely solely upon the socio-political dimensions of life as a resource for theology – it goes beyond seeing liberation as simply confined to the socio-political or economic. If this were not the case then DPT would run the risk of ignoring the metaphysical dimensions of DPT. In other words, the work of God in the world cannot be explained without a dread pneumatology. Dread pneumatology views the work of the Spirit in the world as emancipation-fulfilment. However, no limitations can be placed upon the Spirit. Therefore pneumatology is not confined to the perimeters of the

Church. This means that the Spirit will usher in the work of God in the world even if the Black Church fails to act according to the dictates of the Spirit. As mentioned in the introduction to this study, the Black Church, while driven by the Spirit, is not always willing to be steered in particular socio-political directions.

TRANSFORMATION

Second, because DPT is a concerned with praxis, it goes beyond liberation and calls for transformation.[2] Transformation is holistic reconstruction. The motivation behind transformation is the Kingdom of God. The presence of the Kingdom now provides the revolutionary strength for change in the present. For example, elsewhere I have argued that the kingdom is a focus for Black aspirations and concerns:

> The Kingdom of God provides a space of radical transformation where boundaries, insecurities and impossibilities are overcome. Black rage within the Kingdom is refocused and redirected so that it becomes aligned to both spiritual and socio-political renewal and transformation.[3]

The Kingdom is therefore not some distant future hope, it is also a present reality! The knowledge of the future victory is a driving force for contemporary struggle and joy.[4] There are some pressing needs in Black communities in Britain – the tragic murder of Stephen Lawrence in 1993 and the subsequent inquest reveals the continued subordination of Black life. In addition, there are pressing internal concerns for which Black people must take responsibility. For example, we live in a context where Black men are overrepresented in prisons but underrepresented in institutions of higher education.[5] This suggests that the future of Black (male) Britain is in jeopardy. While these two issues need to be placed alongside the achievements of African Caribbean British men and women, they still identify a pressing need for transformation. What I am proposing is that DPT is a theology of alternation. That is, it seeks to redevelop and reconstruct Black life in Britain. Alternation is intimately linked to the Pentecostal power to witness (Acts 1.8). To be a witness within DPT is to be a conduit of an alternative mode of being for Black communities. Such a task is not accomplished without struggle or difficulty. Such an alternative mode of being must take seriously the reconciling work of Christ. Reconciliation places at its centre love (that is, the unification of all people) under the guidance and inspiration of the Spirit. This means that the liberation project is incomplete without reconciliation. Elsewhere, I have suggested that the strength of Black reconciliation is that it prevents the building up of hostility in future generations:

> Both oppressor and oppressed must be liberated in the quest for justice. Gustavo Gutiérrez provides some insight when he suggests that it is love not freedom that is the ultimate goal of the liberation struggle. This is because without love humans are estranged from both God and each other. Making love a focus in vengeance does not mean that we abandon the quest for concrete justice, but instead refocus our trajectory. Both the older Malcolm X and Martin Luther King realized that their liberation struggles would be transformed by a 'rainbow' alliance of radicals working towards a better society. What I am suggesting is that a God of the 'rahtid' (raged) must have as its ultimate goal a universal and holistic reconciliation.[6]

Therefore, transformation in DPT takes seriously the need for reconciliation. This theme I discuss in greater depth in *God of the Rahtid*.

ESCHATOLOGY

Eschatology is concerned with the study of the last things. However, within DPT, eschatology is not merely consigned to the end of time because eschatology has immediate, historical concerns. Because the 'Kingdom is at hand' God *has* and *is* already breaking into this world, engaging in human transformation. This is a dread event, concerned with power, freedom and uplift. God's reign has implications for Black churches and Black Pentecostals in the *Now*. While there is not sufficient space to explore an eschatological system fully here, there are two immediate issues. First, the promise of future transformation at the end of time victory must be grounded in the contemporary struggle for justice. This means that the DPT cannot encourage any complacency by the Black Church in Britain. We are able to risk all because, as the Pentecostal church song says, 'we have the victory'. Second, the existential or realized eschatological thrust found within DPT legitimates our concern with the political issues stalking Black communities today. Dread eschatology confronts the apocalyptic despair that emerges from the high rates of incarceration, academic failure and racial attacks. Also, dread eschatology celebrates the success of Black people in rising and striving despite the multiple forces of non-being aimed at them in a context of subtle, unrelenting racisms. In such cases, dread eschatology recognizes the *kairos* – God's reign and the destruction of evil forces in the now.

DREAD PENTECOSTAL HERMENEUTICS

DPT has as its central hermeneutical principle (interpretive focus) the theme of emancipation-fulfilment. Above I outlined a hermeneutical method as part of LTP. Here, I want to build upon the method provided by LTP. In order to demonstrate dread hermeneutics, I will begin by outlining the hermeneutics of the Black Church, after which, I will offer a critique of contemporary Black Church hermeneutics through illustrations from Ruach and Mile End. I will end by profiling a dread hermeneutic.

Several studies have attempted to identify the hermeneutics of the Black Church. In Gerloff's analysis the preaching hermeneutic of Black churches relies upon a twofold process. First, biblical imagery is filtered through an African (Caribbean British) understanding of God, gospel, Spirit, worship and community. Consequently, the Bible functions as a resource for holistic living. Second, scripture is reappropriated for today – the narrative is 'alive' and directly transferable for today.[7] MacRobert suggests that as a consequence of this method the Bible is understood as a 'life script' to be placed into the context of the life of the Black Pentecostal. It is primarily understood experientially; the primary task of the Black Pentecostal is therefore to live out the experiences of the Bible because 'present realities of the divine in their lives are simply "located" in the Bible.'[8]

Elsewhere, I have suggested that there is another dimension to interpretation within the Black Church context. For example, within the prayer meeting of Black churches one is exposed to reader-response hermeneutics:

> The version of reader-response that I learned at prayer meetings was always communal. Together, we worked-out, struggled through or stumbled upon the meaning of a passage. The extremes of verbal affirmation or complete silence were a clue to those 'interpreting' that their thoughts were acceptable or errant. Consequently, our re-readings were subject to prescribed reading conventions, that is, the doctrinal affiliations of our Church. As well as being communal our reader-response was also spiritual. We believed that the Holy Spirit was guiding us in the process of applying God's Word. Consequently, I found that when 'in the Spirit' I best understood how to apply Scripture. *Pneumatic hermeneutics* is how one scholar describes this

process. Our reader-response was also dialogical. The emphasis was not exclusively upon the reader or the text. Instead, we inhabited a middle ground, where we would wrestle with the meaning of Scripture. This Scripture – context dialectic began with believers praying for the Spirit of God to lead them into a new understanding of a particular passage of Scripture. Often that new understanding arose from a life-encounter. The life encounter then brought about a new evaluation of the passage. Another feature of prayer meeting hermeneutics was that our reading was intimately related to action. Reading the Bible was geared towards becoming better Christian people. Therefore, new understandings of the Bible were supposed to propel us into a new praxis. Reading was not just about what went on in our heads, but was also deeply connected to transforming existence. The text was pharmacopaeic; had the power to heal.[9]

However, one dimension that was lacking within this reader-response criticism was the political awareness found in the holistic thrust of DPT.

LIMITATIONS ILLUSTRATED

What I want to do in this section is offer a critique in order to show the limitations of hermeneutics in Black churches through an illustration from the preaching at Ruach and Mile End. I have focused on preaching because it is central to the hermeneutical process in Black churches.

Preaching at Ruach and Mile End was dramatic and dynamic, making use of numerous styles and forms characteristic of Black preaching. Pastors used allegory, story and vivid imagery to make the stories in the Bible apply to their congregations. Furthermore, physical touch, call and response, humour and rebuke are all utilized as part of the preacher's expression.

The preachers interpreted the text through their personal framework of experience. This approach ensured that a premium was placed upon an experiential epistemology. For example, in one conversation Davey Johnson (Mile End) reduced the Joseph story to micro-issues such as the family and personal piety:

> When I was talking about Joseph ... I looked at Joseph being a difficult brother to live with ... sibling rivalry ... these are real issues we find in the Bible. We are also talking about an individual who had a problem with pride. ... This is real life.[10]

One negative corollary was that preaching at Ruach and Mile End was also closely tied to the limited subjective spiritual focus that was identified in my analysis of hymnody at these churches. For example, at Ruach on International Women's Day 1998 there was no mention of and no attempt to focus on relating the wider concerns to the women of the Church: the spiritual hermeneutic had pre-eminence over socio-cultural concerns in the community. The net result was a conservative use of texts that failed to address explicit socio-cultural concerns and a devaluing of any wider analysis.

J.S. Croatto describes this process as 'concordism'. Commenting on it he states:

> Another route consists in taking the bible as it is, and seeking 'correspon-dences' between real-life situations and occurrences related in the scriptures. When such a correspondence is found, God is considered to be speaking through the 'archetypal event.'[11]

The danger of concordism occurs when the 'readers' do not acknowl-edge and scrutinize their biases or their motivations. In such cases, readings are severely limited in their capacity to connect the Bible to the wider issues within the social context.

An example of this limitation can be found in a passage from the preaching of John Francis (Ruach) on Genesis 2.1. Here, Francis imposes a personal, patriarchal interpretation divorced from wider historical, structural concerns:

> You were made to be in control of God's creation. Has it hit you yet ... did you understand that when God created the heaven and the earth he had you in mind? If it were not for the women the church would not go on. God I thank you for the women, but we will not get the revival we desire until the men take their place ... God made man first not women first.[12]

In short, this surface reading of the text produces a particular bias. In an attempt to empower men, Francis neglects in part the significance of women's ministry. Men are still deemed more important in the life of the Church and in the 'eyes' of God.

However, both congregation and preacher help to produce such a reading. The oral tradition of 'call and response' ensures a dialogue between the preacher and congregation which might reinforce or modify the subjectivity of the preacher. Through the ethics of 'antiphony'[13] in most Black churches a communal reading is obtained through the dialogue that occurs between the speaker and the congregation. For example, a preacher might have the direction of the sermon challenged or changed by the congregational response to the preacher's message.

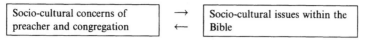

Figure 4. Interaction Between Contexts

Concordism is limited because the multi-dimensional concerns (race, class, gender) inherent within socio-cultural analysis of the text are often not fully appreciated. Therefore the Bible is held captive by the subjectivity of the preacher and congregation. How might the Black Church then engage in an approach that will liberate the Bible?

In Chapter 4, I outlined a theological method that took analysis of the text seriously. I propose that a socio-cultural analysis of both contexts (text and reader) would begin a process whereby complex structural issues within the text could be in dialogue with the social-structural setting of the congregation (Figure 4).

In the majority of cases, only one side (the social context of the believer) is addressed. For example, at one Sunday morning service at Ruach an articulate schoolteacher gave a testimony where she identified structural and personal forms of racialized oppression at her place of work. However, her response was not to explore similarities between her situation and others within the Bible. Instead, holding her Bible aloft, she stated:

> I just need you to pray, I know that this is a spiritual warfare . . . no barrister or solicitor is able to fight it . . . Just keep praying, the Devil is a liar.[14]

There are two possible reasons for her neglect of the structural issues within the text. First there is an avoidance of 'getting political' or using the Bible to defend an explicit political objective or ideology. Second, there is a fear of criticizing the Bible. A high view of the Bible causes suspicion towards many historical-critical studies and their practitioners. This is because it is believed that 'truth' will be accomplished through spiritual readings that emerge from one's heart and not from the intellect. For example, in one sermon Davey Johnson at Mile End, reading the story of Cain and Abel (Genesis 4.1–16) demonstrated how a 'spiritual' reading of this text results in a concern for authentic worship:

> So from the very beginning in scripture worship was an essential thing. In fact, it was not just simply about the quantity of worship but the quality of worship that was important. Very soon after Adam and Eve sinned, in the garden of Eden, they had two sons, Cain and Abel. Genesis Chapter 4 gives us the story of these two people offering up a sacrifice to God. 'Cain

brought an offering of the fruit of the Ground to the Lord, Abel also
brought of the first borne of his flock and of their fats and the Lord respected
Abel and his offering.' Cain got upset because God did not respect his
offering, but there was a difference between the offering that was given, it
was not just a difference in substance, God did not despise Cain's offering
because it was a crop offering . . . but there was a difference in quality. What
Cain did was look at his field and take anything and give it to God. What
Abel did was look at his flock, pick out the best and give it to God. And
there is a difference because God from the beginning of time was trying to
tell us that the quality of worship was important.[15]

In contrast, commenting on the dangers of a 'spiritual' reading of this
passage, Itumeleng J. Mosala shows how a search beneath the surface
of the text can lead to structural questions about its meaning.
Commenting on the historical-critical backdrop to Genesis 4.1–16 he
suggests that there are more sinister ideological issues beneath the
surface:

Genesis 4 represents one such production of the royal scribes of Solomon
and David's monarchy. The question of the division of labour is excellently
inscribed in this text through the struggle between the pastoral sector and
the agricultural sector of the economy. The agenda of this story seems to be
the legitimization of the process of dispossession of freeholding peasants by
the new class of estate holders under the protection of the monarchical State.
Clearly, Cain the tiller of the soil must be seen to represent the freeholding
peasantry who became locked in a life and death struggle with the emergent
royal and latifundiary classes, represented in this story by Abel. Obviously,
the text favours Abel and enlists divine pleasure on his side. The reason
Abel is depicted as a pastoralist must have something to do with the
division of labour mentioned above and the way in which it fed the regional
specialization so important to the ruling classes. Expropriating the land of
the peasant producers for purposes of increasing and intensifying ruling-
class herding, ploughing, viticulture, and orcharding was a practice that is
very well attested in Israelite traditions, not least in Genesis 4. The problem,
of course, is that these traditions must be understood as ideological
productions – spiritual ideological productions certainly, but ideological
productions nonetheless . . . in the case of Genesis 4 roles are changed
around. The story chooses to depict the victorious and successful groups of
the tenth and ninth century BCE, the Israelite monarchy, as the victims and
vice versa, thus lending ideological legitimacy to the process of land-
ifudiazation and peasant land dispossession that took place . . . The class and
ideological commitments of Genesis 4 are unequivocal. This factor,

however, is not immediately obvious to the reader. *It requires a reading that issues out of a firm grounding in the struggle for liberation, as well as a basis in critical theoretical perspectives that can expose the deep structures of a text.*[16] [Note: Use of italics is author's.]

Mosala, reading from a Black South African perspective, suggests that a structural and ideological reading of the text raises issues of dispossession of land and ideological-theological legitimization of oppression – two issues pertinent to the history of the African Caribbean diaspora. However, Mosala's meaning is not necessarily more accurate as it too relies on a degree of speculation. While it may not be possible for every Black pastor to achieve the academic insights of Mosala, what is achievable is a willingness to take all of their concerns, including the socio-political, to the interpretive process. Some progress is being made in respects to this concern. The recent publication of *Preaching with Power: Sermons by Black Preachers* reveals that some Black preachers are beginning to take seriously multi-dimensional analysis of the text.[17]

DREAD HERMENEUTICS

Because DPT is holistic, it represents both a break and continuity with the hermeneutics of the Black Church. It represents *continuity* in that it takes seriously the experiential focus of the Black Church. Therefore, it acknowledges the importance of bringing Black concerns to the text. However, DPT represents a *departure* in that it recognizes the importance of bringing wider socio-political issues to bear upon the text. As a consequence, spiritual/political readings of the text are embodied within a dread hermeneutic. Although none of these scholars uses the term 'dread', such an approach resonates with the work of Black biblical and theological scholars in the USA such as Randall Bailey, Cain Hope Felder, Renita Weems and Delores Williams.[18]

Furthermore, as mentioned above, emancipation-fulfilment realizes that not all scripture is liberative. Therefore it is necessary to employ a critical focus as part of one's hermeneutical weaponry.

At this point I would like to illustrate the outworking of DPT by focusing on Christology. I will attempt to show how the holistic, transformative, eschatological and hermeneutical aspects of DPT are represented in doing theology. I will focus on Christology. Christology is a strategic arena for politicizing theology through DPT.

CHRISTOLOGY

Christology has been a major focus of analysis in studies of Black Pentecostalism in Britain. One of the central concerns has been the significance of the image of Christ. It has been suggested that the image of a White Christ projected on Black people during slavery in the Caribbean is countered in Black Pentecostal worship.

Gerloff argues that through worship the understanding of a White Jesus is altered by a liberating Christ that 'topples the forces of segregation and discrimination' and 'revives ... the worn and weary'. Jesus is therefore presented as a 'liberator who himself carried the pain as well as identifying with the powerless'.[19] This analysis would suggest that in this tradition Jesus sides with the oppressed. But how explicit is the image of Jesus the liberator in Black Pentecostalism?

An answer to this question comes from MacRobert. He suggests that a tension exists between the White Jesus of the missionaries and the Jesus of Black faith. Despite internalizing the image of a White Christ, Black people counter its negative psychological effects through a pneumatic Christ who becomes experientially Black. The Black image prevails because of the primacy of 'experience over ideology in the Black Pentecostal congregations'.[20] The White Christ is therefore 'particularly transformed into a figure which is less easily identified with White hegemony'.[21] MacRobert also suggests that the degree to which the White Christ is really transformed is variable. In his thinking, the more Black the image of Christ the greater the potential for a more explicit Black self-love within the Church.

Alexander identifies a similar continuum as MacRobert. However, she suggests that the tension between the White missionary image and that of Black worship is resolved by a synthesis: the creation of a liberative-conservative Christology which draws upon the passive-resistance motif in African Caribbean Christianity. Here the liberative 'Christ the deliverer' is expressed in language associated with White hegemony:

> It is clear from the research data and observation notes collected that the Black-Led Church's understanding of divine deliverance is an holistic one and yet the starting point for these liberating experiences is, for these believers, the blood of Jesus which washes them 'whiter than snow.' Liberational transformation then, often comes through the symbols of not just literal but ideological Whiteness. Whilst the portraits of a White, blue-eyed Jesus may no longer 'bless the houses' of the younger generation of

believers it is harder to determine the extent to which the realness of such an image has been removed from their consciousness.[22]

What is clear from the analysis of Gerloff, MacRobert, and Alexander is that Black churches have generally failed to develop a Christology that takes seriously emancipation-fulfilment. As a result, in order to demonstrate DPT, I want to construct a dread Christology. First it is necessary to mention some of the dangers involved in constructing a political Christology.

As William Hamilton has pointed out,[23] there are several areas of consideration that must be explored before developing a political Christology. The primary concern is whether the biblical narratives contain a political Jesus or whether Jesus' message, while not explicitly political, still has political significance for today.

Regarding the first school of thought that the gospel is political, there are several presuppositions. First that we know enough about the historical Jesus and his message to construct a coherent political message. Second, Jesus' message was sufficiently dangerous to require his death from the religious establishment.[24] Examples from this school in Black theology in the North Atlantic come from Albert Cleage and James Cone. Cleage argues that Jesus was a Black political leader who came to destroy the White Roman establishment.[25] For Cone, Jesus was political in the sense that his message empowered the poor and outcast. He was crucified because of his challenge to the established religious and political order.[26]

In the second school, the presuppositions are slightly different. Here it is not necessary to have a high view of historical reliability. Neither is it necessary to believe that Jesus' message was explicitly political in its context. Instead, what is important is how the message of Jesus is interpreted today by communities of believers concerned with the political contexts in which they live. Here, eschatology, particularly, Jesus' message of hope in the present, legitimates a concern for change here and now.[27] Within this second school are placed womanist theologians such as Kelly Brown Douglas and Jacquelyn Grant. For example, Douglas states that a womanist Christology seeks to focus on how Christ is understood within the existential context of Black people in struggle.[28] Therefore, the starting point for Christology must be, 'Who is Jesus Christ for us today?'[29] Similarly, Grant argues that Jesus is seen as one who sided with the 'little people' or marginalized.[30] Grant makes no attempt to construct a political gospel, but identifies Black women as today's 'little people'. Hence her christological formulation is the product of the Black women's history. This second school assumes all 'readings' (interpretations) of Jesus are ideological. Therefore, what is at stake is who will benefit from a particular reading.

DPT takes seriously the concerns of both schools but places a premium upon the second school, because the New Testament is not clear on how 'political' Jesus was. But despite the ambivalence of the text, what is important is the relevance to the concrete concerns of marginalized people today.

One way in which I can identify the work of Christ in the world is through symbolic language – in this case, symbols and icons within the African Caribbean community. This is not a new idea, for the Black theology of James Cone and the Womanist theology of Kelly Brown Douglas both use the symbolic as a vehicle for understanding who Jesus is and how he is present today.[31] What I want to suggest here is that a DPT makes use of symbol in its approach to Christology by defining the work of Christ in the world as dread. A dread Christology begins with an understanding of dread as an ontological symbol. Regarding ontological symbols, Paul Tillich argued that humans as finite beings are unable to capture in word the infinity of the divine. The only means of expressing the divine are ontological symbols.

Ontological symbols have at least six significant characteristics:

- They point beyond themselves to the divine.
- They participate in the reality to which they point.
- They 'unlock' aspects of the divine reality that humans would not readily identify.
- They make known 'hidden depths' of human reality.
- They grow out of the individual/collective unconscious.
- They grow when the situation is right for them and die when it is not.[32]

As an ontological symbol, dread signifies a particular type of divine activity. It denotes a God concerned with emancipation-fulfilment. In a similar manner, ontological dreadness describes the practice of emancipation-fulfilment. To call something dread in theological terms is to express such a reality.

Before exploring dread Christology in more detail let us look at some of the difficulties associated with this kind of theologizing. Making dread an ontological symbol raises several issues. First, dread is not a synonym for all divine activity. Dread as emancipation-fulfilment cannot encompass the fullness of the divine. Second, Tillich argues that an ontological symbol must point to something other than itself.

It must point to 'the un-expressive and its relations to us'.[33] Therefore, while dread points to emancipation-fulfilment within the divine, such a proposition will always fail to totally capture the divine. Hence, all that dread can really do is denote in a weak form the nature of the divine.[34] Finally, dread is limited because it has a 'life span'. It will grow and die when the time is right.[35]

Returning to the analysis of dread Christology, a critical question that confronts us is what type of Christ emerges when we apply dread to Christology. In other words, what does it mean to say that this work of Christ is dread?

Elsewhere I have attempted to contour more fully the nature of a dread Christ:

> A *dread* Christ is one who equips Black folk to face and destroy all structures of oppression. Hence, being *'dread'* for the Black Church is to engage in the struggle for Black freedom. Furthermore, to say that Christ is *'dread'* is to unveil a Christ of Black uplift, Black empowerment and Black progress. Similarly, a *'dread'* Christ tells Black British people that the Jesus of history is with them as they protest, fight, boycott, celebrate and progress. In short, a *'dread'* Christ is a Black Christ participating in Black lives and Black struggles. In the context of Britain, a *'dread'* Christ is the focus of our socio-political struggle and the source of joy for our resurrected lives.[36]

Several christological matters arise from this excerpt.

First, the dread Christ is one who equips Black folk to face and destroy all structures of oppression. The dread Christ defies the tension between the 'implicit liberation and external conservatism' of the Black Church and professes a holistic liberation or emancipation-fulfilment. That is, a dread Christ is concerned with oppression in every aspect of human life. While Black Pentecostals have identified adequately the ways in which oppression manifests itself within one's heart and mind, a dread Christ goes further by identifying oppressive structures.

Regarding environmental exploitation, the dread Christ is an 'Ital' Christ. 'Ital' in Rastafarian language describes that which is natural, fair, non-exploitative and wholesome and related to the environment. Ital food was a food policy in Rastafari that was concerned with fair economic production of food. This policy identified an environmentalism within the movement.[37]

Moreover, the idea of a dread Christ recognizes that human liberation occurs on a variety of levels and not just socio-economic or socio-political. While this liberation event is focused on Black people in

Britain, it does not mean that Black people have an exclusive right to the deliverance of Christ. On the contrary, the universal salvific role of Christ (John 3.16) is fully acknowledged within dread Christology. However what I am expressing here is the embodiment of Christ in a dread theology. Such a contextualization is specific and stands in critical dialogue with other ways that Christ has been experienced. In sum, dread Christology takes seriously the incarnation of God in human form but seeks to address the concrete ontological, social and political significance of a Christ within a Black British body.

The second christological issue is that saying that Christ is 'dread' is to unveil a Christ of Black uplift, Black empowerment and Black progress. This informs us of the defining work or what Theo Witvliet calls 'the way' of the dread Christ.[38] A traditional way of phrasing this 'way' is to focus on the meaning of atonement. Typically Black Pentecostalism has ascribed to a traditional view of the atonement where Christ's death and suffering is atonement for the sins of the world. This substitutionary theory places the cross at the centre of Christian experience.

Such a view of the cross is both beneficial and problematic. It is beneficial because it presents Christ as one who understands what it means to suffer at the hands of oppressors. Within African Caribbean history this view of Jesus resonates with the suffering of Africans during slavery and in a different form with the first generation of African Caribbean people in Britain. It is problematic because the cross can also signify unmerited suffering. In recent years several Black theologians from the Black Atlantic context have questioned the over-emphasis within Black church traditions upon Christ as the one who suffers.

As shown above, Delores Williams has argued that the image of the suffering Christ has been mobilized to legitimate the oppression of Black women in the Church. Traditional atonement theories, by encouraging Black women to believe that their suffering is redemptive, necessary and therefore Christ-like, have made it possible for them to accept their subordination as being 'Christ-like'. Williams suggests that for Black women today a more appropriate image is that of Jesus as the 'healer' and the one who gives abundant life. For Williams the cross is a sign of human sinfulness. This change of symbolism is a remedy against manipulation by atonement theology.[39] A similar view is currently being articulated from a Black British womanist perspective by Jillian Brown.[40] In a similar tradition, Karen Baker-Fletcher articulates the view of sacrifice based on Jesus' life. As a result, the concept and symbol of 'blood' is used in such a way that it overturns an otherwise negative atonement symbol into a sign of hope.[41]

The views of Williams and Brown are important in dread Christology. Primarily, a dread Christ must be one that encompasses the life and death of Jesus and finds ways of making sense of the cross of Jesus (atonement) without neglecting or glorifying the cross. While signifying suffering, the cross also signifies that Christ came to give life. A dread answer can be located in one song that Pentecostals sing where the cross is viewed as a dread symbol of healing and life:

> At the cross at the cross where I first saw the light
> And the burdens of my heart rolled away
> It was there by faith I received my sight
> And now I am happy all the day

The binary of the cross as death and life resonates with the central hermeneutical principle of DPT, that is, emancipation-fulfilment. This is because the cross, while a sign of suffering, is also a sign of God's continuing power to heal, restore, celebrate and challenge.

Third, the statement that 'a dread Christ tells Black British people that the Jesus of history is with them as they protest, fight, boycott, celebrate and progress' informs us about the understanding of the historical Jesus in dread Christology. The historical Jesus is understood as one who was concerned with the dispossessed. Despite not constructing a coherent political message, his earthly ministry can be read today as a protest against the ruling order,[42] and an offer from God of a new way of human existence and awareness. This new way is proclaimed when Jesus declares the nature of his ministry:

> The Spirit of the Lord is upon me,
> because he has anointed me to preach good news to the poor.
> He has sent me to proclaim release to the captives
> and recovering of sight to the blind,
> to set at liberty those who are oppressed,
> to proclaim the acceptable year of the Lord.

> (Luke 4.18–19 RSV)

I want to suggest that dread Christology understands the ministry of Jesus as that of holistic redemption. This is not a new or radical idea within Black Pentecostalism. As noted above, within Black Pentecostalism when this Jesus of history is spoken about and experienced in worship he is interpreted as a liberator. This is because

Black Pentecostals realize that the Jesus of history is the one who turns the world upside down so that 'the last shall be first and the first last' (Matthew 20.16). Hence, even within the conservatism of Black Pentecostalism the Jesus of history is a radical figure who transforms human relationships. Emancipation-fulfilment moves the radicality of Christ the liberator beyond the confines of passive radicalism into the arena of active radicalism. Therefore, Christ the liberator is not confined by the limitations of Black Pentecostals, but adheres to a dread agenda shaped by emancipation-fulfilment.

Finally, speaking of a dread Christ as 'a Black Christ participating in Black lives and Black struggles' refers to the ontological significance of Christ. By referring to Christ as 'Black' I imply two things. First, Jesus the first-century Jew was a person of colour (Afro-Asiatic).[43] Second, Jesus is symbolically associated with 'the least of these' (Matthew 25). Therefore a dread Christ is similar to the Black Christ in so much as both are concerned with caring for the dispossessed of the earth. Blackness and dreadness are therefore ontological symbols of God's abiding presence and the potential for emancipation-fulfilment for 'the least of these'.

A dread Christology interrogates all of Black life in search of emancipation-fulfilment. Consequently, even that which is deemed problematic or unseemly (the grotesque) is a legitimate area of enquiry. For example, elsewhere I have suggested that it is important to re-evaluate carnality within the Black Church in order to explore and challenge notions of sex and sexuality.[44]

CONCLUSION

In this chapter, I have attempted to provide a theological system for a dread Pentecostal theology. I showed that as a theological system, dread Pentecostal theology challenged the traditional hermeneutics of the Black Church and offered a more holistic approach to interpreting the Bible. Finally, I showed that Christology is one arena in which a dread Pentecostal theology can be articulated. In the next chapter, I will conclude this study by locating the context for DPT in the contemporary Black Church.

Notes

1. Freire, P. *Pedagogy of the Oppressed.* New York: Herder and Herder, 1970.
2. Baker-Fletcher, K. and Baker-Fletcher, G. *My Brother, My Sister: Xodus and Womanist God Talk,* New York: Orbis, 1997, p. 10.
3. Beckford, R. *God of the Rhatid.* Unpublished conference paper, 1998.
4. See Baker-Fletcher, K and Baker-Fletcher, G.K. op. cit., pp. 269ff.
5. Black men in Britain are over-represented in British prisons and under-represented in institutions of higher education. See Hiro. D. *Black British, White British: A History of Race Relations in Britain.* London: Paladin, 1992, pp. 197ff.
6. Beckford, R. *God of the Rahtid.* London: Darton, Longman & Todd, forthcoming.
7. Gerloff, R. *A Plea for British Black Theologies: The Black Church Movement in Britain in its Transatlantic Cultural and Theological Interaction.* Vol. 1. Frankfurt: Peter Lang, 1992, pp. 12–13.
8. MacRobert, I. *Black Pentecostalism: Its Origins, Functions and Theology.* PhD thesis, University of Birmingham, 1989, p. 506.
9. Beckford, R. *Jesus is Dread, Black Theology and Black Culture.* London: Darton, Longmann and Todd, 1998, p. 168.
10. Johnson, D. Interview with author. 6 March 1998.
11. Croatto, J.S. *Biblical Hermeneutics: Towards a Theory of Reading as the Production of Meaning.* New York: Orbis, 1987, p. 6.
12. Francis, J. *Change My Name.* Ruach promotional tape.
13. This refers to the way in which meaning is changed through the dialogue found in call and response traditions. Gilroy, P. 'It's a Family Affair.' In: Dent, G. (ed.). *Black Popular Culture.* Seattle: Bay Press, 1992, p. 303.
14. Service at Ruach, 22 March 1998.
15. Johnson, D. Sermon, 5 April 1998.
16. Mosala, I.J. *Biblical Hermeneutics and Black Theology in South Africa.* Grand Rapids, Michigan: William B. Eerdmans, 1989, pp. 36–7.
17. Aldred, J. (Ed) *Preaching with Power: Sermons By Black Preachers.* London: Cassell, 1998.
18. See Felder, C.H. *Stony the Road we Trod: African American Biblical Interpretation.* Minneapolis: Fortress Press, 1991
19. Gerloff, R. op. cit., p. 321.

20. MacRobert, I. op. cit., p. 157.

21. ibid.

22. Alexander, V. *'Breaking Every Fetter'? To what Extent Has the Black Led Church in Britain Developed a Theology of Liberation?* PhD thesis, University of Warwick, 1997, p. 223.

23. Hamilton, W. *The Quest for the Post Historical Jesus*. London: SCM Press, 1993, Chapter 6.

24. ibid.

25. See Cleage, A.B. *The Black Messiah*. Kansas City: Sheed, Andrews and McMeel, 1968.

26. See Cone, J. *A Black Theology of Liberation*. New York: Orbis, 1970.

27. Norris, R.A. (trans. and ed.). *The Christological Controversy*. Philadelphia: Fortress Press, 1980, p. 3.

28. Brown-Douglas, K. *The Black Christ*. New York: Orbis, 1994, p. 111.

29. Grant, J. *White Woman's Christ, Black Woman's Jesus: Feminist Christology and Black Women's Response*. Atlanta: Scholars Press, 1988.

30. ibid., pp. 212ff.

31. Cone, J. *A Black Theology of Liberation*, pp. 119ff.

32. Tillich, P. *Dynamics of Faith*. London: George Allen and Unwin Ltd, 1957, pp. 42–3.

33. Tillich, P. *Systematic Theology*. Vol. 1. Chicago: University of Chicago Press, 1967, p. 124.

34. ibid.

35. Beckford, R. *Jesus is Dread*, p. 151.

36. ibid., p. 146.

37. Campbell, H. op. cit., p. 6.

38. Witvliet, T. *The Way of the Black Messiah*. USA: Meyer Stone Books, 1987.

39. Williams, D. *Sisters in the Wilderness*. New York: Orbis, 1993, pp. 164–6.

40. Beckford, R. *Jesus is Dread*, pp. 160ff.

41. Baker-Fletcher, K. and Baker-Fletcher, G. K. op. cit., pp. 111ff.

42. Clevenot, M. *A Materialist Reading of Mark*. New York: Orbis, 1988. Clevenot describes Christ as a non-revolutionary Communist. While this Marxist analysis does not see Christ in strict revolutionary terms it does identify the radical departure that Jesus made from existing modes of spirituality and communality.

43. Felder, C.H. *Troubling Biblical Waters: Race, Class and Family.* New York: Orbis, 1989, pp. 37–48.
44. Beckford, R. 'Does Jesus have a Penis?', *Journal of Theology and Sexuality.* September 1996, No. 5, pp. 10–21.

Conclusion: Outernational

The Context of a Viable Political Theology Within Black Pentecostal Churches in Britain

At the beginning of this study, I showed how the force of diaspora sustains, nurtures and demands the development of a Black political theology from the Black Church. After exploring a genealogy of racism and resistance I was able to develop a theological framework, that is LTP. I then explored the concept of dread as a theological construct in order to build dread Pentecostalism as a theological system able to articulate a political theology concerned with emancipation-fulfilment. Furthermore, through a study of Christology, I have shown that dread Pentecostal theology is a political theology in so much as it is concerned with holistic liberation.

In this final chapter, I want to conclude this study by locating the context for DPT within Britain. This is an important question because as can be seen from the African American context, an inability to successfully locate political theology has major implications for its effectiveness within a given context.[1] In short, I want to argue that a Black political theology must be located within a unique context in order to develop a contextual theological focus. This requires further explanation.

In order to be most effective in the Black British context DPT must be in dialogue with at least three essential contexts. These are the Black community, academia, and the Black Church. As DPT is contextual theology, it places a premium upon the life questions that arise from the Black community. As shown above, these experiences are filtered through analysis and biblical reflection. However, given socio-political and epistemological limitations of the academy and the Black Church as outlined above, it is necessary to find a socio-political location for DPT that provides a context that is both sensitive and responsive to Black existential concerns. Such a location cannot be isolationist, because DPT needs to be in critical dialogue with academia and the Black Church. But, in addition, it must find other sources and influences to maintain its socio-political focus. As shown above, the dread dimension of DPT drives this socio-political requirement, because dread is a catalyst for politicizing and conscientizing Black Pentecostalism.

In order to provide a context for DPT, I want to evaluate DPT in the wider context of a 'reading convention'. My understanding of a reading convention is concerned with more than just the act of reading. A reading convention is the way in which every aspect of life shapes the way we approach, interpret and understand the Bible. Reading conventions reveal the ways in which an individual reading of a text is related to wider social, political and ideological forces. In response to LTP and emancipation-fulfilment, I want to modify my description of a reading convention. I will want to address *thought and action* and *power relationships*.

Thought and Action

Within African Caribbean and diasporan cultures an important ideological relationship exists between *thinking* and *doing*. In short, *thinking* often converges with *doing*. In some circumstances to *think* is also to *do*. The Caribbean sociologist Carolyn Cooper identifies a close connection between *thinking* and *doing* in the reggae music genre. In an analysis of Bob Marley's song 'Chant down Babylon', Cooper argues that an ideological pronouncement (chanting down of the oppressors) converges with political confrontation (burn down Babylon) in Marley's thought.[2]

Moreover, in some Afrocentric epistemologies, truth is verified by the ability to put thought into action or 'personal accountability'. For example, the Black feminist Patricia Hill Collins argues that Black women's counter-hegemonic epistemologies place a premium on putting thought into action.[3]

Moving towards integration between thought and action is not a new idea in this study. In Chapter 4 I showed that LTP promotes a relationship between reflection (*thinking*) and practice (*doing*). The convergence between thinking and doing has implications for the reading convention. In short, this reading convention makes a connection between thinking and doing. *Reading is not divorced from action because it is integral to it.*

Some might think it strange to end a book on political theology with a discussion of Christian outlooks or reading conventions. My reason for doing so is simple. I believe that power relationships are changed from the bottom up. Enabling Black people in pews to change the relationships around them is the route to change. Power is every-where,[4] it is not centralized. Therefore reading conventions enable the individual to begin the process of resisting power relations within their own spheres of influence.

The idea of a reading convention provides a context for a political theology. Before I discuss further the concept of reading conventions, I must first state in brief the theological significance of context.

THEOLOGY AND CONTEXT

Context – our social location and all of its influences – is important in political theology because context influences the production of ideas. Liberation theologians have been most adamant about the causal relationship between context and theology. For example, James Cone argues in *God of the Oppressed* that theology emerges from social context and is shaped by it. Using ideas from the sociology of knowledge, Cone is able to conclude that theology cannot be separated from the social, political and economic realities in which theologians do their work. 'Theologians', he says, 'must face the relativity of their thought processes: their ideas about God are the reflections of social conditioning: their dreams and visions are derived from this world.'[5]

However, our social context brings a variety of influences to bear on our theology. Therefore, it is necessary to relate ideas such as 'race' or 'gender' to our context. For example, as demonstrated above, post-modern Blackness means that the Black context cannot be seen as a singular reality. Hence, in this study, by locating DPT in a particular context, I recognize that context is multi-layered and influenced by a variety of complex factors, some of which will be identified below.

Context is also important because it will affect the ability of a theology to nurture change. Jesus understood this: in the parable of the sower (Luke 8), a good soil (context) produces the best results (salvation). Likewise, a good social location (context) for DPT is vital for achieving results, in this case emancipation-fulfilment (Figure 5).

Interpretation in the Black Church does not occur in a vacuum. Although many testimonies and songs mention the guidance of the Holy Spirit or the influence of Jesus today, a complex process of interpretation is going on. Such is the level of intertextuality that it is difficult to identify where the primary influence is found! Even so, I would like to identify three primary locations/contexts where meaning

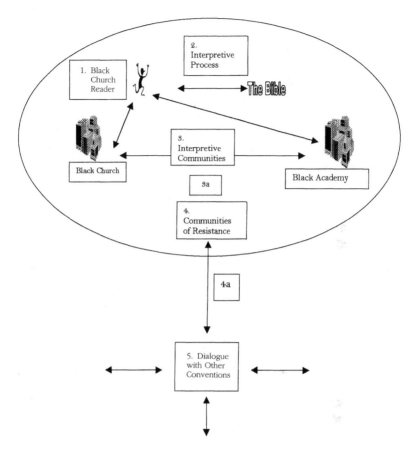

Figure 5. Reading Convention

occurs in the Black Church. These are the *reader*, the *interpretive process* and *interpretive communities*. Through an analysis of these contexts I will suggest a location for DPT. A viable political theology must find a home within the reading convention in order to best effect change. As mentioned above, power relations are changed from the bottom up.

Later I will show that reading conventions are not impermeable. It is possible for a reader to be influenced by more than one convention. This *inter-conventionality* will be addressed later. I begin with the Black church reader.

The Black Church Reader

Some scholars place the stress of interpretation upon the context of the reader (Figure 5, no 1). Of major significance here are the reader's subjective concerns. As I demonstrated in the example of John Francis' preaching (Chapter 5), readers project their interests or 'identity themes' upon the text.[6] Interpretation is not found on the pages of the Bible but instead in the mind of the reader. How the reader regards or interprets himself or herself will affect their interpretation of the text. Despite the subjectivity involved in this reading strategy, readers do not read in isolation, they belong to different communities. Therefore any reading strategy must consider *inter-subjectivity* – the influence of others, particularly 'significant others', on the reader.[7] The wider influences are structural forces and institutions.

Regarding structural forces, I am primarily concerned with how the Black reader understands the role of structural concerns in interpretation. As shown above, within the Black church tradition, little if any effort is made to develop a hermeneutical relationship between the socio-political concerns of the reader and similar concerns within the Bible. The negation of context was partly due to the dissolving of racial and gendered identities into a non-racialized, non-gendered Christian identity. Therefore, the subjective concerns or identity themes that the Black reader brings to the text are viewed as spiritual concerns.

It is significant that the Black church reader encourages DPT to prioritize multi-dimensional focus within the mind. Black church readers must acknowledge structural forces within their worlds as they approach the Bible. According to R.S. Sugirtharajah's analysis of Asian biblical hermeneutics, when we are armed with these presuppositions an explicit political reading of the text is possible.[8]

The stranglehold of the spiritual hermeneutic can only be broken where the reader considers multi-dimensionality as part of the reading process. However, it must be recognized that such a reading strategy is not popular within the context of the Black Church. Even so, this is the task of *transformation* found within DPT. For transformation to occur the role of the Church and the teaching institutions or academia is vital. This last point will be explored further later. Next of concern is the interpretive process.

The Interpretive Process

Some scholars argue that the 'meaning' of a biblical text is found from context rather than within the mind of the reader (Figure 5, no 2). This represents a second location. For example, Stanley Fish has spent much time debating the merits of the text–reader dynamic.[9] In short, meaning is produced through the dialogue between the text and reader. Whether the text or the reader dominates in this process is uncertain.

Within Black Pentecostal circles, reader–text dialogue is primarily a pneumatic experience where the Spirit leads the reader into a deeper understanding of the text. Phenomenologically, Black Pentecostals collapse both reader and text into pneumatology. Hence, meaning is the result of the hermeneutical relationship between the reader and the Spirit:

> As well as being communal our reader-response was also spiritual. We believed that the Holy Spirit was guiding us in the process of applying God's word. Consequently, I found that when I was 'in the spirit' I best understood how to apply scripture.[10]

Spirit-guided interpretation places a premium upon spiritualizing or finding 'revealed' meaning everywhere. For example, it is not uncommon to hear Black Pentecostals even of the second and third generations talking about the presence of God or the Spirit's guidance in every aspect of life. In Black Pentecostalism, everything signifies!

This second focus is also important for DPT because it takes seriously the dialogue between the reader and the text. However, I submit that this process must be invigorated by a dread pneumatology as outlined above. Dread pneumatology is concerned with a holistic focus through asserting a view of the Spirit that prioritizes emancipation-fulfilment. In this interpretive scheme, interpretations of the text are not limited to individual empowerment but also embrace structural dialogue between the reader and the text. I demonstrated such a process in the previous chapter when examining the hermeneutics of the Black Church. Only then will there be an opening for transformation.

Interpretive Communities

Within the Black church context, the reader reads the Bible as part of a community (Figure 5, no 3).[11] Stanley Fish has been central in the application and analysis of 'interpretive communities' as part of literary analysis.[12] Interpretive communities are dynamic and fluid and have an ethical and political character. I want to outline two significant interpretive communities, the Church and academia. The Church and academia are not mutually exclusive. Academia validates the training of the leadership of the Church and the Church legitimates the reading processes within academia (Figure 5, no 3a). In this sense, these locations offer additional levels of interaction.

The Church as a Black urban social movement is characterized by a *passive* and *weak* active radicalism so that liberation is limited and unable to bring about the holistic transformation required by emancipation-fulfilment. The illustrative examples from Ruach and Mile End add weight to this claim. Because most, if not all, readers within Black Pentecostalism are aligned or committed to a church, the doctrinal concerns, church traditions and ethical sensibilities mediate and influence the framework of reading. For example, elsewhere, I have argued that as a member of the Wesleyan Holiness Church, it was not possible to make explicit the socio-political issues perplexing the Black community. This was because the reading convention was influenced by conservative reading strategies deployed from the predominantly White American denomination.[13] In sum, the contemporary Black Church does not yet have the potential to nurture political theology consistent with DPT.

The Black theological academia (the intellectual institutions responsible for theological education) in Britain can be most clearly seen in the projects associated with the BTSG in Birmingham. Like all academies, the BTSG attempts to exert influence in a variety of ways including offering alternative epistemology in order to counter cultural domination. However, as I argued above, while offering a cognitive challenge, the BTSG lacked the structural force necessary for holistic change exemplified in DPT. In this sense, at best, the BTSG offers a space for 'resisting readers'.[14] Resisting readers is a group of 'readers' concerned with specific political reading agendas, such as womanist or Black. However, we have seen that the praxis of the BTSG is primarily cognitive active radicalism, so the BTSG lacks the necessary holism to be able to engage fully with contextual praxis as outlined in LTP and more specifically within DPT. The current Black academia does not have the capacity to meet the demands of DPT. Even so, DPT needs to be in dialogue with the Black academia and the Black Church while it seeks to discover a new 'space' for doing theology.

Transforming Reading Conventions

The critical question for the remainder of this chapter is how to transform the reading convention so that DPT is central to the Black Church. It is necessary to challenge Black Church reading conventions in two ways:

First, communities of resistance must be developed. Communities of resistance (Figure. 5, no 4) are those places where the reading practices and theological insight offered by DPT are taken seriously. These contexts provide an alternative location for 'resisting readers' within the convention. Communities of resistance provide an opportunity for radical voices to remain within the dominant reading convention. For example, not all feminist, Black or other liberation theologians choose to leave their respective churches. Many choose to resist by reforming the present system. With sufficient support, this group can transform aspects of the reading convention from within. To a certain extent, this is the praxis of the BTSG in Birmingham. However, without sufficient critical mass, communities of resistance only manage to offer limited opposition from the inside of the reading convention. Furthermore, by remaining within the reading convention, communities of resistance make their primary reference point the Black Church with all of its inhibitions and limitations. As a consequence, communities of resistance run the risk of being subject to the slow pace of the Church and academia.

The second means of challenging the reading convention is to go beyond the reading convention and engage in dialogue with other conventions (Figure 5, no 5). This process carries greater risk because going beyond the confines of the convention brings sanctions. For example, the reading convention of the Black Church demands allegiance to Christ. Therefore it is difficult to legitimate working with Islamic or Marxist groups who might offer critical insight necessary for transforming the reading convention.[15] The benefit of this second position is that it enables resources from outside the reading convention to be used to challenge the legitimacy of the convention. In Black theology USA and South Africa, it was Black Nationalism that assisted the development of Black theologies. Methodologically, a similar process is at the heart of DPT. The weakness of this position is its distance from the centre of Black church life. Being marginal, it is in danger of having less influence than communities of resistance.

In this study, the use of the concept of 'dread' demonstrates how it is possible to occupy a space between two reading conventions (Rastafari and Christianity) in order to offer a more revolutionary challenge to at least one of them. However, living between two conventions does not necessarily offer the best means of the transformation of one as this location is also beset by the problems associated with marginality. To transform, DPT must be at the centre of the reading convention. What then is an adequate response?

Another option is the formation of a new reading convention. This means forming churches and academies that have dread reading strategies at their centre. This type of activity is not new within the African Caribbean diaspora. Black Christianity in Britain is based upon a desire for autonomy and a new way of being Church compared with the White norm. Furthermore, in African Caribbean history the revolutionary transformation advocated by Marcus Garvey, Rastafari and to some extent the Nation of Islam UK, bear witness to a desire for new reading conventions in the Black community. Further, the sheer force of diaspora demands a viable response from the Black church community.

For example, once such new convention can occur through a critical dialogue between Rastafari and Black Pentecostalism as demonstrated in DPT. This new convention would open a window of opportunity for the construction of various forms of Rastafarian Christianity. Rastafarian Christianity is now being articulated in a variety of locations. For example the Reggae singer Luciano advocates a merging of the two traditions.[16] Similarly, the new wave of ragga-gospel artists such as Spanner and Watchman combine aspects of dread culture with Christian belief.

However, such a task brings both difficulties and benefits. Doctrinal unity would present major problems, particularly, the centrality of Haile Selassie. Hence, to remain Christian in focus, Rastafarian Christianity would better be understood as 'Christafarian' theology. 'Christafari'[17] would ensure that the Jesus encountered in worship provided the necessary strength for emancipation-fulfilment. The benefit would be the formation of a reading convention able to articulate the *rahtid* (wrath) concerns of second- and third-generation African Caribbean people in Britain. However, such a convention must not be exclusionist. It must be cross-cultural, making connections with other radical reading conventions found in other radical Christian traditions. This is because DPT articulates a post-modern, anti-essentialist Blackness where Blackness is concerned with diversity and equality. Hence Christafarian outlook while emerging from a Black location would be essentially cross-cultural and multi-ethnic.

DPT as a new reading convention would not be isolated from other reading conventions. It will be in dialogue with the Black church traditions. While being critical of the Black Church, DTP would also be supportive of the Black Church's quest for renewal and redirection. In other words it would be in critical solidarity with the Black Church. This is what is meant by 'dialogue'.

The major strength of forming a new convention is the freedom to excavate and also create new traditions for the Black Church. For example, very few Black churches are consciously developing a cross-cultural theology from a Black context. Instead, the most vocal quests for cross-cultural theology arise from White churches! For example, the concept of 'inclusive church communities' arises out of the White liberal tradition in Britain. However, the development of inclusive communities is important to DPT. DPT recognizes that Black church history is inherently more multi-cultural than most White church traditions in Britain. Some of the resources for cross-cultural theology lie within.

In contrast, the major weakness that emerges from forming a new convention is that it does not have the necessary resources or credibility to hand. Resources both intellectual and material are necessary for developing academies and communities concerned with DPT. Without sufficient resources the prophetic dimension of DPT is weakened because it cannot be heard. Credibility is related to resources. Without resources DPT lacks credibility. For example, in order to engage in dialogue with the Black Church, DPT needs to be taken seriously. Without intellectual and material resources it will be difficult for this new convention to have sufficient respect and authority.

DREAD AND THE POST-MODERN CRITIQUE

In the last two paragraphs I referred to the relationship between the Black Church and DPT. However, another arena for dialogue for DPT are other conventions situated outside the confines of the Black Church. What I am suggesting is that DPT as a new reading convention is missiological in the sense that the task of transformation concerns the wider world. Therefore, I want to end this section of the conclusion by addressing select concerns of implementing DPT beyond the confines of the Black Church. This what I mean by Outernational: going beyond the prescribed limitations.

In today's world many have lost faith in the ability of emancipatory theories as found in the theological paradigm of DPT. There are two critical fronts.

On the first front, post-modern thought has severely criticized emancipatory theories or 'metanarratives'. Here, metanarratives are problematic because they attempt to impose a collective sense of purpose and understanding upon diverse peoples. Post-modernist thinkers such as Jean-François Lyotard reject metanarratives because metanarratives cannot grasp society in its entirety.[18] The world as we know it has become so complex, varied and multiple that no single theoretical discourse can make sense of all social relationships. In response, post-modern thinkers celebrate plurality and diversity in society.

On the one hand, I must be critical of the Eurocentrism inherent in this project. Not all societies or communities are disillusioned with metanarratives. The rise in religious fundamentalism in many nations weakens this argument. On the other hand, some scholars have attempted to respond positively to the fear of metanarratives. For some, there is a positive political outcome to this thinking. According to Stuart Hall, the increase in marginal ethnic communities or 'new ethnicities' in the social arena promotes a broader democracy.[19] In other words, groups that were once dominant are displaced by those that were once marginal.

A second front is less concerned with emancipatory theories because of the new focus on cultural diversity. Here cultural diversity displaces the once common Black concern with social transformation. One scholar describes the historical movement away from the politics of social change to the politics of difference in Black cultural thought as the shift from the 'right to be equal' to 'the right to be different':

> The shift from campaigning for the 'right to be equal' to proclaiming the 'right to be different' ... is a product of the disillusionment with social change which has become an increasingly prominent feature of post war politics. Campaigning for equality requires one to believe that it is possible to effect social change ... Conversely proclaiming difference requires us to accept society as it is, to accept as given the division and inequalities that characterise our social world.[20]

This movement is important because it suggests that the celebration of cultural diversity risks the loss of a liberation ethic.

Dread responses

The critical focus of post-modern thought has implications for DPT. There are two significant points of reflection. First, although DPT represents a marginal voice, it cannot claim to represent all Black people at all times. DPT recognizes that theology is varied and multiple and that DPT represents one perspective among many. As one convention it seeks dialogue or inter-subjectivity with other conventions in the quest for understanding and social transformation.

Second, despite the importance of social diversity and cultural difference in Black communities, it is vitally important to retain a 'big story' because big stories or totalizing theories still have a purpose:

> A totalising theory provides a framework in which we can decide which facts and interpretations are objectively important or true. We require a standard of significance to distinguish between real or significant facts and irrelevant ones.[21]

Hence, DPT as a metanarrative has an important role to play in attempting to interpret the social world by providing a 'big picture', although the understanding of the big picture is sensitive to dialogue with others.[22] In short, DPT while sensitive to the importance of the 'right to be different' is also concerned with social transformation, 'the right to be equal'.

What I have attempted to do in this chapter is show that the most viable location for political theology within the Black Church is through the formation of new reading convention. These new conventions would 'bridge the gap' between the reading conventions of the Black Church and other relevant reading conventions in order to develop a new space where a Black political theology such as DPT can be located. This is a viable option for two reasons. First, it ensures that the prophetic concerns of DPT are not hindered by the reactive, weak and cognitive active radicalism inherent within the reading convention of the Black Church. Second, it would ensure that DPT is given the necessary impetus and inspiration from outside of the reading convention by being in constant dialogue with other reading conventions outside of the Black Church. Dread Pentecostal Theology occupies this new space in order to offer the Black Church and the wider world a political theology capable of social transformation.

NOTES

1. Cone, J. and Wilmore, G. *Black Theology: A Documentary History, Vol 2.1979–1992.* New York: Orbis, 1992, p. 79.
2. Cooper, C. *Noises in the Blood: Gender, Orality and the Vulgar Body of Jamaican Popular Culture.* North Carolina: Duke University Press, 1995, p. 125.

3. Collins, P.H. *Black Feminist Thought: Knowledge, Consciousness and the Politics of Empowerment.* London: Routledge, 1990, pp. 217ff.

4. See Foucault, M. *The History of Sexuality: An Introduction.* Vol. 1. trans Robert Hurley. New York: Longman Group, 1981, p. 101.

5. Cone, J. *God of the Oppressed.* San Francisco: HarperCollins, 1975, p. 45.

6. Holland, N. 'Unity Identity Text Self'. *PMLA* 1975, 90:813–22, p. 124.

7. See Bleich, D. *The Double Perspective: Language, Literacy and Social Relations.* New York: Oxford University Press, 1988.

8. Sugirtharajah, R.S. *Asian Biblical Hermeneutics and Postcolonialism.* New York: Orbis, 1998, p. xii.

9. See Fish, S. *Surprised by Sin: The Reader in Paradise Lost.* 2nd ed. Berkeley: University of California Press, 1971. Also *Is there a Text in this Class? The Authority of Interpretative Communities.* Cambridge: Harvard University Press, 1980.

10. Beckford, R. *Jesus is Dread: Black Theology and Black Culture in Britain.* London: Darton, Longman and Todd. 1998, p. 168.

11. Beckford, R. op. cit., pp. 166–71.

12. See Fish, S. *Is there a Text in this Class?*

13. Beckford, R. op. cit., p. 169.

14. Fetterley, J. *The Resisting Reader: A Feminist Approach to American Fiction.* Bloomington: Indiana University Press, 1978.

15. See Nathen, R. *New Nation,* 2 November 1998.

16. *The Voice,* 20 April 1998.

17. This is also the name of a Christian reggae band.

18. Lytord, J.-F. *The Post-modern Condition: A Report on Knowledge.* Manchester: Manchester University Press, 1984, p. 23.

19. Hall, S. 'New Ethnicities.' In: Donald, J. and Rattansi, A. (eds). *'Race', Culture and Difference.* London: Sage in association with the Open University, 1992, p. 258.

20. Malik, K. *The Meaning of Race: Race History and Culture in Western Society.* London: Macmillan Press, 1996, p. 262.

21. ibid., p. 256.

22. Landry, D. and McLan, J. 'More on Power and Knowledge.' In: Spivak, G.C. *The Spivak Reader.* London: Routledge, 1992, p. 159.

Index